MATH 308

D1602008

Undergraduate Texts in Mathematics

Editors
J.H. Ewing
F.W. Gehring
P.R. Halmos

Undergraduate Texts in Mathematics

Apostol: Introduction to Analytic Number Theory.
Armstrong: Groups and Symmetry.
Armstrong: Basic Topology.
Bak/Newman: Complex Analysis.
Banchoff/Wermer: Linear Algebra Through Geometry.
Brémaud: Introduction to Probabalistic Modeling.
Bressoud: Factorization and Primality Testing.
Brickman: Mathematical Introduction to Linear Programming and Game Theory.
Cederberg: A Course in Modern Geometries.
Childs: A Concrete Introduction to Higher Algebra.
Chung: Elementary Probabalistic Theory with Stochastic Processes.
Curtis: Linear Algebra: An Introductory Approach.
Dixmier: General Topology.
Driver: Why Math?
Ebbinghaus/Flum/Thomas: Mathematical Logic.
Fischer: Intermediate Real Analysis.
Fleming: Functions of Several Variables. Second edition.
Foulds: Optimization Techniques: An Introduction.
Foulds: Combinatorial Optimization for Undergraduates.
Franklin: Methods of Mathematical Economics.
Halmos: Finite-Dimensional Vector Spaces. Second edition.
Halmos: Naive Set Theory.
Iooss/Joseph: Elementary Stability and Bifuraction Theory. Second edition.
James: Topological and Uniform Spaces.
Janich: Topology.
Kemeny/Snell: Finite Markov Chains.
Klambauer: Aspects of Calculus.
Lang: A First Course in Calculus. Fifth edition.
Lang: Calculus of Several Variables. Third edition.
Lang: Introduction to Linear Algebra. Second editon.
Lang: Linear Algebra. Third edition.
Lang: Undergraduate Algebra.
Lang: Undergraduate Analysis.
Lax/Burstein/Lax: Calculus with Applications and Computing. Volume 1.
LeCuyer: College Mathematics with APL.
Lidl/Pilz: Applied Abstract Algebra.
Macki/Strauss: Introduction to Optimal Control Theory.
Malitz: Introduction to Mathematical Logic.
Marsden/Weinstein: Calculus I, II, III. Second edition.
Martin: The Foundations of Geometry and the Non-Euclidean Plane.
Martin: Transformation Geometry: An Introduction to Symmetry.
Millman/Parker: Geometry: A Metric Approach with Models.
Owen: A First Course in the Mathematical Foundations of Thermodynamics.
Peressini/Sullivan/Uhl: The Mathematics of Nonlinear Programming.
Prenowitz/Jantosciak: Join Geometries.
Priestly: Calculus: An Historical Approach.
Protter/Morrey: A First Course in Real Analysis. Second edition.
Protter/Morrey: Intermediate Calculus.

(continued after Index)

James K. Strayer

Linear Programming and Its Applications

With 95 Illustrations

Springer-Verlag
New York Berlin Heidelberg
London Paris Tokyo Hong Kong

James K. Strayer
Department of Mathematics
Lock Haven University
Lock Haven, PA 17745
USA

Mathematics Subject Classification (1980): 15XX, 90XX

Library of Congress Cataloging-in-Publication Data
Strayer, James K.
  Linear programming and its applications/James K. Strayer.
    p.   cm.—(Undergraduate texts in mathematics)
  Bibliography: p.
  Includes index.
  ISBN 0-387-96930-6
  1. Linear programming. I. Title. II. Series.
T57.74.S82 1989
519.7′2—dc 19   89-30834

Printed on acid-free paper.

Phototypesetting by Thomson Press (India) Limited, New Delhi.
Printed and bound by R.R. Donnelley & Sons, Harrisonburg, Virginia.
Printed in the United States of America.

9 8 7 6 5 4 3 2 1

ISBN 0-387-96930-6 Springer-Verlag New York Berlin Heidelberg
ISBN 3-540-96930-6 Springer-Verlag Berlin Heidelberg New York

Preface

Linear Programming and Its Applications is intended for a first course in linear programming, preferably in the sophomore or junior year of the typical undergraduate curriculum. The emphasis throughout the book is on linear programming skills via the algorithmic solution of small-scale problems, both in the general sense and in the specific applications where these problems naturally occur.

The book arose from lecture notes prepared during the years 1985–1987 while I was a graduate assistant in the Department of Mathematics at The Pennsylvania State University. I used a preliminary draft in a Methods of Management Science class in the spring semester of 1988 at Lock Haven University. Having been extensively tried and tested in the classroom at various stages of its development, the book reflects many modifications either suggested directly by students or deemed appropriate from responses by students in the classroom setting. My primary aim in writing the book was to address common errors and difficulties as clearly and effectively as I could.

The organization of the book attempts to achieve an orderly and natural progression of topics. The first part of the book deals with methods to solve general linear programming problems and discusses the theory of duality that connects these problems. Chapter 1 deals with solving linear programming problems geometrically; it is intended to constitute an intro-duction to the general linear programming problem through familiar geometrical concepts. At the same time, to motivate the study of a more effective procedure, the drawbacks of the geometric method are stressed. Chapter 2 develops the more effective procedure, the simplex algorithm of G. Dantzig. In this respect the book differs from several others in that it uses the condensed tableau of A.W. Tucker to record linear programming problems rather than the classical Dantzig tableau. The smaller size of the

Tucker tableau makes it much more amenable to both hand and computer calculations. Chapter 3 covers certain related problems that are not immediately solvable by the simplex algorithm, but, fortunately, can be easily converted to a form approachable by that method. (Such conversions are especially important in the second part of the book.) Chapter 4 concludes the first part of the book with a treatment of duality theory, a theory that establishes relationships between linear programming problems of maximization and minimization. The Tucker tableau approach makes an elegant presentation of this theory possible.

The second part of the book deals with several applications. These applications, besides being important in their own right, constitute introductions to important fields related to linear programming; the partial intention of this part of the book is the stimulation of the reader's interest in one or more of these fields. Chapter 5 introduces game theory. The methods applied to the games presented here are precisely those discussed in Chapters 2–4. Chapter 6 presents transportation and assignment problems, a large class of problems within operations research. Disadvantages of using the direct simplex algorithm in the solution of such problems are indicated and new algorithms related to it are developed. Finally, Chapter 7 introduces graph theory with a treatment of various network-flow problems. Direct and effective graph-theoretic linear programming algorithms are developed and duality in a specific network-flow problem is discussed in detail.

Appropriately for either a text or a reference book on linear programming, there are many examples and exercises. Virtually every definition is followed by several examples and every algorithm is illustrated in a step-by-step manner. The exercises range from easy computations to more difficult proofs and are chosen to elucidate and complement the exposition. To gain and reinforce comprehension of the material, the reader should attempt as many of these exercises as possible. The answers to all computational exercises appear in the back of the book; complete solutions to all exercises are in a supplementary solutions manual.

I tried to make *Linear Programming and Its Applications* approachable from as many levels (sophomore to graduate) and as many fields (mathematics, computer science, engineering, actuarial science, and economics) as posssible. The basic prerequisite is a knowledge of linear equations including the graphing of lines and planes as well as the solution (without matrices) of systems of simultaneous linear equations. Brief appendices on matrix algebra (for Chapters 2 and 4) and elementary probability (for Chapter 5) are included.

Each chapter of the book, except the introduction, is divided into sections (§'s). The symbol m§n is to be read as "Chapter m, section n." The numbering of definitions, examples, and theorems proceeds sequentially throughout each chapter (i.e., Definition 1, Example 2, Definition 3, Theorem 4, etc.). The scheme is intended to make it easier to find any particular item. The numbering of mathematical statements and diagrams is similar. Any linear programming problem written in non-tableau form such as

$$\begin{aligned}
\text{Maximize} \quad & P(x, y) = 30x + 50y \\
\text{subject to} \quad & 2x + y \le 8 \\
& x + 2y \le 10 \\
& x, y \ge 0
\end{aligned}$$

is referred to by a single number as in

$$\begin{aligned}
\text{Maximize} \quad & P(x, y) = 30x + 50y \\
\text{subject to} \quad & 2x + y \le 8 \\
& x + 2y \le 10 \\
& x, y \ge 0.
\end{aligned} \tag{1}$$

If individual statements in such a problem need to be referred to, decimal numbering will be used, as in

$$\begin{aligned}
\text{Maximize} \quad & P(x, y) = 30x + 50y & (1.1) \\
\text{subject to} \quad & 2x + y \le 8 & (1.2) \\
& x + 2y \le 10 & (1.3) \\
& x, y \ge 0. & (1.4)
\end{aligned}$$

Throughout the book, the following standard notations are used:

> **Z**: the set of integers
> **Q**: the set of rational numbers
> **R**: the set of real numbers
> $\mathbf{R}^n$: n-dimensional real Euclidean space
> $\forall$: "for all" or "for every."

The statement

$$\text{variable} \leftarrow \text{expression}$$

means "evaluate the expression and assign its value to the variable." Unless otherwise stated, all variables in this book represent real numbers.

I would like to express my sincere appreciation to the reviewers of the book as well as the fine staff of Springer-Verlag who assisted in the publication of the book. I must also thank the many students at Penn State University and Lock Haven University who shaped what the book was to become by offering comments, suggestions, and encouragement; the book is dedicated to them.

JAMES K. STRAYER

Contents

Preface v

CHAPTER 0
Introduction 1

Part I: Linear Programming 3

CHAPTER 1
Geometric Linear Programming 5

§0. Introduction.. 5
§1. Two Examples: Profit Maximization and Cost Minimization.................... 5
§2. Canonical Forms for Linear Programming Problems 9
§3. Polyhedral Convex Sets.. 10
§4. The Two Examples Revisited 17
§5. A Geometric Method for Linear Programming...................................... 18
§6. Concluding Remarks 22
    Exercises.. 23

CHAPTER 2
The Simplex Algorithm.. 27

§0. Introduction.. 27
§1. Canonical Slack Forms for Linear Programming Problems; Tucker
    Tableaus.. 27
§2. An Example: Profit Maximization 30
§3. The Pivot Transformation.. 33
§4. An Example: Cost Minimization... 36
§5. The Simplex Algorithm for Maximum Basic Feasible Tableaus.............. 38
§6. The Simplex Algorithm for Maximum Tableaus 49

§7. Negative Transposition; The Simplex Algorithm for Minimum Tableaus   54
§8. Cycling..   58
§9. Concluding Remarks...   63
     Exercises..   64

CHAPTER 3
Noncanonical Linear Programming Problems..   70

§0. Introduction...   70
§1. Unconstrained Variables..   70
§2. Equations of Constraint..   77
§3. Concluding Remarks...   83
     Exercises..   83

CHAPTER 4
Duality Theory..   87

§0. Introduction...   87
§1. Duality in Canonical Tableaus..   87
§2. The Dual Simplex Algorithm..   89
§3. Matrix Formulation of Canonical Tableaus...   94
§4. The Duality Equation...   96
§5. The Duality Theorem...   101
§6. Duality in Noncanonical Tableaus..   105
§7. Concluding Remarks...   109
     Exercises..   109

Part II: Applications..   115

CHAPTER 5
Matrix Games...   117

§0. Introduction...   117
§1. An Example; Two-Person Zero-Sum Matrix Games.................................   117
§2. Linear Programming Formulation of Matrix Games.................................   120
§3. The Von Neumann Minimax Theorem...   124
§4. The Example Revisited...   125
§5. Two More Examples..   127
§6. Concluding Remarks...   135
     Exercises..   135

CHAPTER 6
Transportation and Assignment Problems...   140

§0. Introduction...   140
§1. An Example; The Balanced Transportation Problem................................   140
§2. The Vogel Advanced-Start Method (VAM)..   143
§3. The Transportation Algorithm...   151
§4. Another Example..   157
§5. Unbalanced Transportation Problems..   161

§6. The Assignment Problem 164
§7. Concluding Remarks 177
    Exercises 178

CHAPTER 7
Network-Flow Problems 185

§0. Introduction 185
§1. Graph-Theoretic Preliminaries 185
§2. The Maximal-Flow Network Problem 189
§3. The Max-Flow Min-Cut Theorem; The Maximal-Flow Algorithm 191
§4. The Shortest-Path Network Problem 205
§5. The Minimal-Cost-Flow Network Problem 216
§6. Transportation and Assignment Problems Revisited 228
§7. Concluding Remarks 230
    Exercises 231

APPENDIX A
Matrix Algebra 238

APPENDIX B
Probability 244

Answers to Selected Exercises 249
Bibliography 259
Index 261

CHAPTER 0

Introduction

Many of the problems normally encountered in the real world deal with the maximization or minimization of certain quantities. Frequently, these quantities are profit (in the case of maximization) and cost (in the case of minimization). Linear programming is a collection of procedures for maximizing or minimizing linear functions subject to given linear constraints. Inasmuch as the functions to be optimized are linear, the techniques of calculus imply only that the maximums and/or minimums of these functions lie on the boundaries of the sets determined by the constraints. In this sense, calculus is inadequate for solving linear programming problems. The methods to be discussed in this book take advantage of the linearity of such problems, hence providing effective and direct solution procedures.

The procedures of linear programming have wide applications in many fields. For example, linear programming encompasses many of the main solution techniques in the field commonly referred to as management science or operations research. Although the solution of typical real-life linear programming problems requires the implementation of specific procedures on a computer, it is not this computer programming to which the "programming" of linear programming refers—programming in the linear programming sense means the development of effective algorithms for solving problems. As we will see, the effectiveness of such algorithms is largely dependent upon the particular applications from which the problems arise. Hence, linear programming will not only allow us to solve many different types of problems in many different contexts but will provide deeper insights into the fields in which linear programming finds its utility. After having completed the book, the reader will not only have learned a set of procedures for solving different types of linear programming problems but will also have a sense of the central role of linear programming in areas of mathematics and business.

Part I

Linear Programming

CHAPTER 1

Geometric Linear Programming

§0. Introduction

This chapter is devoted entirely to the solution of linear programming problems by graphical and/or geometrical methods. We introduce linear programming problems, provide a rudimentary procedure for solving linear programming problems, and motivate the need for a better, more efficient algorithm to be discussed in Chapter 2.

§1. Two Examples: Profit Maximization and Cost Minimization

Linear programming problems involve linear functions which are to be maximized or minimized. Frequently, these functions represent profit (in the case of maximization) and cost (in the case of minimization). We begin with two such examples of typical linear programming problems.

EXAMPLE 1. An appliance company manufactures heaters and air conditioners. The production of one heater requires 2 hours in the parts division of the company and 1 hour in the assembly division of the company; the production of one air conditioner requires 1 hour in the parts division of the company and 2 hours in the assembly division of the company. The parts division is operated for at most 8 hours per day and the assembly division is operated for at most 10 hours per day. If the profit realized upon sale is $30 per heater and $50 per air conditioner, how many heaters and air conditioners should the company manufacture per day so as to maximize profits?

We begin by reformulating Example 1 mathematically. We are interested in the number of heaters and air conditioners that the company should manufacture per day so we put

$$x = \text{\# of heaters per day}$$
$$y = \text{\# of air conditioners per day.}$$

The quantity to be maximized, namely profit, is then given by $P(x,y) = 30x + 50y$. The company can not manufacture an unlimited number of heaters and/or air conditioners (and hence can not realize unlimited profits) since it is constrained by the time availability of the parts division and the assembly division. Each heater requires 2 hours in the parts division and each air conditioner requires 1 hour in the parts division. Hence, the total amount of time required from the parts division per day is $2x + y$ hours. Inasmuch as the parts division is available for at most 8 hours per day, we have the constraint

$$2x + y \leq 8.$$

Similar reasoning applied to the assembly division yields the constraint

$$x + 2y \leq 10.$$

Finally, we include the implied constraints

$$x \geq 0$$
$$y \geq 0$$

since a negative number of heaters or air conditioners manufactured per day is not realistic in our problem. We now have the desired mathematical reformulation of Example 1:

$$\begin{aligned}
\text{Maximize} \quad & P(x, y) = 30x + 50y \\
\text{subject to} \quad & 2x + y \leq 8 \\
& x + 2y \leq 10 \qquad\qquad\qquad (1)\\
& x \geq 0 \\
& y \geq 0.
\end{aligned}$$

The set of points (x, y) satisfying all four constraints of (1) is the shaded region below:

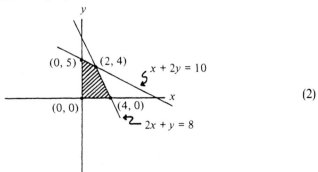

(2)

This region was obtained by graphing the equalities $2x + y = 8$, $x + 2y = 10$, $x = 0$, and $y = 0$, shading the solution sets of the corresponding inequalities, and finding the mutual intersection of all such sets. In other words, the set of points common to the four shaded regions

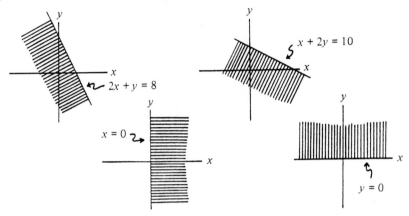

is precisely the shaded region of (2). (1) now asks the following question: Which point(s) (if any) of the shaded region of (2) maximizes P? We leave (1) until its solution in §4 of this chapter.

EXAMPLE 2. An oil company owns two refineries, say refinery A and refinery B. Refinery A is capable of producing 20 barrels of gasoline and 25 barrels of fuel oil per day; refinery B is capable of producing 40 barrels of gasoline and 20 barrels of fuel oil per day. The company requires at least 1000 barrels of gasoline and at least 800 barrels of fuel oil. If it costs $300 per day to operate refinery A and $500 per day to operate refinery B, how many days should each refinery be operated by the company so as to minimize costs?

We begin by reformulating Example 2 mathematically. If we put

$$x = \# \text{ of days for refinery A}$$
$$y = \# \text{ of days for refinery B},$$

then the quantity to be minimized, namely cost, is given by $C(x, y) = 300x + 500y$. Note that the company must incur some positive cost since it is constrained by the minimum petroleum requirements. Refinery A is capable of producing 20 barrels of gasoline per day and refinery B is capable of producing 40 barrels of gasoline per day. Hence, the total amount of gasoline produced is $20x + 40y$ barrels. Inasmuch as at least 1000 barrels of gasoline is required by the company, we have the constraint

$$20x + 40y \geq 1000.$$

Similar reasoning applied to the fuel oil yields the constraint

$$25x + 20y \geq 800.$$

Again, we include the implied constraints

$$x \geqq 0$$
$$y \geqq 0$$

since a negative number of days for either refinery to be operated is not realistic in our problem. We now have the desired reformulation of Example 2:

$$
\begin{aligned}
\text{Minimize} \quad & C(x, y) = 300x + 500y \\
\text{subject to} \quad & 20x + 40y \geqq 1000 \\
& 25x + 20y \geqq 800 \\
& x \geqq 0 \\
& y \geqq 0.
\end{aligned}
\tag{3}
$$

The set of points (x, y) satisfying all four constraints of (3) is the shaded region below:

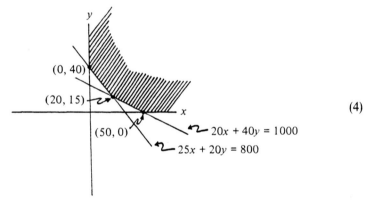

$$\tag{4}$$

This region is precisely the intersection of the four shaded regions

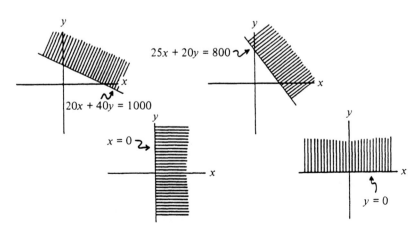

(3) now asks the following question: Which point(s) (if any) of the shaded region of (4) minimizes C? We leave (3) until its solution in §4 of this chapter.

§2. Canonical Forms for Linear Programming Problems

There are two natural or canonical forms taken by linear programming problems, a maximization canonical form and a minimization canonical form. We present these forms now along with some related standard terminology.

Definition 3. (i) The problem

$$\text{Maximize} \quad f(x_1, x_2, \ldots, x_n) = c_1 x_1 + c_2 x_2 + \cdots + c_n x_n - d$$
$$\text{subject to} \quad a_{11} x_1 + a_{12} x_2 + \cdots + a_{1n} x_n \leq b_1$$
$$a_{21} x_1 + a_{22} x_2 + \cdots + a_{2n} x_n \leq b_2$$
$$\vdots$$
$$a_{m1} x_1 + a_{m2} x_2 + \cdots + a_{mn} x_n \leq b_m$$
$$x_1, x_2, \ldots, x_n \geq 0$$

is said to be a *canonical maximization linear programming problem*.
(ii) The problem

$$\text{Minimize} \quad g(x_1, x_2, \ldots, x_n) = c_1 x_1 + c_2 x_2 + \cdots + c_n x_n - d$$
$$\text{subject to} \quad a_{11} x_1 + a_{12} x_2 + \cdots + a_{1n} x_n \geq b_1$$
$$a_{21} x_1 + a_{22} x_2 + \cdots + a_{2n} x_n \geq b_2$$
$$\vdots$$
$$a_{m1} x_1 + a_{m2} x_2 + \cdots + a_{mn} x_n \geq b_m$$
$$x_1, x_2, \ldots, x_n \geq 0$$

is said to be a *canonical minimization linear programming problem*. The first m constraints in each canonical form above are said to be *main constraints*; the second n constraints in each canonical form above are said to be *nonnegativity constraints*.

Note that the profit maximization example (1) and the cost minimization example (3) of §1 are in canonical form. The reason for the (possibly curious) choice of minus sign in front of the constant d in Definition 3 will be made clear in Chapter 2.

Definition 4. The linear functions f and g in Definition 3 above are said to be *objective functions*.

What are the objective functions of (1) and (3) in §1?

Definition 5. The set of all points $(x_1, x_2, \ldots, x_n)$ satisfying the $m + n$ constraints of a canonical maximization or a canonical minimization linear programming problem is said to be the *constraint set* of the problem. Any element of the constraint set is said to be a *feasible point* or *feasible solution*.

The shaded regions of (2) and (4) constitute the constraint sets for (1) and (3) respectively in §1.

Definition 6. Any feasible solution of a canonical maximization (respectively minimization) linear programming problem which maximizes (respectively minimizes) the objective function is said to be an *optimal solution*.

Our immediate goal then is to find optimal solutions for (1) and (3) of §1.

§3. Polyhedral Convex Sets

This section presents the pertinent geometry of $\mathbf{R}^n$ for linear programming problems, culminating in two theorems which will yield a procedure for solving these problems. Throughout this section, the reader should strive to understand the geometrical concepts in the smaller-dimensional spaces, i.e., in $\mathbf{R}^1, \mathbf{R}^2$, and $\mathbf{R}^3$, with the understanding that these concepts have been extended to real spaces of arbitrary finite dimension. Also, no proofs appear in this section; indeed, the geometric linear programming procedure ultimately developed in §5 will be abandoned in Chapter 2 in favor of a better method. This by no means implies that the concepts presented here are not important—they provide a crucial intuitive foundation on which to build our knowledge of linear programming.

Definition 7. Let $\mathbf{x} = (x_1, x_2, \ldots, x_n)$, $\mathbf{y} = (y_1, y_2, \ldots, y_n) \in \mathbf{R}^n$. Then

$$t\mathbf{x} + (1-t)\mathbf{y}, \quad 0 \le y \le 1,$$

is said to be the *line segment* between $\mathbf{x}$ and $\mathbf{y}$ inclusive.

The definition above is an extension of the usual geometric notion of a line segment to higher dimensions. To motivate the fact that this is the usual notion of a line segment in small dimensions, we give an example in $\mathbf{R}^2$.

EXAMPLE 8. Consider $(2, 1), (4, -2) \in \mathbf{R}^2$. The line segment between $(2, 1)$ and $(4, -2)$ is, by the definition above, the collection of all points in $\mathbf{R}^2$ expressible in the form

$$t(2, 1) + (1 - t)(4, -2), \quad 0 \le t \le 1.$$

If $t = 0$, we have

$$t(2, 1) + (1 - t)(4, -2) = 0(2, 1) + 1(4, -2) = (4, -2).$$

If $t = 1$, we have

$$t(2, 1) + (1 - t)(4, -2) = 1(2, 1) + 0(4, -2) = (2, 1).$$

If $t = 1/3$, we have

$$t(2, 1) + (1 - t)(4, -2) = 1/3(2, 1) + 2/3(4, -2) = (10/3, -1).$$

By continuing this process of choosing values of t such that $0 \leq t \leq 1$ and evaluating $t(2, 1) + (1 - t)(4, -2)$, we obtain

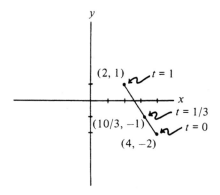

which is the usual geometric notion of the line segment between $(2, 1)$ and $(4, -2)$. Choose some other values of t and verify this for yourself!

Definition 9. Let S be a subset of $\mathbf{R}^n$. S is said to be *convex* if, whenever $\mathbf{x} = (x_1, x_2, \ldots, x_n)$, $\mathbf{y} = (y_1, y_2, \ldots, y_n) \in S$, then

$$t\mathbf{x} + (1 - t)\mathbf{y} \in S, \quad 0 \leq t \leq 1.$$

Stated quite simply, a subset of $\mathbf{R}^n$ is convex if the line segment connecting any two points in the subset also lies entirely within the subset.

EXAMPLE 10.

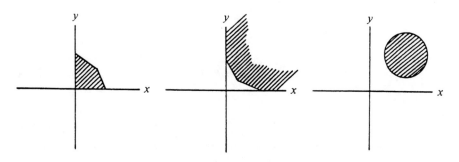

Convex sets in $\mathbf{R}^2$.

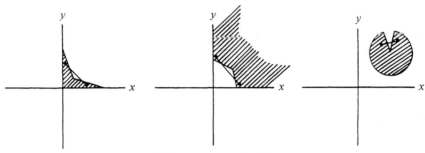

Nonconvex sets in $\mathbf{R}^2$.

Definition 11. The set of points $(x_1, x_2, \ldots, x_n) \in \mathbf{R}^n$ satisfying an equation of the form

$$a_1 x_1 + a_2 x_2 + \cdots + a_n x_n = b$$

is said to be a *hyperplane* of $\mathbf{R}^n$. The set of points $(x_1, x_2, \ldots, x_n) \in \mathbf{R}^n$ satisfying an inequality of the form

$$a_1 x_1 + a_2 x_2 + \cdots + a_n x_n \leq b$$

or

$$a_1 x_1 + a_2 x_2 + \cdots + a_n x_n \geq b$$

is said to be a *closed half-space* of $\mathbf{R}^n$.

EXAMPLE 12. (i) A hyperplane in $\mathbf{R}^1$ is the set of points x_1 satisfying an equation of the form $a_1 x_1 = b$. If a_1 is nonzero, this set is simply the point b/a_1 in $\mathbf{R}^1$ and the closed half-space $a_1 x_1 \leq b$ or $a_1 x_1 \geq b$ is closed ray in $\mathbf{R}^1$.

(ii) A hyperplane in $\mathbf{R}^2$ is the set of points (x_1, x_2) satisfying an equation of the form $a_1 x_1 + a_2 x_2 = b$. If one of a_1 or a_2 is nonzero, this set is a line in $\mathbf{R}^2$ and the closed half-space $a_1 x_1 + a_2 x_2 \leq b$ or $a_1 x_1 + a_2 x_2 \geq b$ is a closed half-plane in $\mathbf{R}^2$.

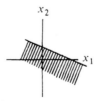

(iii) A hyperplane in $\mathbf{R}^3$ is the set of points (x_1, x_2, x_3) satisfying an equation of the form $a_1 x_1 + a_2 x_2 + a_3 x_3 = b$. If one of a_1, a_2, or a_3 is nonzero, this set is a plane in $\mathbf{R}^3$ and the closed half-space $a_1 x_1 + a_2 x_2 + a_3 x_3 \leq b$ or $a_1 x_1 + a_2 x_2 + a_3 x_3 \geq b$ is a closed half-space in $\mathbf{R}^3$ in the usual sense.

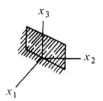

The concept of a hyperplane is an extension of the usual geometric notion of a plane to higher dimensions. A closed half-space is thus all points "lying on one side or the other" of a hyperplane including the hyperplane itself. One could also define the concept of an open half-space (where the boundary hyperplane is not included) by substituting strict inequalities for the weak inequalities in Definition 11. We will have no need for open half-spaces in this book.

The importance of closed half-spaces for linear programming may now be made clear. Since each constraint of a canonical maximization or a canonical minimization linear programming problem describes a closed half-space and since the constraint set of the problem is the intersection of the solution sets of its constraints, we have that the constraint set of a canonical maximization or a canonical minimization linear programming problem is an intersection of closed half-spaces. More is, in fact, true.

Theorem 13. *The constraint set of a canonical maximization or a canonical minimization linear programming problem is convex. Such a set is said to be a* polyhedral convex set.

"Polyhedral" refers to the fact that the boundaries of the constraint set are hyperplanes. In $\mathbf{R}^2$, the boundaries would be lines; in $\mathbf{R}^3$, the boundaries would be planes.

EXAMPLE 14.

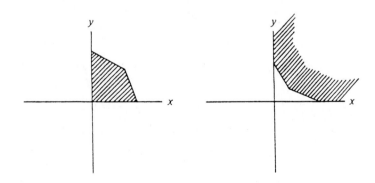

Polyhedral convex sets in $\mathbf{R}^2$.

Can you give an example of a convex set in $\mathbf{R}^2$ that is *not* a polyhedral convex set?

Intuitively, there is a difference between the two polyhedral convex sets in Example 14 above. The first set is bounded on all sides by lines whereas the second set is unbounded. We now make these differences precise for arbitrary polyhedral convex sets.

Definition 15. Let $\mathbf{x} = (x_1, x_2, \ldots, x_n) \in \mathbf{R}^n$. The *norm* of $\mathbf{x}$, denoted $\|\mathbf{x}\|$, is

$$\|\mathbf{x}\| = \sqrt{x_1^2 + x_2^2 + \cdots + x_n^2}.$$

Note that the norm of a point in $\mathbf{R}^n$ is the usual Euclidean distance of that point from the origin.

Definition 16. Let $r \geq 0$. The set of points $\mathbf{x} = (x_1, x_2, \ldots, x_n) \in \mathbf{R}^n$ such that

$$\|\mathbf{x}\| \leq r$$

is said to be the *closed ball of radius r centered at the origin.*

EXAMPLE 17. (i) The closed ball of radius 0 centered at the origin in $\mathbf{R}^n$ is simply the origin of $\mathbf{R}^n$.
(ii) The closed ball of radius $r > 0$ centered at the origin in $\mathbf{R}^1$ is a line segment including the endpoints.

$$\overset{}{\underset{\hspace{1em}r\hspace{1em}0\hspace{1em}r}{\rule{0pt}{0pt}}} \;\; x_1$$

(iii) The closed ball of radius $r > 0$ centered at the origin in $\mathbf{R}^2$ is a circle and its interior.

(iv) The closed ball of radius $r > 0$ centered at the origin in $\mathbf{R}^3$ is a sphere and its interior.

The concept of a closed ball of radius r centered at the origin is an extension of the usual geometric notion of a sphere centered at the origin and its interior to higher dimensions. One could also define the concept of an open ball of radius r centered at the origin by substituting strict inequality for the weak inequality in Definition 16. We will have no need for open balls of radius r centered at the origin in this book.

Definition 18. A subset S of $\mathbf{R}^n$ is said to be *bounded* if there exists $r \geq 0$ such that every element of S is contained in the closed ball of radius r centered at the origin. A subset S of $\mathbf{R}^n$ is said to be *unbounded* if it is not bounded.

EXAMPLE 19.

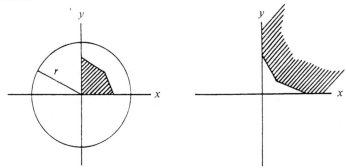

Bounded and unbounded polyhedral convex subsets in $\mathbf{R}^2$ (respectively).

We need but one more geometric definition before our main theorems.

Definition 20. Let S be a convex set in $\mathbf{R}^n$. $\mathbf{e} \in S$ is said to be an *extreme point* of S if there do not exist $\mathbf{x}, \mathbf{y} \in S$ and t with $0 < t < 1$ such that

$$\mathbf{e} = t\mathbf{x} + (1 - t)\mathbf{y}.$$

Recall that $t\mathbf{x} + (1 - t)\mathbf{y}$, $0 \leq t \leq 1$, is the line segment between $\mathbf{x}$ and $\mathbf{y}$ inclusive. Since $t = 0$ implies that

$$t\mathbf{x} + (1 - t)\mathbf{y} = \mathbf{y}$$

and $t = 1$ implies that

$$t\mathbf{x} + (1 - t)\mathbf{y} = \mathbf{x},$$

we have that $t\mathbf{x} + (1 - t)\mathbf{y}$, $0 < t < 1$, is the line segment between $\mathbf{x}$ and $\mathbf{y}$ not including the endpoints $\mathbf{x}$ and $\mathbf{y}$. Hence, a point $\mathbf{e} \in S$ is an extreme point of S if no line segment within S contains $\mathbf{e}$ except at an endpoint. Extreme points in linear programming correspond to "corners" of polyhedral convex sets; however, as the third diagram below shows, such an intuitive definition in general is false.

EXAMPLE 21.

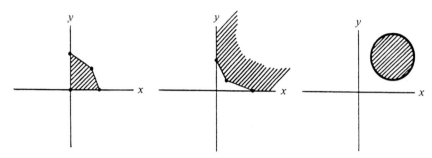

Extreme points of convex sets in $\mathbf{R}^2$ (in bold).

Can you give an example of a convex set in $\mathbf{R}^2$ that has *no* extreme points?
We now state the theorems which will yield a geometrical method for solving linear programming problems.

Theorem 22. *If the constraint set S of a canonical maximization or a canonical minimization linear programming problem is bounded, then the maximum or minimum value of the objective function is attained at an extreme point of S.*

Theorem 23. (i) *If the constraint set S of a canonical maximization linear programming problem is unbounded and there exists $M \in \mathbf{R}$ such that the objective function f satisfies $f(x_1, x_2, \ldots, x_n) \leq M$ for all $(x_1, x_2, \ldots, x_n) \in S$, i.e., f is bounded above (by M), then the maximum value of the objective function is attained at an extreme point of S.*
(ii) *If the constraint set S of a canonical minimization linear programming problem is unbounded and there exists $M \in \mathbf{R}$ such that the objective function g satisfies $g(x_1, x_2, \ldots, x_n) \geq M$ for all $(x_1, x_2, \ldots, x_n) \in S$, i.e., g is bounded below (by M), then the minimum value of the objective function is attained at an extreme point of S.*

We note here that Theorem 22 and Theorem 23 only assert the existence of optimal solutions at extreme points of the constraint set; there may be optimal solutions at points of the constraint set other than extreme points (see Exercise 4).

The existence of the real number M is crucial in Theorem 23 above. For assume that such an M does not exist in (i) of Theorem 23, i.e., f is not bounded above. Then, no matter what real number M is specified, we can find a point $(x_1, x_2, \ldots, x_n)$ of the constraint set S such that $f(x_1, x_2, \ldots, x_n) > M$. But this means that f never attains a maximum value on this set since we can choose larger and larger M. One can employ a similar argument in (ii) of Theorem 23. In such cases, the linear programming problem is said to be *unbounded*. (This should note be confused with the concept of an unbounded constraint set which is different. See Exercise 9.) Unboundedness is a type of pathology in linear programming problems that we will encounter and deal more thoroughly with later.

§4. The Two Examples Revisited

Theorem 22 and Theorem 23 of §3 allow us to solve (1) and (3) of §1.

EXAMPLE 1 (Continued). Recall the profit maximization example (1) and its constraint set (2) from §1:

$$\text{Maximize} \quad P(x, y) = 30x + 50y$$
$$\text{subject to} \quad 2x + y \leq 8$$
$$x + 2y \leq 10 \tag{1}$$
$$x, y \geq 0$$

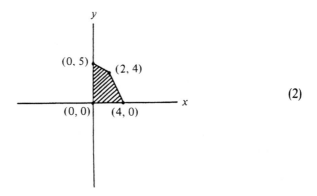

$$(2)$$

Since the constraint set (2) is bounded, Theorem 22 implies that the maximum value of $P(x, y)$ is attained at an extreme point in (2), namely at $(0, 0), (4, 0), (0, 5)$, or $(2, 4)$. Hence we merely need to evaluate P at each of these points and note which evaluation is maximum.

(x, y)	$P(x, y) = 30x + 50y$
$(0, 0)$	0
$(4, 0)$	120
$(0, 5)$	250
$(2, 4)$	260

The maximum is attained at the point $(2, 4)$. Hence the appliance company should manufacture 2 heaters and 4 air conditioners per day so as to obtain a maximum profit of $260 per day.

EXAMPLE 2 (Continued). Recall the cost minimization example (3) and its constraint set (4) from §1:

$$\text{Minimize} \quad C(x, y) = 300x + 500y$$
$$\text{subject to} \quad 20x + 40y \geq 1000 \tag{3}$$
$$25x + 20y \geq 800$$
$$x, y \geq 0$$

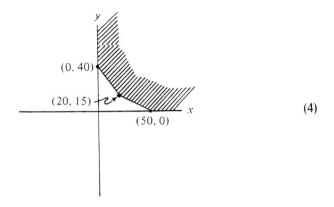

(4)

Since the constraint set (4) is unbounded, before we use Theorem 23(ii), we must show that C is bounded below, i.e., we must find $M \in \mathbf{R}$ such that $C(x, y) = 300x + 500y \geq M$ whenever (x, y) is a point of the shaded region of (4). Now any point of this shaded region, when substituted in $C(x, y)$, will give a positive cost. Hence we may take, for example, $M = 0$. (There are infinitely many different M's that one could choose here; for example, any negative M will work.) Then Theorem 23(ii) implies that the minimum value of $C(x, y)$ is attained at an extreme point in (4), namely at $(50, 0)$, $(0, 40)$, or $(20, 15)$. Hence we merely need to evaluate C at each of these points and note which evaluation is minimum.

(x, y)	$C(x, y) = 300x + 500y$
$(50, 0)$	15000
$(0, 40)$	20000
$(20, 15)$	13500

The minimum is attained at the point $(20, 15)$. Hence the oil company should operate refinery A for 20 days and refinery B for 15 days so as to attain a minimum cost of $\$13500$.

§5. A Geometric Method for Linear Programming

The observant reader will have noticed several limitations of the procedure developed in Theorem 22 and Theorem 23 for solving linear programming problems. One such limitation is that Theorem 22 and Theorem 23 require a knowledge of the extreme points of the constraint set of the problem being considered. This knowledge may be difficult to obtain in some cases. For example, consider the linear programming problem

$$\text{Maximize} \quad f(x, y, z) = 2x + y - 2z$$
$$\text{subject to} \quad x + y + z \leq 1$$
$$y + 4z \leq 2 \tag{5}$$
$$x, y, z \geq 0.$$

Here, the bounding surfaces of the constraint set are planes and, although a visualization of the constraint set is possible, it is more difficult in this three-dimensional case than in the two-dimensional constraint sets of (2) and (4). When we then move to higher dimensions and try to visualize the constraint set of a four-dimensional problem such as

$$\text{Maximize} \quad f(x, y, z, w) = 2x - y + z - w$$
$$\text{subject to} \quad x + w \leq 1$$
$$x - y \leq 2 \tag{6}$$
$$z - 2w \leq 3$$
$$x, y, z, w \geq 0,$$

we find extreme difficulty. Can we somehow find the extreme points of the constraint set of a linear programming problem without actually graphing the constraint set? The answer is YES and we illustrate the method on (5).

The bounding surfaces of the constraint set of (5) are the planes $x + y + z = 1$, $y + 4z = 2$, $x = 0$, $y = 0$, and $z = 0$. Taking these five equations three at a time and solving the resulting systems of linear equations, we obtain

$$\begin{bmatrix} x + y + z = 1 \\ y + 4z = 2 \\ x = 0 \end{bmatrix} \Rightarrow (x, y, z) = (0, 2/3, 1/3)$$

$$\begin{bmatrix} x + y + z = 1 \\ y + 4z = 2 \\ y = 0 \end{bmatrix} \Rightarrow (x, y, z) = (1/2, 0, 1/2)$$

$$\begin{bmatrix} x + y + z = 1 \\ y + 4z = 2 \\ z = 0 \end{bmatrix} \Rightarrow (x, y, z) = (-1, 2, 0)$$

$$\begin{bmatrix} x + y + z = 1 \\ x = 0 \\ y = 0 \end{bmatrix} \Rightarrow (x, y, z) = (0, 0, 1)$$

$$\begin{bmatrix} x + y + z = 1 \\ x = 0 \\ z = 0 \end{bmatrix} \Rightarrow (x, y, z) = (0, 1, 0)$$

$$\begin{bmatrix} x + y + z = 1 \\ y = 0 \\ z = 0 \end{bmatrix} \Rightarrow (x, y, z) = (1, 0, 0)$$

$$\begin{bmatrix} y + 4z = 2 \\ x = 0 \\ y = 0 \end{bmatrix} \Rightarrow (x, y, z) = (0, 0, 1/2)$$

$$\begin{bmatrix} y + 4z = 2 \\ x = 0 \\ z = 0 \end{bmatrix} \Rightarrow (x, y, z) = (0, 2, 0)$$

$$\begin{bmatrix} y + 4z = 2 \\ y = 0 \\ z = 0 \end{bmatrix} \Rightarrow \text{INCONSISTENT}$$

$$\begin{bmatrix} x = 0 \\ y = 0 \\ z = 0 \end{bmatrix} \Rightarrow (x, y, z) = (0, 0, 0).$$

Some of these points may violate one or more of the original constraints of (5). We tabulate each candidate point along with the constraints of (5) violated (if any):

Candidate point	Constraint(s) of (5) violated
$(0, 2/3, 1/3)$	None
$(1/2, 0, 1/2)$	None
$(-1, 2, 0)$	$x \geq 0$
$(0, 0, 1)$	$y + 4z \leq 2$
$(0, 1, 0)$	None
$(1, 0, 0)$	None
$(0, 0, 1/2)$	None
$(0, 2, 0)$	$x + y + z \leq 1$
$(0, 0, 0)$	None

The extreme points of the constraint set of (5) are precisely those points above that violated none of the original constraints. We can verify this by actually graphing the constraint set of (5):

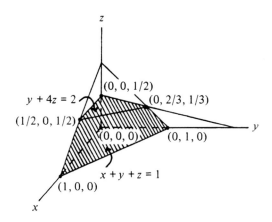

Note that an upper bound for the number of extreme point candidates in this example is given by

$$\binom{5}{3} = \frac{5!}{3!\,2!} = 10$$

since there are five constraints (considered as equations) and since three equations in three unknowns are needed to uniquely determine an ordered triple. Of these 10 candidates, only 6 were actually extreme points of the desired constraint set.

We now seemingly have a geometric method in hand for solving linear programming problems. Unfortunately, there is a snag in our method at present. The snag is alluded to in Theorem 23, namely that a knowledge of the constraint set of a canonical linear programming problem is *not* sufficient to determine an optimal solution for the problem if the constraint set is unbounded. In such a problem, we must additionally show that the objective function on this set is bounded above in the maximization case or bounded below in the minimization case. But how do we know whether or not the constraint set of a linear programming problem is unbounded without graphing it?

Proving that the constraint set of a canonical linear programming problem is bounded or unbounded by a purely analytical argument is largely problem-dependent and may be quite difficult. The crux of such an analysis is to see whether or not one (or more) of the variables of the problem can assume arbitrarily large values and still satisfy all of the constraints. If so, the corresponding constraint set is unbounded provided it is nonempty; other-wise, the constraint set is bounded. (A linear programming problem having an empty constraint set is said to be *infeasible* since it has no feasible solutions. Infeasibility is a type of pathology in linear programming problems that we will encounter and deal more thoroughly with later.) In (5), we see that the main constraint $x + y + z \leq 1$ along with the nonnegativity of x, y, and z implies that $x \leq 1, y \leq 1$, and $z \leq 1$. Hence the corresponding constraint set is bounded (as the preceding graph verifies). In contrast, we see that the modified linear programming problem

$$\begin{aligned}
\text{Maximize} \quad & f(x, y, z) = 2x + y - 2z \\
\text{subject to} \quad & y + 4z \leq 2 \\
& x, y, z \geq 0
\end{aligned} \tag{7}$$

has an unbounded constraint set since the constraint set is nonempty (for example, $(x, y, z) = (0, 0, 0)$ is in the constraint set) and the variable x can grow arbitrarily large and still satisfy all of the constraints.

Now, if the constraint set of a canonical linear programming problem is unbounded, it remains to show that the objective function on this set is bounded above in the maximization case or bounded below in the minimi-zation case. Again, such as analysis is largely problem-dependent and may be quite difficult. We illustrate with analyses for (6) and (7).

In (6), the constraint set is nonempty (for example, $(x, y, z, w) = (0, 0, 0, 0)$ is in the constraint set). Let $x = 0$. Then any nonnegative value of y satisfies all of the constraints. Hence the constraint set is unbounded since y can assume arbitrarily large values and still satisfy all of the constraints. Furthermore,

$$f(x, y, z, w) = 2x - y + z - w = (x + w) + (x - y) + (z - 2w) \leq 1 + 2 + 3 = 6,$$

i.e., the objective function is bounded above by 6 on the constraint set. (Of course, there are infinitely many upper bounds here; for example, any real number greater than 6 will work.) Hence, an optimal solution of (6) is attained at an extreme point of the constraint set by Theorem 23(i).

In (7), we have already noted that the constraint set is unbounded since the constraint set is nonempty and $x \to \infty$ does not violate any of the constraints. Now, fixing any nonnegative values of y and z with $y + 4z \leq 2$ for the moment, we see that $x \to \infty$ implies that $f(x, y, z) = 2x + y - 2z \to \infty$ and hence the objective function of (7) is not bounded above on the constraint set.

We summarize a general geometric method for linear programming. Given a canonical maximization or a canonical minimization linear programming problem having m main constraints and n nonnegativity constraints (see the canonical forms for linear programming problems in §2), the upper bound for the number of extreme point candidates is given by

$$\binom{m + n}{n} = \frac{(m + n)!}{m! \, n!}.$$

These candidates are determined by considering the $m + n$ constraints as equations and solving the systems of linear equations obtained from these constraints by taking the equations n at a time. In general, only a portion of these candidates will then satisfy all of the original constraints of the problem. One must also determine whether the constraint set is bounded or unbounded. If the constraint set is bounded, Theorem 22 may be used directly to solve the problem by testing each of the extreme points in the objective function. If the constraint set is unbounded, one must additionally show that the objective function on this set is bounded above (in the maximization case) or bounded below (in the minimization case) before Theorem 23 is applied in the same manner. One should generally determine the boundedness or unboundedness of the constraint set and, in the latter case, the bounded above or bounded below condition on the objective function *before* finding the extreme points as described above. For if the constraint set is unbounded and the objective function on this set is not bounded above (in the maximization case) or not bounded below (in the minimization case), then the linear programming problem is unbounded and no extreme points need be found at all!

§6. Concluding Remarks

The reader has no doubt realized by now that the geometric procedure discussed in §5 is cumbersome to use as a general technique. There are several disadvantages inherent in solving canonical linear programming problems geometrically. Real-life linear programming problems typically involve hundreds of variables. Hence the geometric visualization of constraint sets is usually impossible. If we rely on the geometric method of §5, we have

$$\binom{m+n}{n} = \frac{(m+n)!}{m!\,n!}$$

as an upper bound for the number of extreme point candidates to be found and tested. This number is generally prohibitively large. For example, if $m = 15$ and $n = 10$ (a relatively small linear programming problem by industrial standards), we have

$$\binom{m+n}{n} = \binom{25}{10} > 3200000;$$

furthermore, finding just one extreme point candidate involves solving a system of 10 linear equations in 10 unknowns! In addition, we need analyses to determine whether the constraint set of the problem is bounded or unbounded and, in the latter case, whether the objective function on this set is bounded above or bounded below. There must be a better way!

Fortunately, there is a method, the simplex algorithm, capable of finding optimal solutions to linear programming problems without finding and testing large numbers of extreme point candidates. In addition, the algorithm will detect pathological behavior such as empty constraint sets and objective functions that are not bounded above or bounded below.

EXERCISES

1. Draw and shade appropriate regions in $\mathbf{R}^2$ as described below. All regions are to be constrained to the first quadrant of the Cartesian plane.

   a. a bounded polyhedral convex subset
   b. an unbounded polyhedral convex subset
   c. a bounded nonconvex subset
   d. an unbounded nonconvex subset
   e. a convex subset that is not a polyhedral convex subset
   f. a convex subset having no extreme points
   g. a polyhedral convex subset having no extreme points
   h. a bounded polyhedral convex subset having exactly one extreme point
   i. an unbounded polyhedral convex subset having exactly one extreme point
   j. an unbounded convex subset having infinitely many extreme points

2. Convert each of the linear programming problems below to canonical form as in Definition 3. [Note: The conversion of a linear programming problem to canonical form will be crucial for the simplex algorithm to be discussed in Chapter 2.]

   a. Maximize $f(x, y) = x + y$
      subject to $x - y \leq 3$
      $2x + y \leq 12$
      $0 \leq x \leq 4$
      $0 \leq y \leq 6$

  b. Minimize $g(x, y) = x - y$
     subject to $2x - y \geq -1$
                  $0 \leq x \leq 2$
                  $y \geq 0$

  c. Maximize $f(x, y) = -2y - x$
     subject to $2x - y \geq -1$
                  $3y - x \leq 8$
                  $x, y \geq 0$

  d. Minimize $g(x, y, z) = x - 2y - z$
     subject to $10x + 5y + 2z \leq 1000$
                  $2y + 4z \leq 800$
                  $x, y, z \geq 0$

3. Solve each of the problems below by sketching the constraint set and applying Theorem 22 or Theorem 23.

  a. Maximize $f(x, y) = 5x + 2y$
     subject to $x + 3y \leq 14$
                  $2x + y \leq 8$
                  $x, y \geq 0$

  b. Minimize $g(x, y) = 5x + 2y$
     subject to $x + 3y \geq 14$
                  $2x + y \geq 8$
                  $x, y \geq 0$

  c. Exercise 2a above
  d. Exercise 2b above
  e. Exercise 2c above

  f. Maximize $f(x, y, z) = x - 2y - z$
     subject to $10x + 5y + 2z \leq 1000$
                  $2y + 4z \leq 800$
                  $x, y, z \geq 0$

  g. Exercise 2d above
  h. A publishing firm prints two magazines, the Monitor and the Recorder, each in units of one hundred. Each unit of the Monitor requires 1 unit of ink, 3 units of paper, and 4 hours of printing press time to print; each unit of the Recorder requires 2 units of ink, 3 units of paper, and 5 hours of printing press time to print. The firm has 20 units of ink, 40 units of paper, and 60 hours of printing press time available. If the profit realized upon sale is $200 per unit of the Monitor and $300 per unit of the Recorder, how many units of each magazine should the firm print so as to maximize profits?
  i. A furniture factory owns two lumber operations. The first lumber operation produces 1/2 ton of usable walnut, 1 ton of usable oak, and 1 ton of usable pine per day. The second lumber operation produces 1 ton of usable walnut, 1 ton of usable oak, and 1/2 ton of usable pine per day. The factory requires at least 10 tons of walnut, 15 tons of oak, and 10 tons of pine. If it costs $300 per day to run the first lumber operation and $350 per day to run the second lumber operation, how many days should each operation be run so as to minimize costs?
  j. A drug company sells three different formulations of vitamin complex and

mineral complex. The first formulation consists entirely of vitamin complex and sells for $1 per unit. The second formulation consists of 3/4 of a unit of vitamin complex and 1/4 of a unit of mineral complex and sells for $2 per unit. The third formulation consists of 1/2 of a unit of each of the complexes and sells for $3 per unit. If the company has 100 units of vitamin complex and 75 units of mineral complex available, how many units of each formulation should the company produce so as to maximize sales revenue?

4. a. Prove that there are infinitely many optimal solutions for Exercise 3j above, only two of which occur at extreme points of the constraint set. [Hint: Find two distinct optimal solutions occurring at extreme points and show that any point on the line segment connecting these points is an optimal solution.]
   b. Graph all optimal solutions of part a on the constraint set diagram of Exercise 3j.

5. Prove (in general) that any point on the line segment connecting two distinct optimal solutions of a canonical linear programming problem is an optimal solution. Deduce that any canonical linear programming problem has either zero, one, or infinitely many optimal solutions.

6. Solve (5) of §5.

7. Find the upper bound for the number of extreme point candidates in (6) of §5.

8. Consider the linear programming problem below:

$$\text{Minimize} \quad g(x, y, z, w) = x - 2y + 3z - 4w$$
$$\text{subject to} \quad -5x - 4y - 3z - 2w \geq -1$$
$$x, y, z, w \geq 0.$$

   a. Show that the constraint set is bounded.
   b. Find all extreme point candidates by considering the five constraints as equations and solving the $\binom{5}{4}$ systems of linear equations obtained from these constraints by taking them four at a time.
   c. Solve the linear programming problem by applying Theorem 22.

9. Consider the linear programming problem below:

$$\text{Minimize} \quad g(x, y, z, w) = x - 2y + 3z - 4w$$
$$\text{subject to} \quad x + 2y + 3z + 4w \geq 5$$
$$-y - 2w \geq -1$$
$$x, y, z, w \geq 0.$$

   a. Show that the constraint set is unbounded.
   b. Show that the objective function is bounded below on the constraint set.
   c. Find all extreme point candidates by considering the six constraints as equations and solving the $\binom{6}{4}$ systems of linear equations obtained from these constraints by taking them four at a time.
   d. Solve the linear programming problem by applying Theorem 23.

10. Show that the linear programming problem

$$\begin{aligned}
\text{Minimize} \quad & g(x, y) = x - 3y \\
\text{subject to} \quad & x + y \geq 2 \\
& x \quad 2y \leq 0 \\
& y - 2x \leq 1 \\
& x, y \geq 0
\end{aligned}$$

is unbounded. [Hint: Graph the constraint set and show that $g(x, y) \to -\infty$ as $y \to \infty$ along the line $x - 2y = 0$.]

11. Label each of the following statements TRUE or FALSE and justify your answers.

  a. Any unbounded linear programming problem has an unbounded constraint set.

  b. Any linear programming problem having an unbounded constraint set is unbounded.

12. Show that the linear programming problem

$$\begin{aligned}
\text{Maximize} \quad & f(x, y) = 3x + 2y \\
\text{subject to} \quad & 2x - y \leq -1 \\
& x - 2y \geq 0 \\
& x, y \geq 0
\end{aligned}$$

is infeasible.

CHAPTER 2

The Simplex Algorithm

§0. Introduction

In this chapter, we present the simplex algorithm, an effective method for solving the canonical maximization and canonical minimization linear programming problems of 1§2. The simplex algorithm was developed in the 1940's by George B. Dantzig. We will employ certain refinements in Dantzig's original technique developed in the 1960's by A.W. Tucker. In particular, we will record our linear programming problems in what is called a Tucker tableau, a more compact version of the original Dantzig tableau and considerably easier to use.

§1. Canonical Slack Forms for Linear Programming Problems; Tucker Tableaus

Consider the canonical maximization linear programming problem of 1§2:

$$\begin{aligned}
\text{Maximize} \quad & f(x_1, x_2, \ldots, x_n) = c_1 x_1 + c_2 x_2 + \cdots + c_n x_n - d \\
\text{subject to} \quad & a_{11} x_1 + a_{12} x_2 + \cdots + a_{1n} x_n \leq b_1 \\
& a_{21} x_1 + a_{22} x_2 + \cdots + a_{2n} x_n \leq b_2 \\
& \qquad\qquad\qquad \vdots \\
& a_{m1} x_1 + a_{m2} x_2 + \cdots + a_{mn} x_n \leq b_m \\
& x_1, x_2, \ldots, x_n \geq 0.
\end{aligned} \tag{1}$$

Let $t_1, t_2, \ldots, t_m \geq 0$ be such that

$$\begin{aligned}
a_{11} x_1 + a_{12} x_2 + \cdots + a_{1n} x_n + t_1 &= b_1 \\
a_{21} x_1 + a_{22} x_2 + \cdots + a_{2n} x_n + t_2 &= b_2 \\
&\ \ \vdots \\
a_{m1} x_1 + a_{m2} x_2 + \cdots + a_{mn} x_n + t_m &= b_m.
\end{aligned}$$

Then

$$a_{11}x_1 + a_{12}x_2 + \cdots + a_{1n}x_n - b_1 = -t_1$$
$$a_{21}x_1 + a_{22}x_2 + \cdots + a_{2n}x_n - b_2 = -t_2$$
$$\vdots$$
$$a_{m1}x_1 + a_{m2}x_2 + \cdots + a_{mn}x_n - b_m = -t_m$$

and we can reformulate (1) as

$$\text{Maximize} \quad f(x_1, x_2, \ldots, x_n) = c_1 x_1 + c_2 x_2 + \cdots + c_n x_n - d$$
$$\text{subject to} \quad a_{11}x_1 + a_{12}x_2 + \cdots + a_{1n}x_n - b_1 = -t_1$$
$$a_{21}x_1 + a_{22}x_2 + \cdots + a_{2n}x_n - b_2 = -t_2$$
$$\vdots \tag{2}$$
$$a_{m1}x_1 + a_{m2}x_2 + \cdots + a_{mn}x_n - b_m = -t_m$$
$$t_1, t_2, \ldots, t_m \geqq 0$$
$$x_1 x_2, \ldots, x_n \geqq 0.$$

Similarly, consider the canonical minimization linear programming problem of 1§2:

$$\text{Minimize} \quad g(x_1, x_2, \ldots, x_n) = c_1 x_1 + c_2 x_2 + \cdots + c_n x_n - d$$
$$\text{subject to} \quad a_{11}x_1 + a_{12}x_2 + \cdots + a_{1n}x_n \geqq b_1$$
$$a_{21}x_1 + a_{22}x_2 + \cdots + a_{2n}x_n \geqq b_2$$
$$\vdots \tag{3}$$
$$a_{m1}x_1 + a_{m2}x_2 + \cdots + a_{mn}x_n \geqq b_m$$
$$x_1, x_2, \ldots, x_n \geqq 0.$$

Let $t_1, t_2, \ldots, t_m \geqq 0$ be such that

$$a_{11}x_1 + a_{12}x_2 + \cdots + a_{1n}x_n = b_1 + t_1$$
$$a_{21}x_1 + a_{22}x_2 + \cdots + a_{2n}x_n = b_2 + t_2$$
$$\vdots$$
$$a_{m1}x_1 + a_{m2}x_2 + \cdots + a_{mn}x_n = b_m + t_m.$$

Then

$$a_{11}x_1 + a_{12}x_2 + \cdots + a_{1n}x_n - b_1 = t_1$$
$$a_{21}x_1 + a_{22}x_2 + \cdots + a_{2n}x_n - b_2 = t_2$$
$$\vdots$$
$$a_{m1}x_1 + a_{m2}x_2 + \cdots + a_{mn}x_n - b_m = t_m$$

and we can reformulate (3) as

$$\text{Minimize} \quad g(x_1, x_2, \ldots, x_n) = c_1 x_1 + c_2 x_2 + \cdots + c_n x_n - d$$
$$\text{subject to} \quad a_{11}x_1 + a_{12}x_2 + \cdots + a_{1n}x_n - b_1 = t_1$$
$$a_{21}x_1 + a_{22}x_2 + \cdots + a_{2n}x_n - b_2 = t_2$$
$$\vdots \tag{4}$$
$$a_{m1}x_1 + a_{m2}x_2 + \cdots + a_{mn}x_n - b_m = t_m$$
$$t_1, t_2, \ldots, t_m \geqq 0$$
$$x_1, x_2, \ldots, x_n \geqq 0.$$

Definition 1. The linear programming problems (2) and (4) above are said to be *canonical slack maximization and canonical slack minimization linear programming problems* respectively. The variables $t_1, t_2, \ldots, t_m$ are said to be *slack variables*.

Slack variables are termed as such because they produce equalities from inequalities—they, in effect, "take up the slack" on one side of the inequality in each type of linear programming problem. We now develop a more concise notation for these canonical slack linear programming problems.

Definition 2. The tables

x_1	x_2	$\cdots$	x_n	-1	
a_{11}	a_{12}	$\cdots$	a_{1n}	b_1	$= -t_1$
a_{21}	a_{22}	$\cdots$	a_{2n}	b_2	$= -t_2$
$\vdots$	$\vdots$		$\vdots$	$\vdots$	$\vdots$
a_{m1}	a_{m2}	$\cdots$	a_{mn}	b_m	$= -t_m$
c_1	c_2	$\cdots$	c_n	d	$= f$

and

	x_1	a_{11}	a_{21}	$\cdots$	a_{m1}	c_1
	x_2	a_{12}	a_{22}	$\cdots$	a_{m2}	c_2
	$\vdots$	$\vdots$	$\vdots$	$\vdots$	$\vdots$	$\vdots$
	x_n	a_{1n}	a_{2n}	$\cdots$	a_{mn}	c_n
	-1	b_1	b_2	$\cdots$	b_m	d
		$= t_1$	$= t_2$	$\cdots$	$= t_m$	$= g$

are said to be *Tucker tableaus* or simply *tableaus* of the canonical slack maximization and the canonical slack minimization linear programming problems respectively. The variables to the north of the maximum tableau and to the west of the minimum tableau are said to be *independent variables* or *nonbasic variables*. The variables to the east of the maximum tableau and to the south of the minimum tableau are said to be *dependent variables* or *basic variables*.

In this book, we will use the terms independent and dependent rather than nonbasic and basic respectively.

Note how the main constraints of each of the canonical slack linear programming problems are recorded in the corresponding Tucker tableaus. The coefficients of the main constraints of (2) appear as rows of the maximum tableau. The ith main constraint may be reconstructed from the ith row of coefficients by multiplying each coefficient by its corresponding independent variable (or multiplying by -1 in the case of b_i), adding all such products, and setting the result equal to the corresponding dependent variable. The objective function of the problem is recorded by the last row of the maximum tableau in the same manner. Similarly, the main constraints and objective function of (4) are recorded in the minimum tableau above as columns instead of rows. (There is a reason for this difference which will be made clear in Chapter 4.) The reason for the choice of minus sign in front of the constant d in the problems (2) and (4) above is now seen to be one of convenience. Note that the nonnegativity constraints of a canonical slack maximization or a canonical slack minimization linear programming problem are *not* recorded in the corresponding Tucker tableaus. The nonnegativity of all variables in a linear programming problem is assumed in the remainder of this chapter. The consequences of relaxing this assumption will be investigated in Chapter 3.

§2. An Example: Profit Maximization

In this section, we present and completely solve a typical canonical maximization linear programming problem. The purpose of this discussion is twofold. First, we will illustrate the concepts just defined in §1. Secondly, and more importantly, our method of solution will correspond to the steps taken by the simplex algorithm to solve the problem. As we proceed toward the solution, these steps will be straightforward but somewhat tedious. For now, attempt only to understand the steps and do not worry about the tedium of the calculations. In §3 of this chapter, we will see that the calculations associated with the simplex algorithm solution of a canonical linear programming problem correspond to easy transformations on Tucker tableaus. We now present our problem.

EXAMPLE 3. An electrical firm manufactures circuit boards in two configurations, say configuration #1 and configuration #2. Each circuit board in configuration #1 requires 1 A component, 2 B components, and 2 C components; each circuit board in configuration #2 requires 2 A components, 2 B components, and 1 C component. The firm has 20 A components, 30 B components, and 25 C components available. If the profit realized upon sale is $200 per circuit board in configuration #1 and $150 per circuit board in configuration #2, how many circuit boards of each configuration should the electrical firm manufacture so as to maximize profits?

Put
$$x_1 = \text{\# of circuit boards in configuration \#1}$$
$$x_2 = \text{\# of circuit boards in configuration \#2.}$$
Then the mathematical reformulation of the problem is

$$\begin{aligned}
\text{Maximize} \quad & P(x_1, x_2) = 200x_1 + 150x_2 \\
\text{subject to} \quad & x_1 + 2x_2 \le 20 \\
& 2x_1 + 2x_2 \le 30 \\
& 2x_1 + x_2 \le 25 \\
& x_1, x_2 \ge 0.
\end{aligned}$$

Put

$$t_A = \text{slack variable for A components}$$
$$t_B = \text{slack variable for B components}$$
$$t_C = \text{slack variable for C components.}$$

Then, from §1, the canonical slack form of the problem is

$$
\begin{aligned}
\text{Maximize} \quad & P(x_1, x_2) = 200x_1 + 150x_2 \\
\text{subject to} \quad & x_1 + 2x_2 - 20 = -t_A \\
& 2x_1 + 2x_2 - 30 = -t_B \\
& 2x_1 + x_2 - 25 = -t_C \\
& t_A, t_B, t_C, x_1, x_2 \geq 0.
\end{aligned}
\tag{5}
$$

(5) is recorded in a Tucker tableau as

x_1	x_2	-1	
1	2	20	$= -t_A$
2	2	30	$= -t_B$
2	1	25	$= -t_C$
200	150	0	$= P$

$\tag{6}$

x_1 and x_2 are independent variables in this tableau while t_A, t_B, and t_C are dependent variables.

We now begin the steps which will ultimately lead to an optimal solution for the problem. Solve the main constraint $2x_1 + x_2 - 25 = -t_C$ for x_1 to obtain

$$x_1 = -1/2t_C - 1/2x_2 + 25/2,$$

i.e.,

$$1/2t_C + 1/2x_2 - 25/2 = -x_1.$$

Now replace every occurrence of x_1 in all other equations of (5) (including the objective function) by $-1/2t_C - 1/2x_2 + 25/2$. Upon simplification, (5) becomes

$$
\begin{aligned}
\text{Maximize} \quad & P(t_C, x_2) = -100t_C + 50x_2 + 2500 \\
\text{subject to} \quad & -1/2t_C + 3/2x_2 - 15/2 = -t_A \\
& -t_C + x_2 - 5 = -t_B \\
& 1/2t_C + 1/2x_2 - 25/2 = -x_1 \\
& t_A, t_B, t_C, x_1, x_2 \geq 0
\end{aligned}
\tag{7}
$$

with corresponding tableau

t_C	x_2	-1	
$-1/2$	$3/2$	$15/2$	$= -t_A$
-1	1	5	$= -t_B$
$1/2$	$1/2$	$25/2$	$= -x_1$
-100	50	-2500	$= P$

$\tag{8}$

It is crucial at this point to notice that any feasible solution of (5) is a feasible solution of (7) and vice versa. No feasible solutions have been created or destroyed in passing from tableau (6) to tableau (8). Note also that the variables x_1 and t_C of tableau (6) have exchanged places in tableau (8), i.e., x_1, originally independent in (6), becomes dependent in (8), and t_C, originally dependent in (6), becomes independent in (8). This exchange will be important in §3.

We now repeat the above procedure with the main constraint $-t_C + x_2 - 5 = -t_B$ of (7). Solve this constraint for x_2 to obtain

$$x_2 = t_C - t_B + 5,$$

i.e.,

$$-t_C + t_B - 5 = -x_2.$$

Upon replacing every occurrence of x_2 in all other equations of (7) by $t_C - t_B + 5$, (7) becomes

$$\begin{aligned}
\text{Maximize} \quad & P(t_C, t_B) = -50t_C - 50t_B + 2750 \\
\text{subject to} \quad & t_C - 3/2t_B = -t_A \\
& -t_C + t_B - 5 = -x_2 \\
& t_C - 1/2t_B - 10 = -x_1 \\
& t_A, t_B, t_C, x_1, x_2 \geq 0
\end{aligned} \quad (9)$$

with corresponding tableau

t_C	t_B	-1	
1	$-3/2$	0	$= -t_A$
-1	1	5	$= -x_2$
1	$-1/2$	10	$= -x_1$
-50	-50	-2750	$= P$

$$(10)$$

Any feasible solution of (7) is a feasible solution of (9) and vice versa. Also, the variables x_2 and t_B of tableau (8) have exchanged places in tableau (10), x_2 going from independent in (8) to dependent in (10) and t_B going from dependent in (8) to independent in (10).

At this point, the optimal solution is contained in tableau (10) and the simplex algorithm would terminate. We will see later that there is an easy way to recognize this point of termination. For now, we content ourselves with finding the optimal solution in (10). First, examine the objective function of (10), namely

$$P(t_C, t_B) = -50t_C - 50t_B + 2750.$$

P decreases with increasing t_C and t_B; since we are trying to maximize P, we would like to set t_C and t_B equal to the smallest values possible. Since $t_C, t_B \geq 0$, we put $t_C = 0$ and $t_B = 0$ to obtain $P(0,0) = 2750$. This profit is optimal since any change in the independent variables t_C and t_B decreases expected profits.

The main constraints of (10) (see also (9)) then give $t_A = 0$, $x_2 = 5$, and $x_1 = 10$. Hence the optimal solution to our problem is

$$x_1 = 10, x_2 = 5, t_A = t_B = t_C = 0, \max P = 2750,$$

i.e., the electrical firm should manufacture 10 circuit boards in configuration #1 and 5 circuit boards in configuration #2 so as to obtain a maximum profit of \$2750. Note also that all available components will be used in this solution since $t_A = t_B = t_C = 0$ implies no "slack" materials. This phenomenon will not always happen of course. After a real-life job is completed, it is reasonable to expect a surplus of one or more of the materials used.

§3. The Pivot Transformation

Recall the sequence of tableaus from Example 3 of §2:

x_1	x_2	-1	
1	2	20	$= -t_A$
2	2	30	$= -t_B$
2	1	25	$= -t_C$
200	150	0	$= P$

$\longrightarrow$

t_C	x_2	-1	
$-1/2$	$3/2$	$15/2$	$= -t_A$
-1	1	5	$= -t_B$
$1/2$	$1/2$	$25/2$	$= -x_1$
-100	50	-2500	$= P$

$\longrightarrow$

t_C	t_B	-1	
1	$-3/2$	0	$= -t_A$
-1	1	5	$= -x_2$
1	$-1/2$	10	$= -x_1$
-50	-50	-2750	$= P$

It would be advantageous to have some direct method for obtaining the second tableau from the first and the third tableau from the second without taking an equation at each step, solving it for a certain variable, and replacing every occurrence of this variable in the other equations of the problem by the resulting expression. Fortunately, there is such a method.

The pivot transformation is the operation by which we transform a tableau into a new tableau having exactly the same feasible solutions as the original. This transformation is crucial to the simplex algorithm, the goal of this chapter. Pivoting implements the cumbersome "solve and replace every occurrence of" procedure alluded to above. Without further ado...

The Pivot Transformation for Maximum and Minimum Tableaus

(1) Choose a nonzero pivot entry p inside the tableau, but not in the objective function row/column or the -1 column/row. (Convention: Pivot entries are noted by a superscripted asterisk (*).)
(2) Interchange the variables corresponding to p's row and column, leaving the signs behind.
(3) Replace p by $1/p$.
(4) Replace every entry q in the same row as p by q/p.
(5) Replace every entry r in the same column as p by $-r/p$.
(6) Every entry s not in the same row and not in the same column as p determines a unique entry q in the same row as p and in the same column as s and a unique entry r in the same column as p and in the same row as s. Replace s by $(ps - qr)/p$.

Note that this algorithm does not tell us how to choose the pivot entry—it only tells us how to obtain a new tableau from an old tableau once a choice has been made. The question of best choices for pivot entries will ultimately be answered by the simplex algorithm. For now, we concentrate purely on the transformation itself given an initial choice of pivot entry.

EXAMPLE 4. Pivot on 5 in the canonical maximum tableau below:

$$
\begin{array}{cc|c|l}
x_1 & x_2 & -1 & \\
\hline
1 & 2 & 3 & = -t_1 \\
4 & 5 & 6 & = -t_2 \\
\hline
7 & 8 & 9 & = f
\end{array}
$$

We first implement steps (1) and (2) of the pivot transformation:

$$
\begin{array}{cc|c|l}
x_1 & t_2 & -1 & \\
\hline
1 & 2 & 3 & = -t_1 \\
4 & 5^* & 6 & = -x_2 \\
\hline
7 & 8 & 9 & = f
\end{array}
$$

By step (3), 5 gets replaced by 1/5. By step (4), 4 gets replaced by 4/5 and 6 gets replaced by 6/5. By step (5), 2 gets replaced by $-2/5$ and 8 gets replaced by $-8/5$. We now implement step (6) of the algorithm. To determine the entry replacing $s = 1$, find the entries q and r described in step (6):

$$
\begin{array}{ccc|c}
x_1 & t_2 & -1 & \\
\hline
s = 1 & r = 2 & 3 & = -t_1 \\
q = 4 & p = 5^* & 6 & = -x_2 \\
\hline
7 & 8 & 9 & = f \\
\end{array}
$$

Now 1 gets replaced by $(ps - qr)/p = ((5)(1) - (4)(2))/5 = -3/5$. Similarly, 3 gets replaced by $((5)(3) - (6)(2))/5 = 3/5$, 7 gets replaced by $((5)(7) - (4)(8))/5 = 3/5$, and 9 gets replaced by $((5)(9) - (6)(8))/5 = -3/5$. Hence, pivoting on 5 in the original tableau yields the new tableau

$$
\begin{array}{cc|c|c}
x_1 & t_2 & -1 & \\
\hline
-3/5 & -2/5 & 3/5 & = -t_1 \\
4/5 & 1/5 & 6/5 & = -x_2 \\
\hline
3/5 & -8/5 & -3/5 & = f \\
\end{array}
$$

Convince yourself of this before reading on!

As stated before, the pivot transformation algorithm simplifies the procedure of "solving and replacing every occurrence of" used in §2. One can verify by computation that the tableau transition above, namely

$$
\begin{array}{cc|c|c}
x_1 & x_2 & -1 & \\
\hline
1 & 2 & 3 & = -t_1 \\
4 & 5^* & 6 & = -t_2 \\
\hline
7 & 8 & 9 & = f \\
\end{array}
\quad\longrightarrow
$$

$$
\begin{array}{cc|c|c}
x_1 & t_2 & -1 & \\
\hline
-3/5 & -2/5 & 3/5 & = -t_1 \\
4/5 & 1/5 & 6/5 & = -x_2 \\
\hline
3/5 & -8/5 & -3/5 & = f \\
\end{array}
$$

is equivalent to solving the equation $4x_1 + 5x_2 - 6 = -t_2$ of the first tableau for x_2 and replacing every occurrence of x_2 in the other equations by the resulting expression. A more general verification appears as Exercise 10.

We should remark that, although pivoting is a powerful tool for linear programming in particular, it is also a powerful tool for the entire field of linear algebra in general. In fact, most of traditional linear algebra can be studied from the point of view of the pivot transformation. (One exception is eigenvalues.) For example, Exercise 11 illustrates how pivoting can be used to invert a matrix.

§4. An Example: Cost Minimization

In this section, we solve a canonical minimization linear programming problem using the pivot transformation of §3. We will still not see how the particular pivot entries are chosen, but such knowledge will follow in due time.

EXAMPLE 5. A feed-mix company is preparing a mixture of three feeds, say feed #1, feed #2, and feed #3. Each unit of feed #1 contains 1 gram of protein, 2 grams of fat, and costs 20 cents; each unit of feed #2 contains 2 grams of protein, 2 grams of fat, and costs 30 cents; each unit of feed #3 contains 2 grams of protein, 1 gram of fat, and costs 25 cents. If the mixture of these three feeds must contain at least 200 grams of protein and at least 150 grams of fat, how many units of each feed should the company use so as to minimize costs?

Put

$$x_1 = \text{\# of units of feed \#1}$$
$$x_2 = \text{\# of units of feed \#2}$$
$$x_3 = \text{\# of units of feed \#3}.$$

Then the mathematical reformulation of the problem is

$$\begin{aligned}
\text{Minimize} \quad & C(x_1, x_2, x_3) = 20x_1 + 30x_2 + 25x_3 \\
\text{subject to} \quad & x_1 + 2x_2 + 2x_3 \geq 200 \\
& 2x_1 + 2x_2 + x_3 \geq 150 \\
& x_1, x_2, x_3 \geq 0;
\end{aligned}$$

if

$$\begin{aligned}
t_P &= \text{slack variable for protein} \\
t_F &= \text{slack variable for fat,}
\end{aligned}$$

then the canonical slack form of the problem is

$$\begin{aligned}
\text{Minimize} \quad & C(x_1, x_2, x_3) = 20x_1 + 30x_2 + 25x_3 \\
\text{subject to} \quad & x_1 + 2x_2 + 2x_3 - 200 = t_P \\
& 2x_1 + 2x_2 + x_3 - 150 = t_F \\
& t_P, t_F, x_1, x_2, x_3 \geq 0.
\end{aligned} \qquad (11)$$

(11) is recorded in a Tucker tableau as

x_1	1	2	20
x_2	2	2	30
x_3	2	1	25
-1	200	150	0
	$= t_P$	$= t_F$	$= C$

We now use the pivot transformation to determine an optimal solution to our canonical slack minimization linear programming problem. Verify the tableau transitions below!

x_1	1	2	20
x_2	2	2	30
x_3	2^*	1	25
-1	200	150	0
	$= t_P$	$= t_F$	$= C$

$\longrightarrow$

x_1	$-1/2$	$3/2$	$15/2$
x_2	-1	1^*	5
t_P	$1/2$	$1/2$	$25/2$
-1	-100	50	-2500
	$= x_3$	$= t_F$	$= C$

$\longrightarrow$

x_1	1	$-3/2$	0
t_F	-1	1	5
t_P	1	$-1/2$	10
-1	-50	-50	-2750
	$= x_3$	$= x_2$	$= C$

(12)

At this point, an optimal solution is contained in tableau (12). The objective function of (12) is $C(x_1, t_F, t_P) = 5t_F + 10t_P + 2750$. C increases with increasing t_F and t_P; since we are trying to minimize C, we would like to set t_F and t_P equal to the smallest values possible. Since $t_F, t_P \geq 0$, we put $t_F = 0$ and $t_P = 0$ to obtain $C(x_1, 0, 0) = 2750$. The main constraints of (12) then give

$$x_1 + 50 = x_3$$
$$-3/2 x_1 + 50 = x_2.$$

Examine the first constraint above. $x_3 \geq 0$ implies that $x_1 + 50 \geq 0$, i.e., $x_1 \geq -50$. Since we already know that $x_1 \geq 0$, no additional information on x_1 is gained from this constraint. Examine the second constraint above. $x_2 \geq 0$ implies that $-3/2x_1 + 50 \geq 0$, i.e., $x_1 \leq 100/3$. Hence $0 \leq x_1 \leq 100/3$ and there are infinitely many optimal solutions to our problem, namely

$$0 \leq x_1 \leq 100/3,$$
$$x_2 = -3/2x_1 + 50,$$
$$x_3 = x_1 + 50,$$
$$t_P = t_F = 0,$$
$$\min C = 2750.$$

A particular optimal solution (obtained by setting $x_1 = 0$) is given by

$$x_1 = 0, x_2 = x_3 = 50, t_P = t_F = 0, \min C = 2750,$$

i.e., a combination of 50 units of feed #2 and 50 units of feed #3 will produce a minimum-cost mixture satisfying the given nutrition requirements. This minimum cost is 2750 cents or $27.50.

We conclude our discussion of this example with an interesting note. Compare the tableau sequence of the cost minimization linear programming problem above with the tableau sequence of the profit maximization linear programming problem of §2. Neglecting notation outside of the tableaus, the minimum tableaus obtained above are exactly the same as the maximum tableaus obtained in §2!! Furthermore, the minimum cost (in cents) above is equal to the maximum profit (in dollars) in §2. This suggests a relationship between canonical maximization and canonical minimization linear programming problems—solving a canonical maximization linear programming problem also solves a related (or dual) canonical minimization linear programming problem and vice versa. A theoretical treatment of this "duality" is presented in Chapter 4.

§5. The Simplex Algorithm for Maximum Basic Feasible Tableaus

In this section, we develop the simplex algorithm for a special type of maximum tableau. In the succeeding sections of this chapter, we will build on this algorithm, culminating in a complete simplex algorithm for canonical maximization and canonical minimization linear programming problems.

Definition 6. Any solution obtained by setting all of the independent variables of a tableau equal to zero is said to be a *basic solution*.

EXAMPLE 7. Consider the tableau sequence in Example 3 of §2:

x_1	x_2	-1	
1	2	20	$= -t_A$
2	2	30	$= -t_B$
2	1	25	$= -t_C$
200	150	0	$= P$

$\longrightarrow$

t_C	x_2	-1	
$-1/2$	$3/2$	$15/2$	$= -t_A$
-1	1	5	$= -t_B$
$1/2$	$1/2$	$25/2$	$= -x_1$
-100	50	-2500	$= P$

$\longrightarrow$

t_C	t_B	-1	
1	$-3/2$	0	$= -t_A$
-1	1	5	$= -x_2$
1	$-1/2$	10	$= -x_1$
-50	-50	-2750	$= P$

The basic solutions of these tableaus are as follows:

First tableau:

$$x_1 = x_2 = 0, t_A = 20, t_B = 30, t_C = 25, P = 0$$

(Note that this solution is feasible since it satisfies all of the constraints of the original problem.)

Second tableau:

$$t_C = x_2 = 0, t_A = 15/2, t_B = 5, x_1 = 25/2, P = 2500$$

(Note that this solution is feasible since it satisfies all of the constraints of the original problem.)

Third tableau:

$$t_C = t_B = 0, t_A = 0, x_2 = 5, x_1 = 10, P = 2750$$

(Note that this solution is the unique optimal solution of the linear programming problem.)

EXAMPLE 8. Consider the tableau sequence in Example 5 of §4:

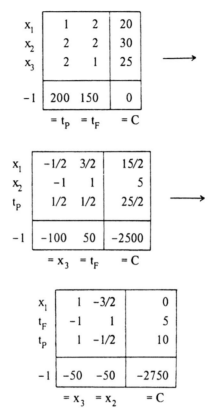

The basic solutions of these tableaus are as follows:

First tableau:

$$x_1 = x_2 = x_3 = 0, t_P = -200, t_F = -150, C = 0$$

(Note that this solution is not feasible since $t_P < 0$ and $t_F < 0$.)

Second tableau:

$$x_1 = x_2 = t_P = 0, x_3 = 100, t_F = -50, C = 2500$$

(Note that this solution is not feasible since $t_F < 0$.)

Third tableau:

$$x_1 = t_F = t_P = 0, x_3 = 50, x_2 = 50, C = 2750$$

(Note that this solution is one of the infinitely many optimal solutions of the linear programming problem.)

In both examples above, the basic solution of the final tableau gives an optimal solution of the linear programming problem. This is, in fact, the goal of the simplex algorithm—to manipulate an initial tableau into a final tableau whose basic solution is optimal. Also, all basic solutions of the maximization example were feasible in direct contrast to the basic solutions of the minimization example. Is this true of maximum tableaus as compared to minimum tableaus in general? The answer is a resounding NO. (See, for example, Exercise 12.) The following definition characterizes those maximum tableaus whose basic solutions are feasible solutions.

Definition 9. Let

$$
\begin{array}{c}
\text{(ind. var.'s)} \qquad -1 \\
\left[\begin{array}{cccc|c}
a_{11} & a_{12} & \cdots & a_{1n} & b_1 \\
a_{21} & a_{22} & \cdots & a_{2n} & b_2 \\
\vdots & \vdots & & \vdots & \vdots \\
a_{m1} & a_{m2} & \cdots & a_{mn} & b_m \\
\hline
c_1 & c_2 & \cdots & c_n & d
\end{array}\right]
\begin{array}{l}
\\
= -(\text{dep. var.'s}) \\
\\
\\
= f
\end{array}
\end{array}
$$

be a tableau of a canonical slack maximization linear programming problem. The tableau is said to be *maximum basic feasible* if $b_1, b_2, \ldots, b_m \geq 0$.

In a maximum basic feasible tableau, the basic solution is a feasible solution. Indeed, upon setting all of the independent variables equal to zero, all of the main constraints reduce to the form

$$- b_i = - (\text{dep. var.}),$$

i.e.,

$$b_i = (\text{dep. var.}).$$

Since $b_i \geq 0$ for all i, we have

$$(\text{dep. var.}) \geq 0$$

for all dependent variables; such a solution satisfies all of the constraints of the original problem and is thus feasible. (What happens if some $b_i < 0$?) A similar argument shows the converse, namely that a maximum tableau whose basic solution is feasible must be a maximum basic feasible tableau. Our goal in this section is to determine what sequence of pivots, if any, will transform a given maximum basic feasible tableau into a final tableau whose basic solution is optimal. The answer is given by the following algorithm.

The Simplex Algorithm for Maximum Basic Feasible Tableaus

(1) The current tableau is maximum basic feasible, i.e., of the form

$$
\begin{array}{c}
\text{(ind. var.'s)} \qquad -1 \\[4pt]
\begin{array}{|cccc|c|}
\hline
a_{11} & a_{12} & \cdots & a_{1n} & b_1 \\
a_{21} & a_{22} & \cdots & a_{2n} & b_2 \\
\vdots & \vdots & & \vdots & \vdots \\
a_{m1} & a_{m2} & \cdots & a_{mn} & b_m \\
\hline
c_1 & c_2 & \cdots & c_n & d \\
\hline
\end{array}
\end{array}
\begin{array}{l}
\\ = -(\text{dep. var.'s}) \\ \\ \\ \\ = f
\end{array}
$$

with $b_1, b_2, \ldots, b_m \geqq 0$.

(2) If $c_1, c_2, \ldots, c_n \leqq 0$, STOP; the basic solution of the current maximum tableau is optimal. (This will be discussed more fully in a moment.) Otherwise, continue.

(3) Choose $c_j > 0$.

(4) If $a_{1j}, a_{2j}, \ldots, a_{mj} \leqq 0$, STOP; the maximization problem is unbounded. (This will be discussed more fully in a moment.) Otherwise, continue.

(5) Compute

$$
\min_{1 \leq i \leq m} \{ b_i/a_{ij} : a_{ij} > 0 \} = b_p/a_{pj},
$$

pivot on a_{pj}, and go to (1).

(Note: There may be more than one value of p for which b_p/a_{pj} is minimum. Choose any such p. (We will say more about this in §8.))

Before illustrating the algorithm above, we look more closely at steps (2) and (4).

Step (2). If we STOP in step (2), the current tableau is of the form

$$
\begin{array}{c}
\text{(ind. var.'s)} \qquad -1 \\[4pt]
\begin{array}{|ccc|c|}
\hline
 & & & \geq 0 \\
 & & & \geq 0 \\
 & & & \vdots \\
 & & & \geq 0 \\
\hline
\leq 0 & \leq 0 \cdots & \leq 0 & d \\
\hline
\end{array}
\end{array}
\begin{array}{l}
\\ = -(\text{dep. var.'s}) \\ \\ \\ = f
\end{array}
\qquad (13)
$$

Since the tableau is maximum basic feasible, the basic solution is a feasible solution. The objective function given by this tableau is of the form

$$
f = (\leqq 0)(\text{ind. var.}) + (\leqq 0)(\text{ind. var.}) + \cdots + (\leqq 0)(\text{ind. var.}) - d;
$$

since we are trying to maximize f, we would like to set those independent variables having negative coefficients equal to the smallest values possible, namely zero. While zero coefficients do not force the corresponding independent variables to be zero, one can always obtain a feasible solution by setting such variables equal to zero anyway. Hence, the basic solution is also an optimal solution since any increase in those independent variables having negative coefficients decreases f. In general, zero coefficients here imply the possible existence of optimal solutions that are not basic since the corresponding independent variables are not forced to be zero. *Moral*: (13) is the tableau form that terminates the simplex algorithm for maximum basic feasible tableaus with a basic solution that is optimal (and possibly other optimal solutions as well).

Step (4). We begin by recalling (and formalizing) a definition from Chapter 1.

Definition 10. A canonical maximization (respectively minimization) linear programming problem is said to be *unbounded* if the constraint set is unbounded and the objective function is not bounded above (respectively not bounded below) on this constraint set.

Hence, an unbounded linear programming problem has no maximum (or minimum) since there are feasible solutions that make the objective function of the problem arbitrarily large (or small). Unboundedness in linear programming problems should be viewed as pathological. Most real-life linear programming problems will have well-defined solutions if properly posed. It is, however, a bonus that our algorithm recognizes such pathology and terminates. If we STOP in step (4), the current tableau is of the form

$$
\begin{array}{c}
 \quad x \qquad\qquad -1 \\
\left.
\begin{array}{|c|c|}
\hline
\leq 0 & \geq 0 \\
\leq 0 & \geq 0 \\
\vdots & \vdots \\
\leq 0 & \geq 0 \\
\hline
> 0 & d \\
\hline
\end{array}
\right.
\begin{array}{l}
= -(\text{dep. var.'s}) \\
\\
\\
= f
\end{array}
\end{array}
\qquad (14)
$$

$$
\underset{j}{\uparrow}
$$

Now set all of the independent variables except x equal to zero. All of the main constraints reduce to the form

$$(\leq 0)x - (\geq 0) = -(\text{dep. var.}),$$

i.e.,

$$(\leq 0)x + (\leq 0) = -(\text{dep. var.}).$$

If x is nonnegative, we have

$$(\leq 0) = -(\text{dep. var.}),$$

i.e.,

$$(\text{dep. var.}) \geq 0;$$

such a solution satisfies all of the constraints of the original problem and is thus feasible. But, as $x \to \infty$, we have

$$f = (> 0)x - d \to \infty,$$

i.e., we can make f arbitrarily large by increasing x. *Moral:* (14) is the tableau form that terminates the simplex algorithm for maximum basic feasible tableaus with an unbounded linear programming problem.

We now illustrate our algorithm with two examples.

EXAMPLE 11. Apply the simplex algorithm above to the maximum tableau

x_1	x_2	-1	
2	1	8	$= -t_1$
1	2	10	$= -t_2$
30	50	0	$= f$

The parenthetical numbers below correspond to the steps of the simplex algorithm for maximum basic feasible tableaus.

(1) The initial tableau is clearly maximum basic feasible.
(2) We proceed to step (3) since $c_1 = 30$ and $c_2 = 50$ are both positive.
(3) We can choose either $c_1 = 30$ or $c_2 = 50$. For definiteness, we choose $c_1 = 30$.
(4) We proceed to step (5) since $a_{11} = 2$ and $a_{21} = 1$ are both positive.
(5) Min $\{b_1/a_{11} = 8/2, b_2/a_{21} = 10/1\} = b_1/a_{11}$.

Pivot on a_{11}:

x_1	x_2	-1	
2*	1	8	$= -t_1$
1	2	10	$= -t_2$
30	50	0	$= f$

$\longrightarrow$

t_1	x_2	-1	
1/2	1/2	4	$= -x_1$
$-1/2$	3/2	6	$= -t_2$
-15	35	-120	$= f$

Go to step (1).

(1) The current tableau is clearly maximum basic feasible.
(2) We proceed to step (3) since $c_2 = 35$ is positive.
(3) We must choose $c_2 = 35$.
(4) We proceed to step (5) since $a_{12} = 1/2$ and $a_{22} = 3/2$ are both positive.
(5) Min $\{b_1/a_{12} = 4/(1/2), b_2/a_{22} = 6/(3/2)\} = b_2/a_{22}$.

Pivot on a_{22}:

t_1	x_2	-1	
1/2	1/2	4	$= -x_1$
$-1/2$	3/2•	6	$= -t_2$
-15	35	-120	$= f$

$\longrightarrow$

t_1	t_2	-1	
2/3	$-1/3$	2	$= -x_1$
$-1/3$	2/3	4	$= -x_2$
$-10/3$	$-70/3$	-260	$= f$

Go to step (1).

(1) The current tableau is clearly maximum basic feasible.
(2) $c_1, c_2 \leq 0$; STOP; the basic solution of the current maximum tableau is optimal. This optimal solution is

$$t_1 = t_2 = 0, x_1 = 2, x_2 = 4, \max f = 260.$$

Example 11 is the simplex algorithm solution of Example 1 of Chapter 1. The constraint set is

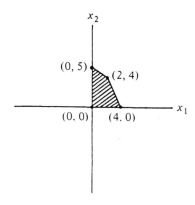

It is interesting to note what the simplex algorithm is doing geometrically here. Consider the x_1 and x_2 values of the basic solutions of the three tableaus in Example 11:

	(x_1, x_2)
Tableau #1	$(0, 0)$
Tableau #2	$(4, 0)$
Tableau #3	$(2, 4)$

We see that the basic solutions correspond to extreme points of the constraint set and that each pivot simulates a movement from one extreme point to an adjacent extreme point along a connecting edge.

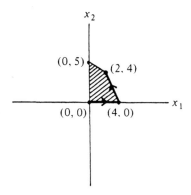

Such facts are true in general for maximum basic feasible tableaus. Basic feasible solutions correspond to extreme points of constraint sets in the geometric sense. The simplex algorithm is designed so that the transition between basic feasible solutions of any two successive maximum tableaus (simulated by movement from one extreme point to another along a connecting edge) does not decrease the value of the objective function. Hence each tableau transition maintains or increases the value of the objective function. Usually, after a finite number of tableau transitions, a maximum value of the objective function is reached or the simplex algorithm detects unboundedness. In rare instances, the objective function may maintain the same value repeatedly without the simplex algorithm terminating with a maximum value or a detection of unboundedness. This phenomenon will be discussed in §8.

EXAMPLE 12. Apply the simplex algorithm above to the maximum tableau

x_1	x_2	-1	
-1	1	1	$= -t_1$
1	-1	3	$= -t_2$
1	2	0	$= f$

The parenthetical numbers below correspond to the steps of the simplex algorithm for maximum basic feasible tableaus.

(1) The initial tableau is clearly maximum basic feasible.
(2) We proceed to step (3) since $c_1 = 1$ and $c_2 = 2$ are both positive.
(3) We can choose either $c_1 = 1$ or $c_2 = 2$. For definiteness, we choose $c_1 = 1$.
(4) We proceed to step (5) since $a_{21} = 1$ is positive.
(5) Min $\{b_2/a_{21} = 3/1\} = b_2/a_{21}$ (obviously!).

Pivot on a_{21}:

x_1	x_2	-1	
-1	1	1	$= -t_1$
$1^\bullet$	-1	3	$= -t_2$
1	2	0	$= f$

$\longrightarrow$

t_2	x_2	-1	
1	0	4	$= -t_1$
1	-1	3	$= -x_1$
-1	3	-3	$= f$

Go to step (1).

(1) The current tableau is clearly maximum basic feasible.
(2) We proceed to step (3) since $c_2 = 3$ is positive.

(3) We must choose $c_2 = 3$.

(4) $a_{12}, a_{22} \leq 0$; STOP; the maximization problem is unbounded.

The constraint set of Example 12 is

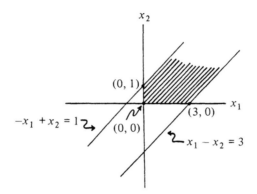

It is clear that the objective function $f(x_1, x_2) = x_1 + 2x_2$ can be made arbitrarily large on this constraint set by considering feasible solutions farther and farther away from the origin. The movement within the constraint set given by the basic solutions of successive tableaus is illustrated below:

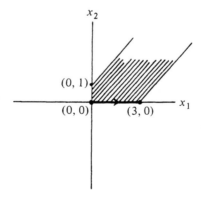

Note that the unboundedness is detected at the point $(3, 0)$. The algorithm terminates because the objective function is not bounded above on the "infinite edge" of the line $x_1 - x_2 = 3$. (On the line $x_1 - x_2 = 3$, we have

$$f(x_1, x_2) = x_1 + 2x_2 = (x_2 + 3) + 2x_2 = 3x_2 + 3.$$

Now $f(x_1, x_2) \to \infty$ as $x_2 \to \infty$.)

We conclude this section with two important notes on the simplex algorithm for maximum basic feasible tableaus. First of all, this algorithm preserves the maximum basic feasibility of a tableau, i.e., if an initial tableau is maximum basic feasible, then every subsequent tableau obtained via this algorithm will also be maximum basic feasible. This fact can be helpful in locating arithmetic mistakes in the b-columns of the tableaus. Secondly, when choosing the positive c_j in step (3), it is advantageous to use some foresight and examine all positive c's and all a's above these c's. If you can find just one positive c corresponding to a column of nonpositive a's, then the linear programming problem is unbounded and the algorithm terminates. *This is true even if there is some other positive c having positive a's in its column!* Exploit the leniency built into this choice of the positive c_j whenever you can!

§6. The Simplex Algorithm for Maximum Tableaus

So far, we have an algorithm for finding optimal solutions, if they exist, of canonical maximization linear programming problems having maximum basic feasible initial tableaus. What if the initial tableau of a canonical maximization problem is not maximum basic feasible? Before we can apply the algorithm of §5, we must convert the maximum tableau into a maximum basic feasible tableau. The algorithm below consists of the algorithm of §5 together with additional preliminary steps which perform the necessary conversion.

The Simplex Algorithm for Maximum Tableaus

(1) The current tableau is of the form

(ind. var.'s)				-1	
a_{11}	a_{12}	$\cdots$	a_{1n}	b_1	
a_{21}	a_{22}	$\cdots$	a_{2n}	b_2	
$\vdots$	$\vdots$		$\vdots$	$\vdots$	$= -(\text{dep. var.'s})$
a_{m1}	a_{m2}	$\cdots$	a_{mn}	b_m	
c_1	c_2	$\cdots$	c_n	d	$= f$

(2) If $b_1, b_2, \ldots, b_m \geq 0$, go to (6). Otherwise, continue.
(3) Choose $b_i < 0$ such that i is maximal.
(4) If $a_{i1}, a_{i2}, \ldots, a_{in} \geq 0$, STOP; the maximization problem is infeasible. (This will be discussed more fully in a moment.) Otherwise, continue.
(5) If $i = m$, choose $a_{mj} < 0$, pivot on a_{mj}, and go to (1). If $i < m$, choose $a_{ij} < 0$, compute

$$\min_{k > i} \left(\{b_i/a_{ij}\} \cup \{b_k/a_{kj} : a_{kj} > 0\} \right) = b_p/a_{pj},$$

pivot on a_{pj}, and go to (1).

(Note: There may be more than one value of p for which b_p/a_{pj} is minimum. Choose any such p, (We will say more about this in §8.))

(6) Apply the simplex algorithm for maximum basic feasible tableaus (§5).

Before illustrating the algorithm above, we look more closely at step (4).

Step (4). We begin by recalling (and formalizing) a definition from Chapter 1.

Definition 13. A canonical maximization or canonical minimization linear programming problem is said to be *infeasible* if it has no feasible solutions.

Hence an infeasible linear programming problem has an empty constraint set. As with unboundedness, infeasibility in linear programming problems should be viewed as pathological. Even though most real-life problems have feasible solutions if properly posed, it is advantageous that our algorithm recognizes the existence of infeasibility and terminates. If we STOP in step (4), the current tableau is of the form

$$
\begin{array}{c}
\text{(ind. var.'s)} \qquad -1 \\[6pt]
i \rightarrow \quad
\begin{array}{|ccccc|c|}
\hline
\geq 0 & \geq 0 & \ldots & \geq 0 & & <0 \\
\hline
& & & & & \\
\hline
\end{array}
\begin{array}{l}
= -x \\[18pt]
= f
\end{array}
\end{array}
\qquad (15)
$$

The equation given by the ith row of this tableau is

$$(\geq 0)(\text{ind. var.}) + (\geq 0)(\text{ind. var.}) + \cdots + (\geq 0)(\text{ind. var.}) - (<0) = -x,$$

i.e.,

$$(\geq 0)(\text{ind. var.}) + (\geq 0)(\text{ind. var.}) + \cdots + (\geq 0)(\text{ind. var.}) + (>0) = -x.$$

Since all of the independent variables are nonnegative in any feasible solution, we have

$$-x > 0,$$

i.e.,

$$x < 0$$

which is impossible since dependent variables are nonnegative in any feasible solution. Hence the maximization problem has no feasible solutions. *Moral*: (15) is the tableau form that terminates the simplex algorithm for maximum tableaus with an infeasible linear programming problem.

We now illustrate our new algorithm with two examples.

EXAMPLE 14. Apply the simplex algorithm above to the maximum tableau

	x_1	x_2	-1	
	-1	-2	-3	$= -t_1$
	1	1	3	$= -t_2$
	1	1	2	$= -t_3$
	-2	4	0	$= f$

The parenthetical numbers below correspond to the steps of the simplex algorithm for maximum tableaus.

(1) The initial tableau is clearly a maximum tableau.
(2) We proceed to step (3) since $b_1 = -3$ is negative.
(3) We must choose $b_1 = -3$.
(4) We proceed to step (5) since $a_{11} = -1$ and $a_{12} = -2$ are both negative.
(5) We can choose either $a_{11} = -1$ or $a_{12} = -2$. For definiteness, we choose $a_{11} = -1$. Since $1 = i < m = 3$, we compute

$$\min\left(\{b_1/a_{11} = -3/-1\} \cup \{b_2/a_{21} = 3/1, b_3/a_{31} = 2/1\}\right) = b_3/a_{31}.$$

Pivot on a_{31}:

	x_1	x_2	-1	
	-1	-2	-3	$= -t_1$
	1	1	3	$= -t_2$
	1^*	1	2	$= -t_3$
	-2	4	0	$= f$

$\longrightarrow$

	t_3	x_2	-1	
	1	-1	-1	$= -t_1$
	-1	0	1	$= -t_2$
	1	1	2	$= -x_1$
	2	6	4	$= f$

Go to step (1).

(1) Obviously!
(2) We proceed to step (3) since $b_1 = -1$ is negative.
(3) We must choose $b_1 = -1$.
(4) We proceed to step (5) since $a_{12} = -1$ is negative.

(5) We must choose $a_{12} = -1$. Since $1 = i < m = 3$, we compute

$$\min(\{b_1/a_{12} = -1/-1\} \cup \{b_3/a_{32} = 2/1\}) = b_1/a_{12}.$$

Pivot on a_{12}:

t_3	x_2	-1	
1	$-1^{\bullet}$	-1	$= -t_1$
-1	0	1	$= -t_2$
1	1	2	$= -x_1$
2	6	4	$= f$

$\longrightarrow$

t_3	t_1	-1	
-1	-1	1	$= -x_2$
-1	0	1	$= -t_2$
2	1	1	$= -x_1$
8	6	-2	$= f$

Go to step (1).

(1) Obviously!
(2) $b_1, b_2, b_3 \geq 0$, i.e., the tableau is maximum basic feasible. Go to step (6).
(6) Apply the simplex algorithm for maximum basic feasible tableaus (§5). (This is left as an exercise for the reader.)

EXAMPLE 15. Apply the simplex algorithm to the maximum tableau

x_1	x_2	-1	
-1	-1	-3	$= -t_1$
1	1	2	$= -t_2$
2	-4	0	$= f$

The parenthetical numbers below correspond to the steps of the simplex algorithm for maximum tableaus.

(1) The initial tableau is clearly a maximum tableau.
(2) We proceed to step (3) since $b_1 = -3$ is negative.
(3) We must choose $b_1 = -3$.
(4) We proceed to step (5) since $a_{11} = -1$ and $a_{12} = -1$ are both negative.

(5) We can choose either $a_{11} = -1$ or $a_{12} = -1$. For definiteness, we choose $a_{11} = -1$. Since $1 = i < m = 2$, we compute

$$\min(\{b_1/a_{11} = -3/-1\} \cup \{b_2/a_{21} = 2/1\}) = b_2/a_{21}.$$

Pivot on a_{21}:

	x_1	x_2	-1	
	-1	-1	-3	$= -t_1$
	1^*	1	2	$= -t_2$
	2	-4	0	$= f$

$\longrightarrow$

	t_2	x_2	-1	
	1	0	-1	$= -t_1$
	1	1	2	$= -x_1$
	-2	-6	-4	$= f$

Go to step (1).

(1) Obviously!
(2) We proceed to step (3) since $b_1 = -1$ is negative.
(3) We must choose $b_1 = -1$.
(4) $a_{11}, a_{12} \geq 0$; STOP; the maximization problem is infeasible.

Hence the constraint set of this canonical maximization linear programming problem is empty. This can be seen without graphing by looking at the main constraints of the original problem, namely

$$-x_1 - x_2 \leq 3$$
$$x_1 + x_2 \leq 2.$$

Multiplying both sides of the first constraint by -1, we obtain

$$x_1 + x_2 \geq 3$$
$$x_1 + x_2 \leq 2.$$

Since a quantity can never by greater than or equal to 3 and less than or equal to 2 simultaneously, this canonical maximization problem is infeasible.

We conclude this section with two important notes on step (3) of the simplex algorithm for maximum tableaus. The choice of $b_i < 0$ with maximal i in this step assures that all nonnegative b's below b_i remain nonnegative in the new tableau after pivoting. This can be helpful in locating arithmetic mistakes in the b-columns of the tableaus. Note, though, that the maximality of i is *unimportant* for the determination of infeasibility in step (4). *Any* row as in (15) implies an infeasible canonical maximization linear programming problem, regardless of its row index. Hence, do not apply step (3) blindly; if you can find just one negative b corresponding to a row of nonnegative a's, the linear programming problem is infeasible and the algorithm terminates. *This is true even if there is some other negative b (possibly with maximal i) having negative a's in its row!* Exploit the fact that the determination of infeasibility is independent of the choice of maximal i in step (3) whenever you can!

§7. Negative Transposition; The Simplex Algorithm for Minimum Tableaus

To obtain a simplex algorithm for canonical minimization linear programming problems, we use a simple trick to convert minimum tableaus into maximum tableaus whence the algorithm of §6 can be implemented. This trick is called negative transposition.

Definition 16. The *negative transpose* of the minimum tableau

$$
\begin{array}{c|cccc|c}
x_1 & a_{11} & a_{21} & \cdots & a_{m1} & c_1 \\
x_2 & a_{12} & a_{22} & \cdots & a_{m2} & c_2 \\
\vdots & \vdots & \vdots & & \vdots & \vdots \\
x_n & a_{1n} & a_{2n} & \cdots & a_{mn} & c_n \\
\hline
-1 & b_1 & b_2 & \cdots & b_m & d \\
\hline
& = t_1 & = t_2 & \cdots & = t_m & = g
\end{array}
\tag{16}
$$

is the maximum tableau

$$
\begin{array}{c|cccc|c|c}
& x_1 & x_2 & \cdots & x_n & -1 & \\
\hline
& -a_{11} & -a_{12} & \cdots & -a_{1n} & -b_1 & = -t_1 \\
& -a_{21} & -a_{22} & \cdots & -a_{2n} & -b_2 & = -t_2 \\
& \vdots & \vdots & & \vdots & \vdots & \vdots \\
& -a_{m1} & -a_{m2} & \cdots & -a_{mn} & -b_m & = -t_m \\
\hline
& -c_1 & -c_2 & \cdots & -c_n & -d & = -g
\end{array}
\tag{17}
$$

and vice versa.

Note that every column of the minimum tableau becomes a negated row in the maximum tableau except for the column outside of the tableau containing the independent variables and -1 which becomes a row but is not negated. By looking at the equations represented by these tableaus, we see that every equation of the minimum tableau has been multiplied by -1 in the maximum tableau. This is the only difference effected by this tableau transition— multiplication of each equation of the minimum tableau by -1 simply gives the form we are accustomed to seeing in a maximum tableau, namely the negated dependent variables to the east.

Now we can solve (17) by using the simplex algorithm for maximum tableaus in §6. (17) maximizes the objective function $-g$; the original minimization problem of (16) was to minimize the objective function g. Is there a relationship between the two quantities $\max(-g)$ and $\min g$? The answer is (not surprisingly) YES—$\min g$ is the negative of $\max(-g)$. Hence we have

The Simplex Algorithm for Minimum Tableaus

(1) The initial tableau is of the form

	a_{11}	a_{21}	$\cdots$	a_{m1}	c_1
	a_{12}	a_{22}	$\cdots$	a_{m2}	c_2
(ind. var.'s)	$\vdots$	$\vdots$		$\vdots$	$\vdots$
	a_{1n}	a_{2n}	$\cdots$	a_{mn}	c_n
-1	b_1	b_2	$\cdots$	b_m	d
	= (dep. var.'s)				= g

(2) Take the negative transpose of the tableau to obtain a maximum tableau.
(3) Apply the simplex algorithm for maximum tableaus (§6).
(4) $\min g = -\max(-g)$.

A remark is in order here. Algorithms for minimum tableaus not involving negative transposition exist. (For example, go back and look at the solution of the cost minimization problem in §4; negative transposition was not used.) We postpone a discussion of these algorithms until Chapter 4. Until then, our approach to solving canonical minimization linear programming problems will be negative transposition to maximum tableau form and the application of the simplex algorithm for maximum tableaus.

EXAMPLE 17. Apply the simplex algorithm above to the minimum tableau

x_1	20	25	300
x_2	40	20	500
-1	1000	800	0
	$= t_1$	$= t_2$	$= g$

The parenthetical numbers below correspond to the steps of the simplex algorithm for minimum tableaus.

(1) The initial tableau is clearly a minimum tableau.

(2)

x_1	20	25	300
x_2	40	20	500
-1	1000	800	0

$= t_1 \quad = t_2 \qquad = g$

$\longrightarrow$

	x_1	x_2	-1	
	-20	-40	-1000	$= -t_1$
	-25	-20	-800	$= -t_2$
	-300	-500	0	$= -g$

(3)

	x_1	x_2	-1	
	-20	-40	-1000	$= -t_1$
	-25	$-20^{\bullet}$	-800	$= -t_2$
	-300	-500	0	$= -g$

$\longrightarrow$

	x_1	t_2	-1	
	$30^{\bullet}$	-2	600	$= -t_1$
	$5/4$	$-1/20$	40	$= -x_2$
	325	-25	20000	$= -g$

$\longrightarrow$

	t_1	t_2	-1	
	$1/30$	$-1/15$	20	$= -x_1$
	$-1/24$	$1/30$	15	$= -x_2$
	$-65/6$	$-10/3$	13500	$= -g$

The optimal solution to the maximization problem is

$$t_1 = t_2 = 0, x_1 = 20, x_2 = 15, \max(-g) = -13500.$$

(4) The optimal solution to the original minimization problem is

$$t_1 = t_2 = 0, x_1 = 20, x_2 = 15, \min g = -\max(-g) = 13500.$$

Example 17 is the simplex algorithm solution of Example 2 of Chapter 1. The constraint set is

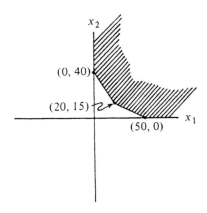

Consider the x_1 and x_2 values of the basic solutions of the three maximum tableaus in step (3) above:

	(x_1, x_2)
Tableau #1	$(0, 0)$
Tableau #2	$(0, 40)$
Tableau #3	$(20, 15)$

The movement exhibited by these basic solutions in the constraint set diagram is illustrated below:

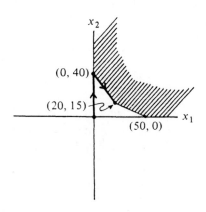

Note that the basic solutions of the second and third tableaus of step (3) are feasible while the basic solution of the first tableau is not feasible. There is a good reason for this—only the second and third tableaus of step (3) are maximum basic feasible tableaus! Recall that, in general, the simplex algorithm transition between maximum basic feasible tableaus is designed so that the objective function ($-g$ in this particular case) is not decreased. Hence each such transition maintains or increases the value of the objective function, usually until either a maximum value is reached or the algorithm detects unboundedness. In rare cases, a phenomenon known as cycling occurs; we discuss this phenomenon now.

§8. Cycling

We begin with an example due to E.M.L. Beale ([B2]).

EXAMPLE 18. Consider the linear programming problem

$$\text{Maximize} \quad f(x_1, x_2, x_3, x_4) = 3/4x_1 - 20x_2 + 1/2x_3 - 6x_4$$
$$\text{subject to} \quad 1/4x_1 - 8x_2 - x_3 + 9x_4 \leq 0$$
$$1/2x_1 - 12x_2 - 1/2x_3 + 3x_4 \leq 0$$
$$x_3 \leq 1$$
$$x_1, x_2, x_3, x_4 \geq 0.$$

Six simplex algorithm pivots are performed below. While it is not intended that you verify these computations, make sure that you see that all pivots have been made in accordance with the simplex algorithm.

x_1	x_2	x_3	x_4	-1	
1/4*	-8	-1	9	0	$= -t_1$
1/2	-12	-1/2	3	0	$= -t_2$
0	0	1	0	1	$= -t_3$
3/4	-20	1/2	-6	0	$= f$

t_1	x_2	x_3	x_4	-1	
4	-32	-4	36	0	$= -x_1$
-2	4	3/2	-15	0	$= -t_2$
0	0	1	0	1	$= -t_3$
-3	4	7/2	-33	0	$= f$

	t_1	t_2	x_3	x_4	-1	
	-12	8	$8^{\bullet}$	-84	0	$= -x_1$
	$-1/2$	$1/4$	$3/8$	$-15/4$	0	$= -x_2$
	0	0	1	0	1	$= -t_3$
	-1	-1	2	-18	0	$= f$

$\longrightarrow$

	t_1	t_2	x_1	x_4	-1	
	$-3/2$	1	$1/8$	$-21/2$	0	$= -x_3$
	$1/16$	$-1/8$	$-3/64$	$3/16^{\bullet}$	0	$= -x_2$
	$3/2$	-1	$-1/8$	$21/2$	1	$= -t_3$
	2	-3	$-1/4$	3	0	$= f$

$\longrightarrow$

	t_1	t_2	x_1	x_2	-1	
	$2^{\bullet}$	-6	$-5/2$	56	0	$= -x_3$
	$1/3$	$-2/3$	$-1/4$	$16/3$	0	$= -x_4$
	-2	6	$5/2$	-56	1	$= -t_3$
	1	-1	$1/2$	-16	0	$= f$

$\longrightarrow$

	x_3	t_2	x_1	x_2	-1	
	$1/2$	-3	$-5/4$	28	0	$= -t_1$
	$-1/6$	$1/3^{\bullet}$	$1/6$	-4	0	$= -x_4$
	1	0	0	0	1	$= -t_3$
	$-1/2$	2	$7/4$	-44	0	$= f$

$\longrightarrow$

	x_3	x_4	x_1	x_2	-1	
	-1	9	$1/4$	-8	0	$= -t_1$
	$-1/2$	3	$1/2$	-12	0	$= -t_2$
	1	0	0	0	1	$= -t_3$
	$1/2$	-6	$3/4$	-20	0	$= f$

Note that the seventh tableau above is the same as the initial tableau up to a rearrangement of the first four columns. Hence the seventh tableau is no closer to an optimal solution than the initial tableau!! (Needless to say, this is quite frustrating!!) Since transitions between maximum basic feasible tableaus maintain or increase the value of the objective function, it is not surprising that the basic solutions of successive tableaus above have not increased the value of the objective function at all—it remains at 0 in all seven tableaus.

The phenomenon in the example above is known as *cycling*. Cycling is rare; in fact, until quite recently, it was thought that cycling never occurred in practical problems, all of the pertinent examples having been artificially constructed. Then, in 1977, Kotiah and Steinberg ([K1]) discovered a nonartificial class of linear programming problems involving queueing theory which cycled. Hence, in this section, we give rules which prevent cycling. Inasmuch as cycling is a rare phenomenon, we make no guarantee of constant adherence to these rules in this book. While anticycling rules should certainly be a part of any computer implementation of the simplex algorithm, we treat cycling as an unfortunate infrequent occurrence rather than something that warrants constant special attention.

In each tableau of Example 18, the pivot choice is not uniquely determined by the simplex algorithm. (For example, 1/2 and 1 are acceptable alternate pivot entries in the initial tableau, 3/2 is an acceptable alternate pivot entry in the second tableau, 3/8 is an acceptable alternate pivot entry in the third tableau, etc.) In a sense, our particular pivot choices contributed to the cycling! We can remedy the phenomenon of cycling by placing additional requirements on the choice of pivot entries in those instances when more than one entry meets the pivoting requirements of the simplex algorithm. These pivoting rules are due to R.G. Bland ([B3]).

Simplex Algorithm Anticycling Rules

List all variables, both independent and dependent, appearing in the initial tableau. (The ordering of the variables in the list is not important as long as the rules below are implemented in a manner consistent with this list.) Any pivot entry is determined uniquely by a pivot row and a pivot column. The rules below determine this row and column.

Rule #1 (Determination of pivot row). Whenever there is more than one possible choice of pivot row in accordance with the simplex algorithm, choose the row corresponding to the variable that appears nearest the top (or front) of the list.

Rule #2 (Determination of pivot column). Whenever there is more than one possible choice of pivot column in accordance with the simplex algorithm, choose the column corresponding to the variable that appears nearest the top (or front) of the list.

A reminder. Don't get too engrossed in the application of these rules—before proceeding with any choice of pivot row or pivot column, examine the tableau for infeasibility or unboundedness.

We now illustrate how the anticycling rules eliminate the problem of cycling in Example 18.

EXAMPLE 19. Apply the simplex algorithm with anticycling rules to the initial maximum tableau of Example 18 below:

x_1	x_2	x_3	x_4	-1	
1/4	-8	-1	9	0	$= -t_1$
1/2	-12	$-1/2$	3	0	$= -t_2$
0	0	1	0	1	$= -t_3$
3/4	-20	1/2	-6	0	$= f$

We choose $x_1, x_2, x_3, x_4, t_1, t_2, t_3$ as our list of variables. In the initial tableau, we have two choices for a pivot column, namely the first column (corresponding to $c_1 = 3/4$) and the third column (corresponding to $c_3 = 1/2$). Since the first column corresponds to the variable x_1 and the third column corresponds to the variable x_3, we choose the first column as our pivot column in accordance with Rule #2 of the anticycling rules. We now have two choices for the pivot row, namely the first row ($b_1/a_{11} = 0/(1/4) = 0$) and the second row ($b_2/a_{21} = 0/(1/2) = 0$). Since the first row corresponds to the variable t_1 and the second row corresponds to the variable t_2, we choose the first row as our pivot row in accordance with Rule #1 of the anticycling rules. Hence we pivot on 1/4 as in Example 18 to obtain the second tableau

t_1	x_2	x_3	x_4	-1	
4	-32	-4	36	0	$= -x_1$
-2	4^*	3/2	-15	0	$= -t_2$
0	0	1	0	1	$= -t_3$
-3	4	7/2	-33	0	$= f$

In this new tableau, we have two choices for a pivot column, namely the second column (corresponding to $c_2 = 4$) and the third column (corresponding to $c_3 = 7/2$). Since the second column corresponds to the variable x_2 and the third column corresponds to the variable x_3, we choose the second column as our pivot column in accordance with Rule #2 of the anticycling rules. The choice for the pivot row is then determined by the simplex algorithm and we pivot on 4 as in Example 18 to obtain the third tableau

t_1	t_2	x_3	x_4	-1	
-12	8	8	-84	0	$= -x_1$
$-1/2$	$1/4$	$3/8$	$-15/4$	0	$= -x_2$
0	0	1	0	1	$= -t_3$
-1	-1	2	-18	0	$= f$

In this new tableau, the choice for the pivot column is determined by the simplex algorithm but there are two choices for the pivot row, namely the first row ($b_1/a_{13} = 0/8 = 0$) and the second row ($b_2/a_{23} = 0/(3/8) = 0$). Since the first row corresponds to the variable x_1 and the second row corresponds to the variable x_2, we choose the first row as our pivot row in accordance with Rule #1 of the anticycling rules. Hence we pivot on 8 as in Example 18 to obtain the fourth tableau

t_1	t_2	x_1	x_4	-1	
$-3/2$	1	$1/8$	$-21/2$	0	$= -x_3$
$1/16$	$-1/8$	$-3/64$	$3/16$	0	$= -x_2$
$3/2$	-1	$-1/8$	$21/2$	1	$= -t_3$
2	-3	$-1/4$	3	0	$= f$

In this new tableau, we have two choices for a pivot column, namely the first column (corresponding to $c_1 = 2$) and the fourth column (corresponding to $c_4 = 3$). Since the first column corresponds to the variable t_1 and the fourth column corresponds to the variable x_4, we choose the fourth column as our pivot column in accordance with Rule #2 of the anticycling rules. The choice for the pivot row is then determined by the simplex algorithm and we pivot on 3/16 as in Example 18 to obtain the fifth tableau

t_1	t_2	x_1	x_2	-1	
2	-6	$-5/2$	56	0	$= -x_3$
$1/3$	$-2/3$	$-1/4$	$16/3$	0	$= -x_4$
-2	6	$5/2$	-56	1	$= -t_3$
1	-1	$1/2$	-16	0	$= f$

In this new tableau, we have two choices for a pivot column, namely the first column (corresponding to $c_1 = 1$) and the third column (corresponding to $c_3 = 1/2$). Since the first column corresponds to the variable t_1 and the third column corresponds to the variable x_1, we choose the third column as our pivot column in accordance with Rule #2 of the anticycling rules. (Note that the first column was chosen as the pivot column at this point in Example 18.)

The choice for the pivot row is then determined by the simplex algorithm and we pivot on 5/2 (instead of 2 as in Example 18) to obtain the sixth tableau

t_1	t_2	t_3	x_2	-1	
0	0	1	0	1	$= -x_3$
2/15	$-1/15$	1/10	$-4/15$	1/10	$= -x_4$
$-4/5$	12/5	2/5	$-112/5$	2/5	$= -x_1$
7/5	$-11/5$	$-1/5$	$-24/5$	$-1/5$	$= f$

The pivot in this new tableau is uniquely determined by the simplex algorithm so that no anticycling rules are necessary. The reader should verify that a pivot on $a_{21} = 2/15$ results in a tableau whose basic solution is optimal. Hence, the cycling problem of Example 18 has been remedied.

§9. Concluding Remarks

We have now developed the simplex algorithm with anticycling rules, a complete procedure for solving canonical maximization and canonical minimization linear programming problems. Canonical maximization and canonical minimization linear programming problems fall into four classes:

(i) infeasible linear programming problems,
(ii) unbounded linear programming problems,
(iii) linear programming problems having bounded constraint sets for which the optimal values of the objective functions are attained at extreme points, and
(iv) linear programming problems having unbounded constraint sets for which the optimal values of the objective functions are attained at extreme points.

The simplex algorithm with anticycling rules effectively handles all four classes above. In classes (i) and (ii), the algorithm terminates with a tableau indicating the infeasibility or unboundedness; in classes (iii) and (iv), the algorithm terminates with a tableau whose basic solution is optimal irrespective of the boundedness or unboundedness of the constraint set. In addition, the simplex algorithm is much more efficient than the geometric approach of Chapter 1. For example, the geometric approach of Chapter 1 applied to a canonical linear programming problem with 15 main constraints and 10 variables would involve finding and testing up to

$$\binom{25}{10} > 3200000$$

candidates for extreme points. The simplex algorithm, on the other hand, would only require between about 13 and 50 pivot steps. The simplex algorithm is also easily implemented on a computer.

EXERCISES

1. Consider the canonical maximum tableau below:

$$
\begin{array}{cc}
x & y & -1 \\
\end{array}
$$

x	y	−1	
1	2	3	$= -t_1$
4	5	6	$= -t_2$
7	8	9	$= f$

a. In the notation of (1) of §1, state the canonical maximization linear programming problem represented by the tableau above.

b. Explain why the initial tableau for the simplex algorithm solution of the linear programming problem

$$
\begin{aligned}
\text{Maximize} \quad & f(x, y) = 7x + 8y - 9 \\
\text{subject to} \quad & x + 2y \geq 3 \\
& 4x + 5y \geq 6 \\
& x, y \geq 0
\end{aligned}
$$

is *not* the tableau above.

c. Pivot on 4 in the tableau above.

d. Describe the tableau transition of part c in terms of the "solving and replacing every occurrence of" procedure demonstrated in §2.

2. Consider the canonical minimum tableau below:

	x	1	2	3
	y	4	5	6
−1		7	8	9
		$= t_1$	$= t_2$	$= g$

a. In the notation of (3) of §1, state the canonical minimization linear programming problem represented by the tableau above.

b. Explain why the initial tableau for the simplex algorithm solution of the linear programming problem

$$
\begin{aligned}
\text{Minimize} \quad & g(x, y) = 3x + 6y - 9 \\
\text{subject to} \quad & x + 4y \leq 7 \\
& 2x + 5y \leq 8 \\
& x, y \geq 0
\end{aligned}
$$

is *not* the tableau above.

c. Pivot on 4 in the tableau above.

d. Describe the tableau transition of part c in terms of the "solving and replacing every occurrence of" procedure demonstrated in §2.

3. a. Describe the tableau transitions in Example 5 in terms of the "solving and replacing every occurrence of" procedure demonstrated in §2.
   b. Interpret the condition $t_P = t_F = 0$ in the optimal solutions of Example 5.

4. Solve each of the linear programming problems in Exercise 3 of Chapter 1 by using the simplex algorithm. In each problem, illustrate the movement in the constraint set diagram exhibited by the basic solutions of successive tableaus. [Note: When illustrating the movement in a minimization problem, ignore the negative transposition step to maximum tableau form.]

5. Solve each of the canonical linear programming problems below by using the simplex algorithm.

a. Maximize $f(x, y) = x$
   subject to $x + y \leq 1$
   $$x - y \geq 1$$
   $$y - 2x \geq 1$$
   $$x, y \geq 0$$

b. Minimize $g(x, y) = y - 5x$
   subject to $x - y \geq 1$
   $$y \leq 8$$
   $$x, y \geq 0$$

c. Minimize $g(x, y, z) = -x - y$
   subject to $3x + 6y + 2z \leq 6$
   $$y + z \geq 1$$
   $$x, y, z \geq 0$$

d.

	x	y	-1	
	1	-1	3	$= -t_1$
	-2	1	2	$= -t_2$
	2	-1	0	$= f$

e.

	x	y	-3
x	-2	1	-3
y	1	-2	-2
-1	1	0	0

$= t_1 \quad = t_2 \quad = g$

f.

	x	y	-1	
	-1	-1	-2	$= -t_1$
	1	-2	0	$= -t_2$
	-2	1	1	$= -t_3$
	-1	3	0	$= f$

6. a. Solve the canonical linear programming problem below by using the simplex algorithm with anticycling rules corresponding to the list x, y, t_1, t_2, t_3.

	x	y	-1	
	3	2	1	$= -t_1$
	-9	-2	0	$= -t_2$
	3	1	0	$= -t_3$
	3	2	1	$= f$

b. Sketch the constraint set corresponding to the problem in part a and illustrate the movement in the constraint set diagram exhibited by the basic solutions of the successive tableaus in part a.

7. The canonical programming problem below (due to H.W. Kuhn and given in [B1]) will cycle after six particular simplex algorithm pivots. (The ambitious reader is invited to find these pivots and confirm this.) Solve the problem by using the simplex algorithm with anticycling rules.

x_1	x_2	x_3	x_4	-1	
-2	-9	1	9	0	$= -t_1$
1/3	1	-1/3	-2	0	$= -t_2$
2	3	-1	-12	2	$= -t_3$
2	3	-1	-12	0	$= f$

8. Each of the canonical linear programming problems below has infinitely many optimal solutions. Solve each of the linear programming problems by using the simplex algorithm and find all optimal solutions. [Note: In the exercises of Chapter 3 and Chapter 4, an increasing emphasis will be made on finding *all* optimal solutions of linear programming problems having infinitely many optimal solutions. For this reason, complete discussions of the problems below may be found in the answers section in the back of this book.]

a.

x	y	z	w	-1	
0	1	1	-1	3	$= -t_1$
1	1	1	-1	3	$= -t_2$
1	2	2	-4	0	$= f$

b.

	-1	-1	-1
x	-1	-1	-1
y	-1	1	-1
-1	-2	1	0
	$= t_1$	$= t_2$	$= g$

9. Solve each of the linear programming problems below.

   a. A nut company makes three different mixtures of nuts having the following compositions and profits per pound:

	Peanuts	Cashews	Pecans	Profit
Mixture 1	100%	0%	0%	$2
Mixture 2	80%	15%	5%	$1.50
Mixture 3	60%	30%	10%	$1

   The management of the company decides that it wants to produce at least twice as much of mixture 3 as of mixture 2 and at least twice as much of mixture 2 as of mixture 1. The company has 500 pounds of peanuts, 250 pounds of cashews, and 100 pounds of pecans available. If all production can be sold, how many pounds of each mixture should be produced so as to maximize profits?

   b. A hotel rental service needs to have clean towels for each day of a three-day period. Some of the clean towels may be purchased new and some may be dirty towels from previous days that have been washed by a laundry service. The cost of new towels is $1 per towel, the cost of a fast one-day laundry serice is 40¢ per towel, and the cost of a slow two-day laundry service is 25¢ per towel. If the rental service needs 300, 200, and 400 clean towels for each of the next three days (respectively), how many towels should the rental service buy new and how many should the rental service have washed by the different laundry services so as to minimize total costs?

10. Consider the canonical maximum tableau below:

$$
\begin{array}{cc|c|l}
x_1 & x_2 & -1 & \\
\hline
a_{11} & a_{12} & b_1 & = -t_1 \\
a_{21} & a_{22} & b_2 & = -t_2 \\
\hline
c_1 & c_2 & d & = f
\end{array}
$$

If $a_{ij} \neq 0$, prove that pivoting on a_{ij} is equivalent to solving the ith equation of the tableau for the jth variable and replacing every occurrence of this variable in the other equations of the tableau by the resulting expression.

11. (This problem is an application of the pivot transformation to linear algebra.) Let $A = [a_{ij}]_{n \times n}$ be a square matrix. Form the tableau

$$
\begin{array}{cccc|c|l}
x_1 & x_2 & \cdots & x_n & -1 & \\
\hline
a_{11} & a_{12} & \cdots & a_{1n} & 0 & = -t_1 \\
a_{21} & a_{22} & \cdots & a_{2n} & 0 & = -t_2 \\
\vdots & \vdots & & \vdots & \vdots & \vdots \\
a_{n1} & a_{n2} & \cdots & a_{nn} & 0 & = -t_n \\
\hline
0 & 0 & \cdots & 0 & 0 & = f
\end{array}
$$

Then it is a fact that it is possible to transform the tableau above into the tableau

t_1	t_2	$\cdots$	t_n	-1	
a_{11}'	a_{12}'	$\cdots$	a_{1n}'	0	$= -x_1$
a_{21}'	a_{22}'	$\cdots$	a_{2n}'	0	$= -x_2$
$\vdots$	$\vdots$		$\vdots$	$\vdots$	$\vdots$
a_{n1}'	a_{n2}'	$\cdots$	a_{nn}'	0	$= -x_n$
0	0	$\cdots$	0	0	$= f$

via a sequence of pivot transformations and possibly a rearrangement of rows and/or columns if and only if $A' = [a_{ij}']_{nxn} = A^{-1}$. Use this fact to invert the matrices below if possible. [Note: Do not use the simplex algorithm here to determine pivot entries; choose pivot entries that will move the x's from north to east and the t's from east to north. Also, since the last row and the last column of all tableaus will always be zero, they may be deleted without any harm.]

a. $\begin{bmatrix} 1 & 1 & 0 \\ 0 & 1 & 1 \\ 1 & 0 & 1 \end{bmatrix}$

b. $\begin{bmatrix} 1 & -1 & 0 \\ 0 & 1 & 1 \\ 1 & 0 & 1 \end{bmatrix}$

c. $\begin{bmatrix} 0 & 1 & 2 & 3 \\ 1 & 2 & 3 & 2 \\ 2 & 3 & 2 & 1 \\ 3 & 2 & 1 & 0 \end{bmatrix}$

12. a. Find a necessary and sufficient condition for the minimum tableau

	a_{11}	a_{21}	$\cdots$	a_{m1}	c_1
x_1	a_{11}	a_{21}	$\cdots$	a_{m1}	c_1
x_2	a_{12}	a_{22}	$\cdots$	a_{m2}	c_2
$\vdots$	$\vdots$	$\vdots$		$\vdots$	$\vdots$
x_n	a_{1n}	a_{2n}	$\cdots$	a_{mn}	c_n
-1	b_1	b_2	$\cdots$	b_m	d
	$= t_1$	$= t_2 \cdots$		$= t_m$	$= g$

to have a feasible basic solution.
b. Does the tableau satisfying the condition in part a but viewed as a maximum tableau necessarily have a feasible basic solution?
c. Find a necessary and sufficient condition for the tableau

$$
\begin{array}{c|cccc|c|l}
 & x_1 & x_2 & \cdots & x_n & -1 & \\
\hline
y_1 & a_{11} & a_{12} & \cdots & a_{1n} & b_1 & = -t_1 \\
y_2 & a_{21} & a_{22} & \cdots & a_{2n} & b_2 & = -t_2 \\
\vdots & \vdots & \vdots & & \vdots & \vdots & \\
y_m & a_{m1} & a_{m2} & \cdots & a_{mn} & b_m & = -t_m \\
\hline
-1 & c_1 & c_2 & \cdots & c_n & d & = f \\
\hline
 & = s_1 & = s_2 & \cdots & = s_n & = g &
\end{array}
$$

viewed as a maximum tableau to have a feasible basic solution *and* viewed as a minimum tableau to have a feasible basic solution.

13. In the simplex algorithm for maximum basic feasible tableaus, the choice of positive c_j in step (3) is unrestricted. It is shown in [R2] that restrictions on the choice of positive c_j in this step effectively reduce the number of pivoting operations required in the simplex algorithm, especially for large linear programming problems. Two such restrictions are discussed below.

   a. Replace step (3) of the simplex algorithm for maximum basic feasible tableaus with

   (3′) Choose the most positive $c_j > 0$.

   Apply this new simplex algorithm for maximum basic feasible tableaus to the linear programming problem of Example 11. Illustrate the movement in the constraint set exhibited by the basic solutions of successive tableaus above and compare this movement with the movement exhibited in Example 11.

   b. Replace step (3) of the simplex algorithm for maximum basic feasible tableaus with

   (3′) For each $c_j > 0$, compute

$$
\mu_j = \min_{1 \le i \le m} \{b_i/a_{ij} : a_{ij} > 0\}.
$$

   Choose the c_j for which $\mu_j c_j$ is most positive.

   Apply this new simplex algorithm for maximum basic feasible tableaus to the canonical linear programming problem below:

$$
\begin{array}{c|ccc|c|l}
 & x & y & z & -1 & \\
\hline
 & 1 & 2 & 1 & 4 & = -t_1 \\
 & 2 & 1 & 5 & 5 & = -t_2 \\
 & 3 & 2 & 0 & 6 & = -t_3 \\
\hline
 & 1 & 2 & 3 & 0 & = f
\end{array}
$$

CHAPTER 3

Noncanonical Linear Programming Problems

§0. Introduction

The simplex algorithm discussed in Chapter 2 solves canonical maximization and canonical minimization linear programming problems. The important properties that characterize a canonical linear programming problem (in this book at least) are the nonnegativity of the initial independent variables and the inequality form of the main constraints. However, easy modifications of the algorithms of Chapter 2 enable the solution of certain noncanonical linear programming problems. The concern of this chapter is the formalization of these modifications. Our linear programming solution procedure will consequently apply to a broader class of problems. In addition, the solution of the noncanonical problems here will be crucial to our first application in Chapter 5.

§1. Unconstrained Variables

Definition 1. A real variable in a linear programming problem is said to be *unconstrained* if there is no nonnegativity constraint on the variable.

The first type of noncanonical linear programming problem has canonical maximization or canonical minimization form except that there may not be nonnegativity constraints on all of the independent variables, i.e., some of these variables may be unconstrained. Fortunately, such a problem is easily transformed into an equivalent linear programming problem in canonical form plus a number of filed equations. We illustrate with several examples.

EXAMPLE 2.

$$\text{Maximize} \quad f(x, y) = x + 3y$$
$$\text{subject to} \quad x + 2y \leq 10$$
$$- 3x - y \leq - 15.$$

In this problem, both x and y are unconstrained. Before we illustrate the solution procedure, we sketch the constraint set of this problem:

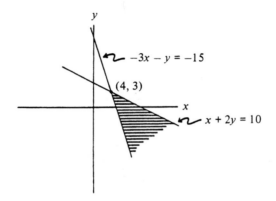

On the basis of this constraint set, can you guess the outcome of the problem?

We begin by recording the problem in a Tucker tableau as usual. To record the fact that x and y are unconstrained, we circle those variables.

ⓧ	ⓨ	-1	
1	2	10	= -t_1
-3	-1	-15	= -t_2
1	3	0	= f

Note that slack variables are always constrained to be nonnegative. Our goal now is to pivot each unconstrained independent variable down to the east. Since the tableau represents a noncanonical linear programming problem, the simplex algorithm of Chapter 2 is *not* used for this. The simplex algorithm only applies to canonical linear programming problems! The acceptable pivot entries are a_{11}, a_{12}, a_{21}, and a_{22}; in a noncanonical maximum tableau (or canonical maximum tableau for that matter), *never* pivot on any entry in the -1 column or the objective function row. The most convenient of these pivots for our purposes is $a_{11} = 1$ or $a_{22} = -1$ since all tableau entries will remain integral after pivoting. We choose $a_{11} = 1$ for definiteness; pivoting on 1 moves x down to the east:

x	y	-1	
1^*	2	10	$= -t_1$
-3	-1	-15	$= -t_2$
1	3	0	$= f$

pivot
x
down

t_1	y	-1	
1	2	10	$= -\,\boxed{x}$
3	5	15	$= -t_2$
-1	1	-10	$= f$

Since x is unconstrained, the equation represented by the first row of the new tableau represents no constraint on t_1 or y. Notice, however, that this equation will enable us to solve for x if we know t_1 and y. We hence file the equation corresponding to the x row (for future use) and delete that row from the tableau:

file equation
$t_1 + 2y - 10 = -x$;
delete x row

t_1	y	-1	
3	5	15	$= -t_2$
-1	1	-10	$= f$

To pivot y down to the east, we must use $a_{12} = 5$:

t_1	y	-1	
3	5^*	15	$= -t_2$
-1	1	-10	$= f$

pivot
y
down

t_1	t_2	-1	
3/5	1/5	3	$= -\,\boxed{y}$
$-8/5$	$-1/5$	-13	$= f$

Since y is unconstrained, the equation represented by the first row of the new tableau represents no constraint on t_1 or t_2. Notice, however, that this equation will enable us to solve for y if we know t_1 and t_2. We hence file the equation corresponding to the y row (for future use) and delete that row from the tableau:

	t_1	t_2	-1	
	$-8/5$	$-1/5$	-13	$= f$

file equation
$3/5t_1 + 1/5t_2 - 3 = -y$;
delete y row

This tableau is now in canonical form since all independent variables are constrained to be nonnegative. (Remember: slack variables are always constrained to be nonnegative!) At this point, we would ordinarily use the simplex algorithm to manipulate this canonical tableau into basic solution optimal form. However, the basic solution of the final tableau above is clearly optimal since any change in t_1 or t_2 would decrease f. Hence, the optimal solution to the noncanonical maximization linear programming problem is given by

$$t_1 = t_2 = 0, \quad \max f = 13,$$
$$y = 3 \text{ (from second filed equation)},$$
$$x = 4 \text{ (from first filed equation)}.$$

In view of the constraint set for this problem, this seems like a natural answer since the only extreme point is located at $(4, 3)$. But one must be careful with predictions as the following example illustrates.

EXAMPLE 3.

$$\text{Maximize} \quad f(x, y) = x + 3y$$
$$\text{subject to} \quad x + 2y \leq 10$$
$$3x + y \leq 15.$$

As in Example 2, both x and y are unconstrained. The constraint set of this problem is sketched below:

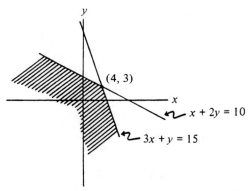

Can you guess the outcome of this problem?

Again, we record the problem in a Tucker tableau, pivot on a convenient entry that moves an unconstrained independent variable to the east, file the equation corresponding to the row of the unconstrained variable pivoted, and delete that row from the tableau:

$$t_1 + 2y - 10 = -x;$$
delete x row

Now pivot y down to the east, file the equation corresponding to the y row, and delete that row from the tableau:

file equation
$$3/5t_1 - 1/5t_2 - 3 = -y;$$
delete y row

t_1	t_2	-1	
$-8/5$	$1/5$	-13	$= f$

The final tableau above is in canonical form since all independent variables are constrained to be nonnegative. (Remember: Slack variables are always constrained to be nonnegative!) As in Example 2, we would ordinarily use the simplex algorithm at this point to manipulate this canonical tableau into basic solution optimal form. But the objective function f can clearly be made as large as we please by putting $t_1 = 0$ and letting $t_2 \to \infty$. Hence, the noncanonical maximization linear programming problem is unbounded. This may be a surprise in view of the constraint set. The linear programming problem does *not* have an optimal solution at the lone extreme point of the constraint set as in Example 2. How could one move in the constraint set so as to force $f(x, y) = x + 3y$ to get arbitrarily large? One answer is sketched below:

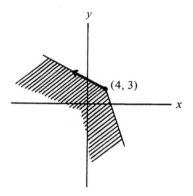

Since we are moving on the line $x + 2y = 10$, we have $x = 10 - 2y$ and

$$f(x, y) = x + 3y = (10 - 2y) + 3y = 10 + y.$$

Now, if we move as above, we have $y \to \infty$ whence $f(x, y) \to \infty$.

EXAMPLE 4. Solve the following modification of Example 3 above:

$$\text{Maximize} \quad f(x, y) = x + 3y$$
$$\text{subject to} \quad x + 2y \le 10$$
$$3x + y \le 15$$
$$x \ge 0.$$

Here, only y is unconstrained. The constraint set of the problem is sketched below:

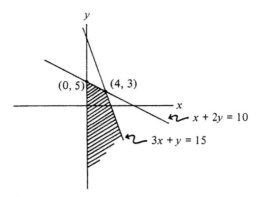

On the basis of Example 3, the outcome of this problem should be obvious. By requiring that x be nonnegative, we have effectively removed the unboundedness from Example 3 since points having larger and larger y values have been removed from the constraint set. Hence, in view of the movement which produced unboundedness in Example 3, we would conjecture that this modified problem should now have an optimal solution at the extreme point $(0, 5)$. We now substantiate our conjecture.

$$
\begin{array}{c c}
& x \quad \textcircled{y} \quad -1 \\
\begin{array}{|c c|c|}
\hline
1 & 2 & 10 \\
3 & 1^{*} & 15 \\
\hline
1 & 3 & 0 \\
\hline
\end{array}
&
\begin{array}{l}
= -t_1 \\
= -t_2 \\[4pt]
\xrightarrow{\quad\quad} \\
\text{pivot} \\
y \\
\text{down}
\end{array}
\\
= f
\end{array}
$$

$$
\begin{array}{c c}
& x \quad t_2 \quad -1 \\
\begin{array}{|c c|c|}
\hline
-5 & -2 & -20 \\
3 & 1 & 15 \\
\hline
-8 & -3 & -45 \\
\hline
\end{array}
&
\begin{array}{l}
= -t_1 \\
= -\textcircled{y} \\[4pt]
\xrightarrow{\quad\quad} \\
\text{file equation} \\
3x + t_2 - 15 = -y; \\
\text{delete } y \text{ row}
\end{array}
\\
= f
\end{array}
$$

$$
\begin{array}{c}
x \quad t_2 \quad -1 \\
\begin{array}{|c c|c|}
\hline
-5 & -2 & -20 \\
\hline
-8 & -3 & -45 \\
\hline
\end{array}
\end{array}
\begin{array}{l}
= -t_1 \\[10pt]
= f
\end{array}
$$

Note that the final tableau above is in canonical form since all independent variables are constrained to be nonnegative. Hence, we apply the simplex algorithm:

$$
\begin{array}{ccc}
x & t_2 & -1 \\
\end{array}
$$

-5 $-2^{\bullet}$	-20	$= -t_1$
-8 -3	-45	$= f$

simplex
algorithm

(Note that there are two pivot choices in the tableau above. What pivot choice would we have made if we were using the anticycling rules with corresponding list x, t_1, t_2?)

$$
\begin{array}{ccc}
x & t_1 & -1 \\
\end{array}
$$

$5/2$ $-1/2$	10	$= -t_2$
$-1/2$ $-3/2$	-15	$= f$

The basic solution of the tableau above is optimal. Hence the optimal solution of the noncanonical maximization linear programming problem is given by

$$x = t_1 = 0, \quad t_2 = 10, \quad \max f = 15,$$
$$y = 5 \text{ (from filed equation)}$$

and our conjecture is proved.

Minimization linear programming problems with unconstrained independent variables are handled similarly. Each unconstrained independent variable in the minimum tableau is pivoted down to the south and corresponding *columns* are filed and deleted. Once a canonical minimum tableau is obtained, the simplex algorithm is applied.

§2. Equations of Constraint

The second type of noncanonical linear programming problem has canonical maximization or canonical minimization form except that there may be some equality constraints among the initial variables instead of inequality constraints only. When we say equality constraints, we mean equations prior to the introduction of slack variables. Such equations of constraint are assigned slack "variable" 0 when written in slack form; this 0 is then exploited to obtain an equivalent linear programming problem in canonical form. We illustrate with several examples.

EXAMPLE 5.

$$
\begin{aligned}
\text{Maximize} \quad & f(x, y, z) = 2x + y - 2z \\
\text{subject to} \quad & x + y + z \leq 1 \\
& y + 4z = 2 \\
& x, y, z \geq 0.
\end{aligned}
$$

Note the equation of constraint $y + 4z = 2$. This equation can be rewritten in the form

$$y + 4z - 2 = -0;$$

this form corresponds to the usual slack form of a main constraint of a canonical maximization linear programming problem except that the slack "variable" is 0. It is highly recommended that the sign in front of the 0 be included; as with the sign of any other slack variable, this sign will stay behind when variables are interchanged during pivoting. We now record the problem in a Tucker tableau:

x	y	z	−1	
1	1	1	1	$= -t_1$
0	1	4	2	$= -0$
2	1	−2	0	$= f$

We wish to pivot the 0 up to the north. As with unconstrained variables, the simplex algorithm of Chapter 2 is *never* applied to a noncanonical tableau. Hence, we merely need to choose the most convenient pivot for our purposes. The acceptable pivot entries are a_{22} and a_{23}; again, *never* pivot on any entry in the −1 column or the objective function row of any maximum tableau. The most convenient of these pivots is $a_{22} = 1$ since all tableau entries will remain integral after pivoting:

x	y	z	−1	
1	1	1	1	$= -t_1$
0	1•	4	2	$= -0$
2	1	−2	0	$= f$

pivot
0
up

x	0	z	−1	
1	−1	−3	−1	$= -t_1$
0	1	4	2	$= -y$
2	−1	−6	−2	$= f$

Now the second column of the new tableau above never enters into the main constraints or objective function of this tableau since every entry is multiplied by 0. We may then delete this column without any loss of information:

		x z	−1	
		1 −3	−1	= −t_1
		0 4	2	= −y
		2 −6	−2	= f

→ delete
0
column

This tableau is now in canonical form since all 0 slack "variables" have been removed from the tableau. Hence, we apply the simplex algorithm:

x z	−1	
1 −3•	−1	= −t_1
0 4	2	= −y
2 −6	−2	= f

→ simplex
algorithm

x t_1	−1	
−1/3 −1/3	1/3	= −z
4/3 4/3	2/3	= −y
0 −2	0	= f

The basic solution of the final tableau above is optimal. Hence an optimal solution of the noncanonical maximization linear programming problem is given by

$$x = t_1 = 0, \quad z = 1/3, \quad y = 2/3, \quad \max f = 0.$$

The constraint set (which is a bounded region in the plane $y + 4z = 2$) and the basic optimal solution of this problem are sketched below:

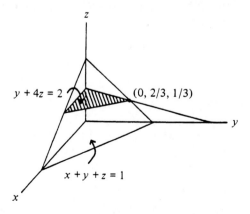

EXAMPLE 6.

$$\text{Maximize} \quad f(x, y, z) = x + 4y + 2z$$
$$\text{subject to} \quad x + 2y + 3z \leq 6$$
$$4x - 7y = 28$$
$$x, y, z \geq 0.$$

We record the problem in a Tucker tableau, pivot on the most convenient entry that moves the slack "variable" 0 to the north, and delete the column corresponding to this 0:

	x	y	z	−1	
	1	2	3	6	$= -t_1$
	4*	−7	0	28	$= -0$
	1	4	2	0	$= f$

pivot
0
up

	0	y	z	−1	
	−1/4	15/4	3	−1	$= -t_1$
	1/4	−7/4	0	7	$= -x$
	−1/4	23/4	2	−7	$= f$

delete
0
column

	y	z	−1	
	15/4	3	−1	$= -t_1$
	−7/4	0	7	$= -x$
	23/4	2	−7	$= f$

The final tableau above is in canonical form since all 0 slack "variables" have been removed from the tableau. The simplex algorithm applied to this tableau immediately yields infeasibility by the first row. Hence, the noncanonical maximization linear programming problem is infeasible. The constraint set (which must be empty since the linear programming problem has no feasible solutions) is sketched below:

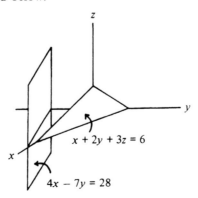

$x + 2y + 3z = 6$

$4x - 7y = 28$

Minimization linear programming problems with equations of constraint
are handled similarly. Each equation of constraint in the minimum tableau is
associated with an $= 0$ column; each such slack "variable" 0 is pivoted up to
the west and corresponding *rows* are deleted. Once a canonical minimum
tableau is obtained, the simplex algorithm is applied.

We conclude this section with an example of a noncanonical linear
programming problem which combines the two types of noncanonical
behavior discussed in this chapter.

EXAMPLE 7.

$$\text{Maximize} \quad f(x, y, z) = x + 2y + z$$
$$\text{subject to} \quad x + y + z = 6$$
$$x + y \leq 1$$
$$x, z \geq 0.$$

In this problem, we have an equation of constraint given by $x + y + z = 6$
and an unconstrained independent variable y. Not surprisingly, we simultaneously use both of the methods that have been developed in this chapter.
Recording the problem in a Tucker tableau, we obtain

x	y	z	-1	
1	1	1	6	$= -0$
1	1	0	1	$= -t_1$
1	2	1	0	$= f$

Now, our goal is to pivot the unconstrained independent variable y down to
the east and the slack "variable" 0 up to the north. We can accomplish both of
these at the same time by choosing the correct pivot, namely $a_{12} = 1$. (Under
what circumstances would we *not* be able to pivot an unconstrained
independent variable down to the east and a slack "variable" 0 up to the north
at the same time?) Then the filing and deletion of the y row and the deletion of
the 0 column proceed as before. The complete solution of the noncanonical
maximization linear programming problem follows.

x	y	z	-1	
1	1*	1	6	$= -0$
1	1	0	1	$= -t_1$
1	2	1	0	$= f$

$\longrightarrow$

pivot y down;
pivot 0 up

x	0	z	-1	
1	1	1	6	$= -\text{\textcircled{y}}$
0	-1	-1	-5	$= -t_1$
-1	-2	-1	-12	$= f$

file equation
$x + z - 6 = -y;$
delete y row;
delete 0 column

x	z	-1	
0	-1*	-5	$= -t_1$
-1	-1	-12	$= f$

simplex
algorithm

x	t_1	-1	
0	-1	5	$= -z$
-1	-1	-7	$= f$

The basic solution of the final tableau above is optimal. Hence the optimal
solution of the noncanonical maximization linear programming problem is
given by

$$x = t_1 = 0, \quad z = 5, \quad \max f = 7,$$
$$y = 1 \text{ (from filed equation).}$$

The constraint set (which is an unbounded region in the plane $x + y + z = 6$)
and the optimal solution of this problem are sketched below:

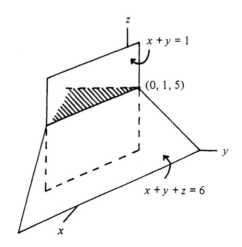

§3. Concluding Remarks

We summarize the crucial ideas of §1 and §2.

(i) Unconstrained independent variables in noncanonical tableaus always get pivoted down—from north to east in maximum tableaus and from west to south in minimum tableaus. (Remember: *Never* pivot on any entry in the -1 column/row or the objective function row/column of any tableau.)

(ii) Slack "variables" of 0 (corresponding to equations of constraint) in noncanonical tableaus always get pivoted up—from east to north in maximum tableaus and from south to west in minimum tableaus. (Again, *never* pivot on any entry in the -1 column/row or the objective function row/column of any tableau.)

(iii) In noncanonical maximum tableaus, rows corresponding to pivoted unconstrained variables are filed and deleted. In noncanonical minimum tableaus, columns corresponding to pivoted unconstrained variables are filed and deleted.

(iv) In noncanonical maximum tableaus, columns corresponding to slack "variables" of 0 are deleted. In noncanonical minimum tableaus, rows corresponding to slack "variables" of 0 are deleted.

(v) *Never* apply the simplex algorithm until the noncanonical tableau has been transformed into a canonical tableau. A canonical tableau is a tableau having no unconstrained independent variables and no slack "variables" of 0.

Exercises

1. Solve each of the noncanonical linear programming problems below. If a linear programming problem has infinitely many optimal solutions, find all optimal solutions.

   a. Maximize $f(x, y, z) = x - y + z$
      subject to $x + y \geq 2$
      $$z - y \geq 3$$
      $$2x + z \leq 8$$

   b. Maximize $f(x, y, z) = x + y + z$
      subject to $x - y - z \leq 2$
      $$y - z \geq 1$$

   c. Minimize $g(x, y, z) = 3x + y + 2z$
      subject to $x + 2y + 3z \geq 24$
      $$2x + 4y + 3z = 36$$
      $$x, y, z \geq 0$$

   d. Minimize $g(x, y, z) = 3x + y + 2z$
      subject to $x + 2y + 3z \geq 24$
      $$2x + 4y + 3z = 36$$
      $$y, z \geq 0$$

    e. Maximize $\quad f(x, y, z) = x + y + z$

       subject to $\quad x + y + z \leq 3$

$$x + y \leq 1$$
$$y + 2z = 2$$
$$x, y \geq 0$$

    f. Maximize $\quad f(x, y, z) = 3x - 2y + 3z$

       subject to $\quad x - y + 2z = 6$

$$x + 2z = 8$$
$$y + 2z \geq 2$$
$$y, z \geq 0$$

    g. Minimize $\quad g(x, y, z) = -5x + y - 2z$

       subject to $\quad 2x + z = 0$

$$x - y \geq 1$$
$$3x - y + z \leq 3$$

    h. Maximize $\quad f(x, y) = x + y$

       subject to $\quad 2x + y = 5$

$$x - y = -2$$
$$x + 3y = 6$$
$$x, y \geq 0$$

2. Label each of the following statements TRUE or FALSE. If the statement is FALSE, provide a counterexample.

    a. A noncanonical linear programming problem with more unconstrained independent variables than constraints is unbounded. (See, for example, part b of Exercise 1 above.)

    b. A noncanonical linear programming problem with more equations of constraint than independent variables is infeasible. (See, for example, part h of Exercise 1 above.)

3. The noncanonical linear programming problem of Example 5 has infinitely many optimal solutions. Find all optimal solutions and graph these optimal solutions on the constraint set diagram of Example 5.

4. Show that the noncanonical linear programming problem

$$\text{Maximize} \quad f(x, y, z) = 2x + y - 2z$$
$$\text{subject to} \quad x + y + z = 1$$
$$y + 4z \leq 2$$
$$x, y, z \geq 0$$

has the same optimal solution as that of (5) in Chapter 1. Sketch the constraint set and indicate this optimal solution.

5. Sketch the constraint set for each noncanonical linear programming problem below. On the basis of this constraint set, formulate a conjecture as to whether or not the solution of the given problem is the same as the solution of the associated canonical linear programming problem where all independent variables are constrained to be nonnegative. Verify your conjecture by solving both linear programming problems.

a. Maximize $f(x, y) = x + y$
   subject to $x + 4y \le 12$
   $\qquad\qquad x - 4y \le -4$

b. Minimize $g(x, y) = x + 2y$
   subject to $x + y \ge 1$
   $\qquad\qquad 4x - 4y \ge 1$

c. Maximize $f(x, y) = -x + 2y$
   subject to $-x + y \le -1$
   $\qquad\qquad 2x - y \le -2$

d. Minimize $g(x, y) = -x - y$
   subject to $-x + 2y \ge 1$
   $\qquad\qquad x - y \ge 1$

6. An alternate method for transforming a linear programming problem with unconstrained independent variables into canonical form is to replace every unconstrained independent variable by the difference of two independent variables constrained to be nonnegative. This produces an equivalent canonical linear programming problem which is solved by using the simplex algorithm. For example, the linear programming problem of Example 4, namely

$$\text{Maximize} \quad f(x, y) = x + 3y$$
$$\text{subject to} \quad x + 2y \le 10$$
$$3x + y \le 15 \tag{1}$$
$$x \ge 0,$$

is noncanonical since the variable y is unconstrained. Put $y = y^+ - y^-$ with $y^+, y^- \ge 0$. Replacing every y in (1) by $y^+ - y^-$, we obtain the equivalent canonical linear programming problem

$$\text{Maximize} \quad f(x, y^+, y^-) = x + 3y^+ - 3y^-$$
$$\text{subject to} \quad x + 2y^+ - 2y^- \le 10$$
$$3x + y^+ - y^- \le 15 \tag{2}$$
$$x, y^+, y^- \ge 0,$$

which is solved by using the simplex algorithm.

a. Solve (2) above.
b. Use the solution of (2) along with $y = y^+ - y^-$ to solve (1). Compare your solution with that obtained in Example 4.

7. An alternate method for transforming a linear programming problem with equations of constraint into canonical form is to replace every equation of constraint by two inequality constraints. This produces an equivalent canonical linear programming problem which is solved by using the simplex algorithm. For example, the linear programming problem of Example 5, namely

$$\text{Maximize} \quad f(x, y, z) = 2x + y - 2z$$
$$\text{subject to} \quad x + y + z \le 1$$
$$y + 4z = 2$$
$$x, y, z \ge 0,$$

is noncanonical due to the equation of constraint $y + 4z = 2$. Replacing this equation by the two inequality constraints $y + 4z \leq 2$ and $y + 4z \geq 2$, we obtain the equivalent canonical linear programming problem

$$
\begin{aligned}
\text{Maximize} \quad & f(x, y, z) = 2x + y - 2z \\
\text{subject to} \quad & x + y + z \leq 1 \\
& y + 4z \leq 2 \\
& y + 4z \geq 2 \\
& x, y, z \geq 0
\end{aligned}
\tag{3}
$$

which is solved by using the simplex algorithm. Solve (3) by using the simplex algorithm and compare your solution with that obtained in Example 5.

8. Solve Example 7 by using the methods of Exercise 6 and Exercise 7 above.

9. Discuss some disadvantages of the methods of Exercise 6 and Exercise 7 above.

CHAPTER 4

Duality Theory

§0. Introduction

The concept of duality is of fundamental importance in linear programming. This chapter is devoted to a theoretical treatment of duality with the goal of gaining a greater understanding of the relationships that exist between dual linear programming problems. These relationships, although interesting from a purely mathematical viewpoint, are crucial to many applications, some of which are investigated more deeply in Chapter 5, Chapter 6, and Chapter 7. The treatment of duality presented here is, in large part, due to A.W. Tucker.

§1. Duality in Canonical Tableaus

Recall that the canonical maximization linear programming problem of 2§2 had initial tableau

x_1	x_2	-1	
1	2	20	$= -t_A$
2	2	30	$= -t_B$
2	1	25	$= -t_C$
200	150	0	$= P$

and that the canonical minimization linear programming problem of 2§4 had initial tableau

$$
\begin{array}{c|cc|c}
x_1 & 1 & 2 & 20 \\
x_2 & 2 & 2 & 30 \\
x_3 & 2 & 1 & 25 \\
\hline
-1 & 200 & 150 & 0 \\
& = t_P & = t_F & = C
\end{array}
$$

Furthermore, exactly the same pivot steps solved both linear programming problems (although, at this point, we would use a different procedure than that in 2§4 to solve the minimization problem) and max P was equal to min C. This suggests an intimate relationship between these two linear programming problems. Do similar relationships exist in general? The answer to this question is a resounding YES; it is the purpose of this chapter to examine these relationships.

Any canonical tableau can be interpreted both as a canonical maximization linear programming problem and a canonical minimization linear programming problem. For example, the canonical tableau

$$
\begin{array}{c|cccc|c|l}
 & x_1 & x_2 & \cdots & x_n & -1 & \\
\hline
y_1 & a_{11} & a_{12} & \cdots & a_{1n} & b_1 & = -t_1 \\
y_2 & a_{21} & a_{22} & \cdots & a_{2n} & b_2 & = -t_2 \\
\vdots & \vdots & \vdots & & \vdots & \vdots & \vdots \\
y_m & a_{m1} & a_{m2} & \cdots & a_{mn} & b_m & = -t_m \\
\hline
-1 & c_1 & c_2 & \cdots & c_n & d & = f \\
 & = s_1 & = s_2 & \cdots & = s_n & = g &
\end{array}
$$

represents the canonical slack maximization linear programming problem given by the variables to the north and east (ignoring the variables to the west and south) *and* the canonical slack minimization linear programming problem given by the variables to the west and south (ignoring the variables to the north and east).

Definition 1. Any pair of canonical maximization and canonical minimization linear programming problems corresponding to the same tableau as above are said to exhibit *duality* or be *duals* of one another. The tableau of dual canonical linear programming problems is said to be a *dual canonical tableau.*

Questions concerning the behavior of dual canonical linear programming problems instantly arise; we conclude this section with some questions that will be answered in forthcoming sections. Consider an arbitrary canonical maximization linear programming problem and its dual canonical minimization linear programming problem. If one of these linear programming problems has an optimal solution, must the other linear programming problem also have an optimal solution? More generally, what combinations are possible? (For example, a given canonical maximization linear programming problem can have an optimal solution, be infeasible, or be unbounded. The same is true for a given canonical minimization linear programming problem. Now, how many of the $3^2 = 9$ different combinations are possible?) If both linear programming problems have optimal solutions, does the optimal value of the maximum objective function have to equal the optimal value of the minimum objective function? On the basis of your knowledge at present, formulate answers to these questions. Your intuition may prove to be correct!

§2. The Dual Simplex Algorithm

The simplex algorithm of Chapter 2 views all canonical linear programming problems from the perspective of canonical maximization linear programming problems, i.e., canonical maximization linear programming problems are handled directly and canonical minimization linear programming problems are transformed into equivalent canonical maximization linear programming problems by negative transposition. It is possible, however, to view all canonical linear programming problems from the perspective of canonical minimization linear programming problems and transform canonical maximization linear programming problems into equivalent canonical minimization linear programming problems by negative transposition. What follows is this dual form of the simplex algorithm of Chapter 2. It is *not* suggested that this dual simplex algorithm be committed to memory. It does, however, have certain important theoretical ramifications as we will see. For now, be content with noticing the obvious similarity and duality of the algorithms.

Definition 2. Let

a_{11}	a_{12}	$\cdots$	a_{1n}	b_1
a_{21}	a_{22}	$\cdots$	a_{2n}	b_2
$\vdots$	$\vdots$		$\vdots$	$\vdots$
a_{m1}	a_{m2}	$\cdots$	a_{mn}	b_m
c_1	c_2	$\cdots$	c_n	d

(ind. var.'s) on the left, -1 on the bottom left, $=$ (dep. var.'s) below, $= g$ at bottom right.

be a tableau of a canonical slack minimization linear programming problem. The tableau is said to be *minimum basic feasible* if $c_1, c_2, \ldots, c_n \leq 0$.

In a minimum basic feasible tableau, the basic solution is a feasible solution (see Exercise 12a in Chapter 2).

The Dual Simplex Algorithm for Minimum Tableaus

(1) The current tableau is of the form

	a_{11} a_{12} $\cdots$ a_{1n}	b_1
(ind. var.'s)	a_{21} a_{22} $\cdots$ a_{2n}	b_2
	$\vdots$ $\quad \vdots$ $\qquad \vdots$	$\vdots$
	a_{m1} a_{m2} $\cdots$ a_{mn}	b_m
-1	c_1 $\quad c_2$ $\cdots$ c_n	d
	= (dep. var.'s)	= g

(2) If $c_1, c_2, \ldots c_n \leq 0$, go to (6). Otherwise, continue.
(3) Choose $c_j > 0$ such that j is maximal.
(4) If $a_{1j}, a_{2j}, \ldots, a_{mj} \leq 0$, STOP; the minimization problem is infeasible.
Otherwise, continue.
(5) If $j = n$, choose $a_{in} > 0$, pivot on a_{in}, and go to (1). If $j < n$, choose $a_{ij} > 0$,
compute

$$\min_{k>j} (\{c_j/a_{ij}\} \cup \{c_k/a_{ik} : a_{ik} < 0\}) = c_p/a_{ip},$$

pivot on a_{ip}, and go to (1).
(6) The current tableau is minimum basic feasible, i.e., of the form

	a_{11} a_{12} $\cdots$ a_{1n}	b_1
(ind. var.'s)	a_{21} a_{22} $\cdots$ a_{2n}	b_2
	$\vdots$ $\quad \vdots$ $\qquad \vdots$	$\vdots$
	a_{m1} a_{m2} $\cdots$ a_{mn}	b_m
-1	c_1 $\quad c_2$ $\cdots$ c_n	d
	= (dep. var.'s)	= g

with $c_1, c_2, \ldots, c_n \leq 0$.
(7) If $b_1, b_2, \ldots, b_m \geq 0$, STOP; the basic solution of the current minimum
tableau is optimal. Otherwise, continue.
(8) Choose $b_i < 0$.
(9) If $a_{i1}, a_{i2}, \ldots, a_{in} \geq 0$, STOP; the minimization problem is unbounded.
Otherwise, continue.
(10) Compute

$$\min_{1 \leq j \leq n} \{c_j/a_{ij} : a_{ij} < 0\} = c_p/a_{ip},$$

pivot on a_{ip}, and go to (6).

The Dual Simplex Algorithm for Maximum Tableaus

(1) The current tableau is of the form

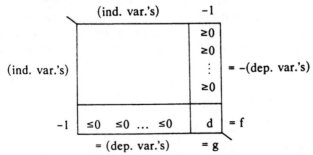

(2) Take the negative transpose of the tableau to obtain a minimum tableau.
(3) Apply the dual simplex algorithm for minimum tableaus.
(4) Max $f = -\min(-g)$.

In some sense, it would be foolish to spend time learning the dual simplex algorithm above, primarily since it is simply a restatement of the simplex algorithm of Chapter 2 in dual form. However, the dual simplex algorithm is of prime theoretical significance. Assume that we have a pair of dual canonical linear programming problems recorded in a dual canonical tableau. Note that any single pivot transformation transforms the maximization problem into an equivalent maximization problem having the same feasible solutions as the original *and* transforms the minimization problem into an equivalent minimization problem having the same feasible solutions as the original. Assume that the maximization problem is not infeasible or unbounded. If the simplex algorithm of Chapter 2 is applied to this maximization problem and we make sure that variables corresponding to pivot entries are interchanged in the dual minimization problem as well as the maximization problem, the algorithm terminates in a basic optimal solution for the maximization problem with the tableau in the form

But the basic solution of the minimization problem is also optimal since the dual simplex algorithm terminates with the tableau in the same form! Hence the existence of an optimal solution for a canonical maximization linear programming problem implies the existence of an optimal solution for its dual canonical minimization linear programming problem. The converse is true;

simply "dualize" the above argument. (Assume that we have a pair of dual canonical linear programming problems recorded in a dual canonical tableau and assume that the minimization problem is not infeasible or unbounded. If the dual simplex algorithm is applied to this minimization problem and we make sure that variables corresponding to pivot entries are interchanged in the dual maximization problem as well as the minimization problem, the algorithm terminates in a basic optimal solution for the minimization problem with the tableau in the form above. But the basic solution of the maximization problem is also optimal since the simplex algorithm of Chapter 2 terminates with the tableau in the same form! Hence the existence of an optimal solution for a canonical minimization linear programming problem implies the existence of an optimal solution for its dual canonical maximization linear programming problem.) Hence, the existence of an optimal solution for one canonical linear programming problem implies the existence of an optimal solution for its dual linear programming problem. Now assume that we have a pair of optimal solutions of dual canonical linear programming problems. Since all optimal solutions of a linear programming problem yield the same objective function value (otherwise, some of the solutions would not be optimal!) and since one such pair of optimal solutions for the maximization and minimization problems arises from the basic solutions of a dual canonical tableau in the form above, we have $f = g = d$. We have just proven the following theorem.

Theorem 3. *If a canonical maximization linear programming problem has an optimal solution, then the dual canonical minimization linear programming problem has an optimal solution and vice versa. Furthermore, dual canonical linear programming problems with optimal solutions have $f = g$ at these solutions.*   □

As an additional consequence of the agreement of the tableau forms that terminate both the simplex algorithm of Chapter 2 and the dual simplex algorithm of this chapter in optimal solutions, we note that canonical minimization linear programming problems with optimal solutions can be solved directly by applying the simplex algorithm of Chapter 2 to the dual canonical maximization linear programming problem—*no negative transposition is required*. Two linear programming problems are being solved for the price of one! Nice!

EXAMPLE 4. The tableau sequence

	x_1	x_2	-1	
y_1	1	2	20	$= -t_1$
y_2	2	2	30	$= -t_2$
y_3	2^*	1	25	$= -t_3$
-1	200	150	0	$= f$
	$= s_1$	$= s_2$	$= g$	

	t_3	x_2	-1	
y_1	$-1/2$	$3/2$	$15/2$	$= -t_1$
y_2	-1	$1^\bullet$	5	$= -t_2$
s_1	$1/2$	$1/2$	$25/2$	$= -x_1$
-1	-100	50	-2500	$= f$
	$= y_3$	$= s_2$	$= g$	

$\longrightarrow$

	t_3	t_2	-1	
y_1	1	$-3/2$	0	$= -t_1$
s_2	-1	1	5	$= -x_2$
s_1	1	$-1/2$	10	$= -x_1$
-1	-50	-50	-2750	$= f$
	$= y_3$	$= y_2$	$= g$	

solves the linear programming problems of 2§2 and 2§4 simultaneously without negative transposition. (Note the notation change from 2§2 and 2§4.) Verify for yourself that the simplex algorithm of Chapter 2 is being implemented in the maximization linear programming problem.

EXAMPLE 5. Solve the dual canonical linear programming problems below:

	x_1	x_2	-1	
y_1	20	25	300	$= -t_1$
y_2	40	20	500	$= -t_2$
-1	1000	800	0	$= f$
	$= s_1$	$= s_2$	$= g$	

We apply the simplex algorithm of Chapter 2 to the maximization linear programming problem, making sure that variables corresponding to pivot entries are interchanged in the dual minimization problem as well as the maximization problem.

	x_1	x_2	-1	
y_1	20	25	300	$= -t_1$
y_2	$40^\bullet$	20	500	$= -t_2$
-1	1000	800	0	$= f$
	$= s_1$	$= s_2$	$= g$	

$\longrightarrow$

	t_2	x_2	-1	
y_1	$-1/2$	15^*	50	$=-t_1$
s_1	$1/40$	$1/2$	$25/2$	$=-x_1$
-1	-25	300	-12500	$=f$
	$=y_2$	$=s_2$	$=g$	

	t_2	t_1	-1	
s_2	$-1/30$	$1/15$	$10/3$	$=-x_2$
s_1	$1/24$	$-1/30$	$65/6$	$=-x_1$
-1	-15	-20	-13500	$=f$
	$=y_2$	$=y_1$	$=g$	

The basic solution of each linear programming problem in the final tableau above is optimal:

$$t_2 = t_1 = 0, \quad x_2 = 10/3, \quad x_1 = 65/6, \quad \max f = 13500,$$
$$s_2 = s_1 = 0, \quad y_2 = 15, \quad y_1 = 20, \quad \min g = 13500.$$

A remark is in order here. The minimization linear programming problem above is the same as that in 2§7. (Note the notation change from 2§7.) The simplex algorithm for minimum tableaus applied there required negative transposition and only solved one linear programming problem. In contrast, we have solved *two* linear programming problems above and have eliminated the negative transposition step. More solutions with less work!

A consequence of the fact that the existence of an optimal solution for a canonical linear programming problem implies the existence of an optimal solution for its dual canonical linear programming problem is that, if a canonical linear programming problem is infeasible or unbounded, then the dual canonical linear programming problem must be infeasible or unbounded. Are all four combinations of pathology possible? Experiment with some examples and formulate some conjectures!

§3. Matrix Formulation of Canonical Tableaus

Consider the dual canonical tableau

	x_1	x_2	$\cdots$	x_n	-1	
y_1	a_{11}	a_{12}	$\cdots$	a_{1n}	b_1	$=-t_1$
y_2	a_{21}	a_{22}	$\cdots$	a_{2n}	b_2	$=-t_2$
$\vdots$	$\vdots$	$\vdots$		$\vdots$	$\vdots$	
y_m	a_{m1}	a_{m2}	$\cdots$	a_{mn}	b_m	$=-t_m$
-1	c_1	c_2	$\cdots$	c_n	d	$=f$
	$=s_1$	$=s_2$	$\cdots$	$=s_n$	$=g$	

(1)

Letting

$$A = \begin{bmatrix} a_{11} & a_{12} & \cdots & a_{1n} \\ a_{21} & a_{22} & \cdots & a_{2n} \\ \vdots & \vdots & & \vdots \\ a_{m1} & a_{m2} & \cdots & a_{mn} \end{bmatrix}, \quad B = \begin{bmatrix} b_1 \\ b_2 \\ \vdots \\ b_m \end{bmatrix}, \quad C = [c_1 \quad c_2 \quad \cdots \quad c_n], \quad D = [d],$$

$$X = [x_1 \quad x_2 \quad \cdots \quad x_n], \quad Y = \begin{bmatrix} y_1 \\ y_2 \\ \vdots \\ y_m \end{bmatrix}, \quad T = \begin{bmatrix} t_1 \\ t_2 \\ \vdots \\ t_m \end{bmatrix}, \quad \text{and}$$

$$S = [s_1 \quad s_2 \quad \cdots \quad s_n],$$

we have that (1) becomes

	X	−1	
Y	A	B	= −T
−1	C	D	= f
	= S	= g	

(2)

We can now reformulate the dual canonical linear programming problems of (2) in terms of matrix equations:

Matrix reformulation of canonical maximization linear programming problem of (2):

$$\text{Maximize} \quad f = CX^t - D$$
$$\text{subject to} \quad AX^t - B = -T$$
$$X, T \geq 0.$$

Matrix reformulation of canonical minimization linear programming problem of (2):

$$\text{Minimize} \quad g = Y^t B - D$$
$$\text{subject to} \quad Y^t A - C = S$$
$$Y, S \geq 0.$$

Here, $'$ denotes the transpose of a matrix. Also, a matrix being greater than or equal to zero is to be interpreted as every entry of that matrix being greater than or equal to zero. These matrix reformulations allow concise and accurate representations of dual canonical linear programming problems which are useful in the theory of duality that follows. Before continuing, make sure that you can clearly see how these matrix equations represent the canonical slack forms of the maximization and minimization linear programming problems of (1). Substitute the relevant matrices and perform the indicated operations!

(For example, $f = CX^t - D$ if and only if

$$f = \lfloor c_1 \quad c_2 \quad \cdots \quad c_n \rfloor [x_1 \quad x_2 \quad \cdots \quad x_n]^t - [d]$$

$$= [c_1 \quad c_2 \quad \cdots \quad c_n] \begin{bmatrix} x_1 \\ x_2 \\ \vdots \\ x_n \end{bmatrix} - [d]$$

$$= c_1 x_1 + c_2 x_2 + \cdots + c_n x_n - d$$

which is the maximization objective function of (1). Also, $AX^t - B = -T$ if and only if

$$\begin{bmatrix} a_{11} & a_{12} & \cdots & a_{1n} \\ a_{21} & a_{22} & \cdots & a_{2n} \\ \vdots & \vdots & & \vdots \\ a_{m1} & a_{m2} & \cdots & a_{mn} \end{bmatrix} [x_1 \quad x_2 \quad \cdots \quad x_n]^t - \begin{bmatrix} b_1 \\ b_2 \\ \vdots \\ b_m \end{bmatrix} = - \begin{bmatrix} t_1 \\ t_2 \\ \vdots \\ t_m \end{bmatrix}$$

if and only if

$$\begin{bmatrix} a_{11} & a_{12} & \cdots & a_{1n} \\ a_{21} & a_{22} & \cdots & a_{2n} \\ \vdots & \vdots & & \vdots \\ a_{m1} & a_{m2} & \cdots & a_{mn} \end{bmatrix} \begin{bmatrix} x_1 \\ x_2 \\ \vdots \\ x_n \end{bmatrix} - \begin{bmatrix} b_1 \\ b_2 \\ \vdots \\ b_m \end{bmatrix} = - \begin{bmatrix} t_1 \\ t_2 \\ \vdots \\ t_m \end{bmatrix}$$

if and only if

$$a_{11} x_1 + a_{12} x_2 + \cdots + a_{1n} x_n - b_1 = -t_1$$
$$a_{21} x_1 + a_{22} x_2 + \cdots + a_{2n} x_n - b_2 = -t_2$$
$$\vdots$$
$$a_{m1} x_1 + a_{m2} x_2 + \cdots + a_{mn} x_n - b_m = -t_m$$

which are the main maximization constraints of (1).)

§4. The Duality Equation

Much of the theory of duality presented in this book relies on the following theorem due to A.W. Tucker known as the duality equation. In what follows, we assume all notation developed in §3.

Theorem 6 (The Duality Equation). *For any pair of feasible solutions of dual canonical linear programming problems, we have*

$$g - f = SX^t + Y^t T.$$

Before proving this theorem, we illustrate it with an example.

EXAMPLE 7. Consider the dual canonical tableau

$$
\begin{array}{c|cc|c|l}
 & x_1 & x_2 & -1 & \\
\hline
y_1 & 1 & 2 & 3 & = -t_1 \\
y_2 & 4 & 5 & 6 & = -t_2 \\
\hline
-1 & 7 & 8 & 9 & = f \\
\end{array}
$$

$$= s_1 \quad = s_2 \quad = g$$

We first construct a feasible solution to the canonical maximization linear programming problem. Let $x_1 = 1$ and $x_2 = 1/3$ (for example). Then $t_1 = 4/3$ by the first row of the tableau and $t_2 = 1/3$ by the second row of the tableau. Since all of x_1, x_2, t_1, and t_2 are nonnegative, this solution to the canonical maximization linear programming problem is feasible. The value of f at this feasible solution is 2/3 from the third row of the tableau. Next, we construct a feasible solution to the canonical minimization linear programming problem. Let $y_1 = 1$ and $y_2 = 2$ (for example). Then $s_1 = 2$ by the first column of the tableau and $s_2 = 4$ by the second column of the tableau. Since all of y_1, y_2, s_1, and s_2 are nonnegative, this solution to the canonical minimization problem is feasible. The value of g at this feasible solution is 6 from the third column of the tableau. Now

$$g - f = 6 - 2/3 = 16/3$$

and

$$SX' + Y'T = [s_1 \quad s_2] \begin{bmatrix} x_1 \\ x_2 \end{bmatrix} + [y_1 \quad y_2] \begin{bmatrix} t_1 \\ t_2 \end{bmatrix}$$

$$= [2 \quad 4] \begin{bmatrix} 1 \\ 1/3 \end{bmatrix} + [1 \quad 2] \begin{bmatrix} 4/3 \\ 1/3 \end{bmatrix}$$

$$= 2 + 4/3 + 4/3 + 2/3$$

$$= 16/3,$$

i.e.,

$$g - f = SX' + Y'T!!$$

We now prove Theorem 6.

PROOF (of Theorem 6). From the matrix reformulations of the canonical maximization and the canonical minimization linear programming problems in §3, we obtain the equations

$$f = CX' - D$$
$$B = AX' + T$$
$$g = Y'B - D$$
$$C = Y'A - S.$$

Now

$$g - f = (Y'B - D) - (CX' - D)$$
$$= Y'B - CX'$$

$$= Y^t(AX^t + T) - (Y^tA - S)X^t$$
$$= Y^tAX^t + Y^tT - Y^tAX^t + SX^t$$
$$= Y^tT + SX^t$$
$$= SX^t + Y^tT. \qquad \square$$

Note that only the matrix forms of the objective function and the main constraints were used in the proof of the duality equation above; the nonnegativity constraints were *not* used. Hence the duality equation is also true for solutions to dual canonical linear programming problems that are infeasible in terms of the nonnegativity constraints only, i.e., solutions which satisfy all main constraints but which violate one or more nonnegativity constraints. The duality equation does not hold if an infeasible solution violates a main constraint!

The duality equation has several corollaries which begin to address the questions at the end of §1.

Corollary 8. *For any pair of feasible solutions of dual canonical linear programming problems, we have*

$$g \geq f.$$

(Note that this is certainly true for Example 7!)

PROOF. Since the solutions of the dual canonical linear programming problems are feasible, every entry of S, X^t, Y^t, and T is nonnegative. Hence, $SX^t + Y^tT \geq 0$. Since

$$g - f = SX^t + Y^tT$$

by the duality equation, we have $g - f \geq 0$ or $g \geq f$. $\qquad \square$

Corollary 9. (i) *If a canonical maximization linear programming problem is unbounded, then the dual canonical minimization linear programming problem is infeasible.*
(ii) *If a canonical minimization linear programming problem is unbounded, then the dual canonical maximization linear programming problem is infeasible.*

PROOF. (i) Assume, by way of contradiction, that the maximization linear programming problem is unbounded and that the dual minimization linear programming problem has a feasible solution. By Corollary 8, this feasible solution must yield a value for g that is greater than or equal to the value of f for any feasible solution to the maximization problem. But since the maximization problem is unbounded, feasible solutions for this problem exist for which $f \to \infty$. Hence no such feasible solution corresponding to a value for g can exist and the minimization linear programming problem is infeasible.
(ii) The proof is similar to (i). $\qquad \square$

Note that Corollary 9 rules out the possibility of ever encountering dual unbounded canonical linear programming problems.

Corollary 10. *Any pair of feasible solutions of dual canonical linear programming problems for which $f = g$ are optimal solutions.*

PROOF. No other feasible solution can increase the value of f since, if it could, we would have $f > g$, contradicting Corollary 8. Similarly, no other feasible solution can decrease the value of g. Hence the given feasible solutions are optimal solutions.   □

A caution is in order here. Corollary 10 does *not* say that, if a canonical linear programming problem has an optimal solution, then the dual canonical linear programming problem also has an optimal solution. It does not even guarantee that dual canonical linear programming problems both having optimal soluions will necessarily have $f = g$ at these solutions. Both of these statements are, however, true by Theorem 3. Corollary 10 only assures the converse of this latter statement, namely that any pair of feasible solutions of dual canonical linear programming problems which yield the same values at the canonical maximization and the canonical minimization objective functions must be optimal solutions.

We conclude this section with a brief discussion of the topic of complementary slackness. Complementary slackness is an important consideration in sensitivity analysis (not discussed in this book; see, for example, [R2]) and has played an important role in the development of many algorithms in the field of linear programming.

Definition 11. Any pair of feasible solutions of the dual canonical linear programming problems

	X	−1	
Y	A	B	= −T
−1	C	D	= f
	= S	= g	

(notation as in §3) for which

(i) $x_j \neq 0 \Rightarrow s_j = 0, \ j = 1, 2, \ldots, n$, and
(ii) $y_i \neq 0 \Rightarrow t_i = 0, \ i = 1, 2, \ldots, m$,

are said to exhibit *complementary slackness.*

EXAMPLE 12. Consider the pair of optimal solutions of the dual canonical linear programming problems of Example 4 in §2. The dual tableau

	x_1	x_2	-1	
y_1	1	2	20	$= -t_1$
y_2	2	2	30	$= -t_2$
y_3	2	1	25	$= -t_3$
-1	200	150	0	$= f$
	$= s_1$	$= s_2$	$= g$	

has optimal maximization solution $x_1 = 10, x_2 = 5, t_1 = t_2 = t_3 = 0, \max f = 2750$ and optimal minimization solution $y_1 = 0, y_2 = y_3 = 50, s_1 = s_2 = 0$, $\min g = 2750$. Whenever x_j is not equal to zero, s_j is equal to zero and similarly for y_i and t_i. Hence complementary slackness is exhibited in these optimal solutions.

EXAMPLE 13. Consider the pair of optimal solutions of the dual canonical linear programming problems of Example 5 in §2. The dual tableau

	x_1	x_2	-1	
y_1	20	25	300	$= -t_1$
y_2	40	20	500	$= -t_2$
-1	1000	800	0	$= f$
	$= s_1$	$= s_2$	$= g$	

has optimal maximization solution $x_1 = 65/6, x_2 = 10/3, t_1 = t_2 = 0, \max f = 13500$ and optimal minimization solution $y_1 = 20, y_2 = 15, s_1 = s_2 = 0$, $\min g = 13500$. Whenever x_j is not equal to zero, s_j is equal to zero and similarly for y_i and t_i. Hence complementary slackness is exhibited in these optimal solutions.

The examples above motivate two questions. First of all, does every pair of optimal solutions of dual canonical linear programming problems exhibit complementary slackness? Secondly, is it possible for a feasible nonoptimal pair of solutions of dual canonical linear programming problems to exhibit complementary slackness? The answers to these questions are provided by the following theorem.

Theorem 14. *A pair of feasible solutions of dual canonical linear programming problems exhibit complementary slackness if and only if they are optimal solutions.*

(So the answers to the questions above are yes and no respectively.)

PROOF. ($\Rightarrow$) Assume that a pair of feasible solutions of dual canonical linear programming problems exhibit complementary slackness. Then

$$s_j x_j = 0, \quad j = 1, 2, \cdots, n,$$

and

$$y_i t_i = 0, \quad i = 1, 2, \cdots, m.$$

Now

$$SX^t = [s_1 \quad s_2 \quad \cdots \quad s_n] \begin{bmatrix} x_1 \\ x_2 \\ \vdots \\ x_n \end{bmatrix} = \sum_{j=1}^{n} s_j x_j = 0,$$

and

$$Y^t T = [y_1 \quad y_2 \quad \cdots \quad y_m] \begin{bmatrix} t_1 \\ t_2 \\ \vdots \\ t_m \end{bmatrix} = \sum_{i=1}^{m} y_i t_i = 0,$$

i.e., $SX^t + Y^t T = 0$. But $g - f = SX^t + Y^t T$ by the duality equation so $g - f = 0$, i.e., $f = g$. By Corollary 10, the given feasible solutions are optimal solutions.

($\Leftarrow$) Assume that we have a pair of optimal solutions of dual canonical linear programming problems. Then $f = g$ at these solutions by Theorem 3. Hence $SX^t + Y^t T = 0$ by the duality equation. Now, since every entry of the matrices S, X^t, Y^t, and T must be nonnegative, we have $SX^t = Y^t T = 0$, i.e.,

$$SX^t = \sum_{j=1}^{n} s_j x_j = 0$$

and

$$Y^t T = \sum_{i=1}^{m} y_i t_i = 0.$$

Again, since s_j, x_j, y_i, and t_i are nonnegative for all i and j, we have that at least one of the factors in every term of each summation must be zero. This is equivalent to complementary slackness. $\square$

§5. The Duality Theorem

At the end of §1, we asked the following question: Since a given canonical maximization or canonical minimization linear programming problem can have an optimal solution, be infeasible, or be unbounded, how many of the $3^2 = 9$ combinations are possible for dual canonical linear programming problems? Below we give a chart containing the nine combinations and a summary of our knowledge at present.

Maximization problem	Minimization problem	Possible?
Optimal solution	Optimal solution	Yes
Optimal solution	Infeasible	No (see §2)
Optimal solution	Unbounded	No (see §2)
Infeasible	Optimal solution	No (see §2)
Infeasible	Infeasible	?
Infeasible	Unbounded	Yes (see Corollary 9)
Unbounded	Optimal solution	No (see §2)
Unbounded	Infeasible	Yes (see Corollary 9)
Unbounded	Unbounded	No (see Corollary 9)

The following theorem, known as the duality theorem, provides an exhaustive list of the possible behaviors of dual canonical linear programming problems, hence completing and summarizing the chart above.

Theorem 15 (The Duality Theorem). *Given dual canonical linear programming problems, exactly one of the following is true:*

(i) *both problems have optimal solutions; for these solutions, $f = g$;*
(ii) *the maximization problem is unbounded and the minimization problem is infeasible;*
(iii) *the minimization problem is unbounded and the maximization problem is infeasible;*
(iv) *both problems are infeasible (such problems exist; see Example 17).*

PROOF. We have essentially already proved this theorem. If a canonical maximization linear programming problem has an optimal solution, then the dual canonical minimization linear programming problem also has an optimal solution and $f = g$ at these solutions by Theorem 3. This is (i). If a canonical maximization linear programming problem is unbounded, then the dual canonical minimization linear programming problem is infeasible by Corollary 9. This is (ii). If a canonical maximization linear programming problem is infeasible, then the dual canonical minimization linear programming problem does not have an optimal solution by Theorem 3 and, therefore, must be infeasible or unbounded. This is (iv) and (iii) (respectively). □

If the simplex algorithm of Chapter 2 is applied to the canonical maximization linear programming problem of dual canonical linear programming problems and if the maximization problem has an optimal solution or is unbounded, then the dual canonical minimization linear programming problem is immediately solved (it has an optimal solution in the former case (Theorem 3) and is infeasible in the latter case (Corollary 9)). However, if the canonical maximization linear programming problem is infeasible, you only know that the dual canonical minimization linear programming problem is infeasible *or* unbounded. To detect which type of pathology is displayed by the minimization problem, one must either resort to negative transposition or use the dual simplex algorithm of §2. We will use negative transposition. We conclude this section with two examples.

EXAMPLE 16. Solve the dual canonical linear programming problems below:

	x_1	x_2	-1	
y_1	-1	-1	-3	$= -t_1$
y_2	1	1	2	$= -t_2$
-1	2	-4	0	$= f$
	$= s_1$	$= s_2$	$= g$	

	x_1	x_2	-1	
y_1	-1	-1	-3	$= -t_1$
y_2	1^*	1	2	$= -t_2$
-1	2	-4	0	$= f$
	$= s_1$	$= s_2$	$= g$	

$\longrightarrow$

	t_2	x_2	-1	
y_1	1	0	-1	$= -t_1$ $\leftarrow$ max infeasible
s_1	1	1	2	$= -x_1$
-1	-2	-6	-4	$= f$
	$= y_2$	$= s_2$	$= g$	

neg. trans.
for min
$\longrightarrow$

	y_1	s_1	-1	
	-1	-1	2	$= -y_2$
	0	-1	6	$= -s_2$
	1	-2	4	$= -g$

$\uparrow$
min
unbounded

EXAMPLE 17. Solve the dual canonical linear programming problems below:

	x_1	x_2	-1	
y_1	-1	1	-1	$= -t_1$
y_2	1	-1	-1	$= -t_2$
-1	1	1	0	$= f$
	$= s_1$	$= s_2$	$= g$	

	x_1	x_2	-1	
y_1	-1	1	-1	$= -t_1$
y_2	1	-1^*	-1	$= -t_2$
-1	1	1	0	$= f$
	$= s_1$	$= s_2$	$= g$	

$\longrightarrow$

	x_1	t_2	-1	
y_1	0	1	-2	$= -t_1$ ← max infeasible
s_2	-1	-1	1	$= -x_2$
-1	2	1	-1	$= f$
	$= s_1$	$= y_2$	$= g$	

$\longrightarrow$
neg. trans.
for min

	y_1	s_2	-1	
	0	1	-2	$= -s_1$ ← min infeasible
	-1	1	-1	$= -y_2$
	2	-1	1	$= -g$

In both examples above, the dual canonical minimization linear programming problem was immediately solved after negative transposition. This will not happen in general—it may be necessary to perform pivots on the transposed tableau in order to determine the type of pathology exhibited by the minimization problem.

§6. Duality in Noncanonical Tableaus

The duality theory presented in the preceding sections can be extended to accommodate dual noncanonical tableaus corresponding to the noncanonical linear programming problems of Chapter 3. Although we will not reprove any of this theory here (but see Exercise 14), this theory does remain true and is the foundation for the solution procedure applied to such tableaus. We will be content in this section with giving the form of a dual noncanonical tableau and illustrating, via examples, the solution procedure for reducing it to a dual canonical tableau.

Definition 18. A *dual noncanonical tableau* is a noncanonical tableau of the form

	$\textcircled{x_1}$	$\cdots$	$\textcircled{x_j}$	x_{j+1}	$\cdots$	x_n	-1	
$\textcircled{y_1}$	a_{11}	$\cdots$	a_{1j}	$a_{1\,j+1}$	$\cdots$	a_{1n}	b_1	$= -0$
$\vdots$	$\vdots$		$\vdots$	$\vdots$		$\vdots$	$\vdots$	$\vdots$
$\textcircled{y_i}$	a_{i1}	$\cdots$	a_{ij}	$a_{i\,j+1}$	$\cdots$	a_{in}	b_i	$= -0$
y_{i+1}	$a_{i+1\,1}$	$\cdots$	$a_{i+1\,j}$	$a_{i+1\,j+1}$	$\cdots$	$a_{i+1\,n}$	b_{i+1}	$= -t_{i+1}$
$\vdots$	$\vdots$		$\vdots$	$\vdots$		$\vdots$	$\vdots$	$\vdots$
y_m	a_{m1}	$\cdots$	a_{mj}	$a_{m\,j+1}$	$\cdots$	a_{mn}	b_m	$= -t_m$
-1	c_1	$\cdots$	c_j	c_{j+1}	$\cdots$	c_n	d	$= f$
	$= 0$	$\cdots$	$= 0$	$= s_{j+1}$	$\cdots$	$= s_n$	$= g$	

Note that each unconstrained independent variable in the maximization linear programming problem corresponds to an equation of constraint in the dual minimization linear programming problem and each unconstrained independent variable in the minimization linear programming problem corresponds to an equation of constraint in the dual maximization linear programming problem. These unconstrained variables and 0 slack "variables" lie opposite each other in the tableau. This property is crucial and allows one to solve dual noncanonical linear programming problems by using the techniques developed in Chapter 3. We illustrate with two examples.

EXAMPLE 19. Solve the dual noncanonical linear programming problems below:

	$\textcircled{x_1}$	$\textcircled{x_2}$	x_3	-1	
$\textcircled{y_1}$	1	-1	2	1	$= -0$
y_2	2	0	2	-1	$= -t_1$
y_3	0	1	-1	-1	$= -t_2$
-1	1	-1	3	0	$= f$
	$= 0$	$= 0$	$= s_1$	$= g$	

We apply the techniques of Chapter 3 to the dual noncanonical tableau, making sure that unconstrained independent variables and 0 slack "variables" are handled accordingly in both problems.

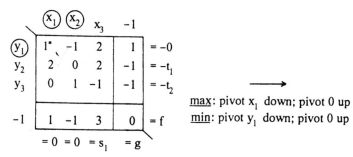

$$\underline{max}:\ \text{pivot } x_1 \text{ down; pivot 0 up}$$
$$\underline{min}:\ \text{pivot } y_1 \text{ down; pivot 0 up}$$

Second tableau:

	0	x_2	x_3	-1	
0	1	-1	2	1	$= - \ x_1$
y_2	-2	2	-2	-3	$= -t_1$
y_3	0	1	-1	-1	$= -t_2$
-1	-1	0	1	-1	$= f$
	$= y_1$	$=0$	$= s_1$	$= g$	

$$\underline{max}:\ \text{file } -x_2 + 2x_3 - 1 = -x_1;$$
$$\text{delete } x_1 \text{ row; delete 0 column}$$
$$\underline{min}:\ \text{file } -2y_2 + 1 = y_1;$$
$$\text{delete } y_1 \text{ column; delete 0 row}$$

Third tableau:

	x_2	x_3	-1	
y_2	2	-2	-3	$= -t_1$
y_3	1^*	-1	-1	$= -t_2$
-1	0	1	-1	$= f$
	$=0$	$= s_1$	$= g$	

$$\underline{max}:\ \text{pivot } x_2 \text{ down}$$
$$\underline{min}:\ \text{pivot 0 up}$$

Fourth tableau:

	t_2	x_3	-1	
y_2	-2	0	-1	$= -t_1$
0	1	-1	-1	$= - \ x_2$
-1	0	1	-1	$= f$
	$= y_3$	$= s_1$	$= g$	

$$\underline{max}:\ \text{file } t_2 - x_3 + 1 = -x_2;$$
$$\text{delete } x_2 \text{ row}$$
$$\underline{min}:\ \text{delete 0 row}$$

	t_2	x_3	-1	
y_2	-2^*	0	-1	$= -t_1$
-1	0	1	-1	$= f$
	$= y_3 = s_1$		$= g$	

$\longrightarrow$ simplex algorithm

	t_1	x_3	-1	
y_3	$-1/2$	0	$1/2$	$= -t_2$
-1	0	1	-1	$= f$
	$= y_2 = s_1$		$= g$	

$\uparrow$

max
unbounded
$\therefore$ min
infeasible

EXAMPLE 20. Solve the dual noncanonical linear programming problems below:

	x_1	x_2	x_3	-1	
y_1	0	-1	-1	-1	$= -0$
y_2	-1	-3	4	0	$= -t_1$
y_3	-1	2	-3	0	$= -t_2$
-1	-1	0	0	0	$= f$
	$= 0 = s_1$	$= s_2$		$= g$	

Again, we apply the techniques of Chapter 3 to the dual noncanonical tableau, making sure that unconstrained independent variables and 0 slack "variables" are handled accordingly in both problems. Since the un-constrained independent variable x_1 and the 0 slack "variable" can not be interchanged at the same time in the maximization problem (similarly, the unconstrained independent variable y_1 and the 0 slack "variable" in the minimization problem), we must perform two separate pivots to implement this interchange.

$$
\begin{array}{c|ccc|c}
 & \boxed{x_1} & x_2 & x_3 & -1 \\
\hline
\boxed{y_1} & 0 & -1 & -1 & -1 & = -0 \\
y_2 & -1 & -3 & 4 & 0 & = -t_1 \\
y_3 & -1 & 2 & -3 & 0 & = -t_2 \\
\hline
-1 & -1 & 0 & 0 & 0 & = f \\
\hline
 & = 0 & = s_1 & = s_2 & = g
\end{array}
$$

$\longrightarrow$

max: pivot 0 up
min: pivot y_1 down

$$
\begin{array}{c|ccc|c}
 & \boxed{x_1} & 0 & x_3 & -1 \\
\hline
s_1 & 0 & -1 & 1 & 1 & = -x_2 \\
y_2 & -1 & -3 & 7 & 3 & = -t_1 \\
y_3 & -1 & 2 & -5 & -2 & = -t_2 \\
\hline
-1 & -1 & 0 & 0 & 0 & = f \\
\hline
 & = 0 & = \boxed{y_1} & = s_2 & = g
\end{array}
$$

$\longrightarrow$

max: delete 0 column
min: file $-s_1 - 3y_2 + 2y_3 = y_1$;
delete y_1 column

$$
\begin{array}{c|cc|c}
 & \boxed{x_1} & x_3 & -1 \\
\hline
s_1 & 0 & 1 & 1 & = -x_2 \\
y_2 & -1 & 7 & 3 & = -t_1 \\
y_3 & -1^* & -5 & -2 & = -t_2 \\
\hline
-1 & -1 & 0 & 0 & = f \\
\hline
 & = 0 & = s_2 & = g
\end{array}
$$

$\longrightarrow$

max: pivot x_1 down
min: pivot 0 up

$$
\begin{array}{c|cc|c}
 & t_2 & x_3 & -1 \\
\hline
s_1 & 0 & 1 & 1 & = -x_2 \\
y_2 & -1 & 12 & 5 & = -t_1 \\
0 & -1 & 5 & 2 & = -\boxed{x_1} \\
\hline
-1 & -1 & 5 & 2 & = f \\
\hline
 & = y_3 & = s_2 & = g
\end{array}
$$

$\longrightarrow$

max: file $-t_2 + 5x_3 - 2 = -x_1$;
delete x_1 row
min: delete 0 row

MBFT MT

min $\{t, \frac{5}{12}\}$

$= \frac{2}{12}$

$\Rightarrow 12$

$$
\begin{array}{c|cc|c}
 & t_2 & x_3 & -1 \\
\hline
s_1 & 0 & 1 & 1 & = -x_2 \\
y_2 & -1 & 12^* & 5 & = -t_1 \\
\hline
-1 & -1 & 5 & 2 & = f \\
\hline
 & = y_3 & = s_2 & = g
\end{array}
$$

$\longrightarrow$

simplex
algorithm

	t_2	t_1	-1	
s_1	$1/12$	$-1/12$	$7/12$	$=-x_2$
s_2	$-1/12$	$1/12$	$5/12$	$=-x_3$
-1	$-7/12$	$-5/12$	$-1/12$	$=f$
	$=y_3$	$=y_2$	$=g$	

The basic solution of each linear programming problem in the final tableau above is optimal:

$$t_2 = t_1 = 0, \quad x_2 = 7/12, \quad x_3 = 5/12, \quad \max f = 1/12,$$
$$x_1 = -1/12 \text{ (from second filed equation)},$$
$$s_1 = s_2 = 0, \quad y_3 = 7/12, \quad y_2 = 5/12, \quad \min g = 1/12,$$
$$y_1 = -1/12 \text{ (from first filed equation)}.$$

§7. Concluding Remarks

The concept of duality occurs throughout mathematics. Being seekers of patterns by nature, mathematicians are interested in the relationships that exist between structurally similar problems. Duality sometimes provides the needed connection. The theoretical and computational significance of duality in the area of linear programming is (hopefully) clear and will be exploited again and again in forthcoming chapters.

EXERCISES

1. Consider the canonical maximization linear programming problem below:

$$\text{Maximize} \quad f(x_1, x_2) = x_1 + x_2$$
$$\text{subject to} \quad x_1 + 2x_2 \leq 4$$
$$3x_1 + x_2 \leq 6$$
$$x_1, x_2 \geq 0.$$

   a. State the dual canonical minimization linear programming problem.
   b. Sketch the constraint sets for both problems above.
   c. Solve both problems above by applying the simplex algorithm to a dual tableau. Indicate the movement in both constraint set diagrams exhibited by the basic solutions of successive tableaus.
   d. Is complementary slackness exhibited in the solutions above? Why or why not?

2. Consider the canonical minimization linear programming problem below:

$$\text{Minimize} \quad g(y_1, y_2) = -y_2$$
$$\text{subject to} \quad y_1 - y_2 \geq 1$$
$$-y_1 + y_2 \geq 2$$
$$y_1, y_2 \geq 0.$$

    a. State the dual canonical maximization linear programming problem.

    b. Sketch the constraint sets for both problems above.

    c. Solve both problems above. (Be clever—the simplex algorithm is unnecessary here.)

3. Consider the canonical maximization linear programming problem below:

$$\text{Maximize} \quad f(x_1, x_2) = x_1$$
$$\text{subject to} \quad x_1 + x_2 \leq 1$$
$$x_1 - x_2 \geq 1$$
$$x_2 - 2x_1 \geq 1$$
$$x_1, x_2 \geq 0.$$

    a. State the dual canonical minimization linear programming problem.

    b. Sketch the constraint sets for both problems above.

    c. Solve both problems above. (Be clever—the simplex algorithm is unnecessary here.)

4. a. Solve Example 5 of Chapter 2 by using the dual simplex algorithm.

    b. Solve Example 3 of Chapter 2 by using the dual simplex algorithm.

    [Note: The intent of this exercise is to familiarize the reader with the dual simplex algorithm. As stated before, it is *not* suggested that this algorithm be used in general since the techniques of this chapter applied to the simplex algorithm of Chapter 2 suffice.]

5. Solve each of the dual canonical linear programming problems below. If a linear programming problem has infinitely many optimal solutions, find all optimal solutions.

a.

	x_1	x_2	-1	
y_1	1	-1	-1	$= -t_1$
y_2	-1	-1	-1	$= -t_2$
-1	1	-2	0	$= f$
	$= s_1$	$= s_2$	$= g$	

b.

	x_1	x_2	-1	
y_1	-2	1	-2	$= -t_1$
y_2	1	-1	-1	$= -t_2$
-1	1	1	0	$= f$
	$= s_1$	$= s_2$	$= g$	

c.

	x_1	x_2	-1	
y_1	2	-2	-1	$= -t_1$
y_2	-1	1	-1	$= -t_2$
-1	2	1	0	$= f$
	$= s_1$	$= s_2$	$= g$	

d.

	x_1	x_2	-1	
y_1	9	-2	0	$= -t_1$
y_2	3	2	1	$= -t_2$
y_3	3	1	0	$= -t_3$
-1	3	2	0	$= f$
	$= s_1$	$= s_2$	$= g$	

e.

	x_1	x_2	x_3	-1	
y_1	2	-1	1	-3	$= -t_1$
y_2	-1	2	1	1	$= -t_2$
-1	0	-1	2	0	$= f$
	$= s_1$	$= s_2$	$= s_3$	$= g$	

f.

	x_1	x_2	-1	
y_1	-1	0	-2	$= -t_1$
y_2	-2	1	1	$= -t_2$
y_3	-1	-1	-3	$= -t_3$
-1	1	-1	0	$= f$
	$= s_1$	$= s_2$	$= g$	

6. a. Find b_1, b_2, c_1, and c_2 such that the maximization problem of the dual canonical tableau

	x_1	x_2	-1	
y_1	1	0	b_1	$= -t_1$
y_2	0	2	b_2	$= -t_2$
-1	c_1	c_2	3	$= f$
	$= s_1$	$= s_2$	$= g$	

is in basic solution optimal form and such that both the maximization and minimization problems have infinitely many solutions.

   b. Characterize all such b_1, b_2, c_1, and c_2 for which the conditions of part a hold.

7. a. Prove (ii) of Corollary 9.

   b. Label the following statement TRUE or FALSE and justify your answer.

   If a canonical minimization linear programming problem is infeasible, then the dual canonical maximization linear programming problem is unbounded.

8. Prove that no dual canonical linear programming problems of the form

have the optimal solutions

$$x_1 = 0, \quad x_2 = 2, \quad x_3 = 1, \quad t_1 = 0, \quad t_2 = 0, \quad \max f = 2.$$
$$y_1 = 1, \quad y_2 = 0, \quad s_1 = 1, \quad s_2 = 0, \quad s_3 = 1, \quad \min g = 2.$$

9. a. Prove that any feasible solutions of dual canonical linear programming problems for which $f = g$ exhibit complementary slackness.
   b. Does part a remain true if we replace "feasible solutions" by "solutions which satisfy all main constraints but violate one or more nonnegativity constraints"? If so, prove it. If not, explain.
   c. Prove that any feasible solutions of dual canonical linear programming problems exhibiting complementary slackness have $f = g$.
   d. Does part c remain true if we replace "feasible solutions" by "solutions which satisfy all main constraints but violate one or more nonnegativity constraints"? If so, prove it. If not, explain.

10. Consider the dual canonical tableau below:

Assume, without loss of generality, that $a > 0$.

a. If $b > 0$ and $c > 0$, which of the four types of behavior for dual canonical linear programming problems as given by the duality theorem is exhibited above? Prove your assertion.
b. Repeat part a under the assumptions that $b > 0$ and $c < 0$.
c. Repeat part a under the assumptions that $b < 0$ and $c > 0$.
d. Repeat part a under the assumptions that $b < 0$ and $c < 0$.

11. Consider the noncanonical maximization linear programming problem below:

$$\text{Maximize} \quad f(x_1, x_2, x_3) = x_1 + x_2 - x_3$$
$$\text{subject to} \quad x_1 - x_2 + x_3 = -1$$
$$-x_1 - x_2 + x_3 = 1 \qquad (1)$$
$$-x_1 + x_2 + x_3 \leq 1$$
$$x_2, x_3 \geq 0.$$

a. State the dual noncanonical minimization linear programming problem.

b. Solve both problems above by using a dual noncanonical tableau. If either problem has infinitely many optimal solutions, find all optimal solutions.

c. Is complementary slackness exhibited in the solutions above? Why or why not?

d. If x_1 were constrained to be nonnegative in (1), would the solution to (1) be the same as that obtained in part b? Explain.

12. Consider the noncanonical minimization linear programming problem below:

$$\text{Minimize} \quad g(y_1, y_2, y_3) = y_1 + 2y_2 + 3y_3$$
$$\text{subject to} \quad y_1 + y_2 + y_3 \geq 1$$
$$2y_2 + y_3 = 1 \tag{2}$$
$$y_1 + y_3 \geq 1$$
$$y_1, y_3 \geq 0.$$

a. State the dual noncanonical maximization linear programming problem.

b. Solve both problems above by using a dual noncanonical tableau. If either problem has infinitely many optimal solutions, find all optimal solutions.

c. Is complementary slackness exhibited in the solutions above? Why or why not?

d. If y_2 were constrained to be nonnegative in (2), would the solution to (2) be the same as that obtained in part b? Explain.

13. Solve each of the dual noncanonical linear programming problems below. If a linear programming problem has infinitely many optimal solutions, find all optimal solutions.

a.

	x_1	x_2	-1	
y_1	2	-1	-1	$= -0$
y_2	-1	1	-1	$= -t_1$
-1	2	1	0	$= f$
	$= 0 = s_2$	$= g$		

b.

	x_1	x_2	-1	
y_1	1	2	2	$= -0$
y_2	-1	-2	-2	$= -t_1$
-1	-1	-2	0	$= f$
	$= 0 = s_2$	$= g$		

c.

	x_1	x_2	-1	
y_1	1	-1	-2	$= -0$
y_2	-2	2	-1	$= -t_1$
-1	0	1	0	$= f$
	$= 0 = s_2$	$= g$		

d.

	x_1	x_2	x_3	-1	
y_1	1	-1	1	-1	$= -0$
y_2	-1	-1	1	1	$= -t_1$
y_3	-1	1	1	1	$= -t_2$
-1	1	1	-1	0	$= f$
	$= 0$	$= 0$	$= s_2$	$= g$	

14. State and prove the analogue of Corollary 8 for dual noncanonical linear programming problems.

Part II

Applications

CHAPTER 5

Matrix Games

§0. Introduction

Our first application of linear programming occurs in the area of game theory, specifically, two-person zero-sum matrix games. Although we barely scratch the surface of the broad field of game theory, the matrix games discussed here serve as a more than adequate introduction to the subject. In addition, we see firsthand how the analysis of a matrix game leads to dual noncanonical linear programming problems, culminating in optimal strategies for the players of the game.

§1. An Example; Two-Person Zero-Sum Matrix Games

We begin with a typical example of a matrix game along with a preliminary analysis leading to a simplification of the game.

EXAMPLE 1. Two players, say an "even" player and an "odd" player, each secretly think of an integer between 1 and 3 inclusive. Both players reveal their numbers simultaneously. If the sum of the numbers is even, the "even" player wins a number of dollars from the "odd" player equal to the difference of the numbers provided that the numbers are distinct. If the numbers are the same (in which case the sum is also even), the "even" player wins a number of dollars from the "odd" player equal to the sum of the numbers. If the sum of the numbers is odd, the "odd" player wins $3 from the "even" player.
  Given this game, which player (if any) has the advantage? How much of an

advantage (if any) does this player have? Is there an optimal strategy for each player, i.e., does each player have a strategy whereby he can maximize his winnings or minimize his losses? We will obtain the answers to these questions in forthcoming sections. For now, formulate your own conjectures!

Note that, in any round of the game, each player has three choices, a 1, a 2, or a 3. By using a matrix to tabulate all of the possible combinations of choices by the players as well as the payoffs associated with these choices, we can obtain a payoff matrix for the game. This payoff matrix, in terms of winnings for the "even" player (i.e., negative entries in the matrix are interpreted as losses for the "even" player or, equivalently, winnings for the "odd" player), is given by

$$
\begin{array}{c}
\text{"ODD"}\\
\text{PLAYER'S}\\
\text{CHOICE}\\
\begin{array}{ccc} 1 & 2 & 3 \end{array}
\end{array}
$$

$$
\begin{array}{cc}
\text{"EVEN"} & 1\\
\text{PLAYER'S} & 2\\
\text{CHOICE} & 3
\end{array}
\begin{bmatrix}
2 & -3 & 2\\
-3 & 4 & -3\\
2 & -3 & 6
\end{bmatrix}
$$

For example, if the "even" player chooses 1 (first row) and the "odd" player chooses 1 (first column), the "even" player wins $2 from the "odd" player since $1 + 1 = 2$. This is recorded as a 2 (since the "even" player wins $2) in the first row and first column of the payoff matrix. If the "even" player chooses 1 (first row) and the "odd" player chooses 2 (second column), the "odd" player wins $3 from the "even" player since $1 + 2 = 3$ is odd. This is recorded as a -3 (since the "even" player loses $3) in the first row and second column of the payoff matrix. If the "even" player chooses 1 (first row) and the "odd" player chooses 3 (third column), the "even" player wins $2 from the "odd" player since $3 - 1 = 2$. This is recorded as a 2 (since the "even" player wins $2) in the first row and third column of the payoff matrix. This completes the computation of the entries of the payoff matrix in the first row; the other entries of the payoff matrix are computed similarly. Before reading further, make sure that you verify *all* entries of the payoff matrix above. Also, study this matrix and make a guess as to which player (if any) is favored by this game.

The 3×3 payoff matrix above can be reduced somewhat. Notice that the "even" player should never choose 1 since he can always do as well or better by choosing 3 *no matter what number the "odd" player chooses*. In other words, the first row of the payoff matrix is term-by-term less than or equal to the third row of the payoff matrix. Hence, we delete the first row from the payoff matrix:

$$
\begin{array}{c}
\text{"ODD"}\\
\text{PLAYER'S}\\
\text{CHOICE}\\
\begin{array}{ccc} 1 & 2 & 3 \end{array}
\end{array}
$$

$$
\begin{array}{cc}
\text{"EVEN"} & 2\\
\text{PLAYER'S} & \\
\text{CHOICE} & 3
\end{array}
\begin{bmatrix}
-3 & 4 & -3\\
2 & -3 & 6
\end{bmatrix}
$$

Now, by applying similar reasoning to the reduced payoff matrix, the "odd" player should never choose 3 since he can always do as well or better by choosing 1 *no matter what number the "even" player chooses*. In other words, the third column of the reduced payoff matrix is term-by-term greater than or equal to the first column of the reduced payoff matrix. Hence, we delete the third column from the reduced payoff matrix:

$$
\begin{array}{c}
\text{``ODD''} \\
\text{PLAYER'S} \\
\text{CHOICE} \\
\begin{array}{cc} 1 & \quad 2 \end{array}
\end{array}
$$

$$
\begin{array}{cc}
\begin{array}{c}
\text{``EVEN''} \quad 2 \\
\text{PLAYER'S} \\
\text{CHOICE} \quad 3
\end{array}
&
\begin{bmatrix} -3 & 4 \\ 2 & -3 \end{bmatrix}
\end{array}
$$

We now leave our game until its solution in §4. Do you care to revise your prediction as to which player (if any) is favored by this game?

The game of Example 1 above is a typical example of a *two-person zero-sum matrix game* (hereafter referred to simply as a *matrix game*). The terminology is obvious except perhaps for "zero-sum" which refers to the fact that one player's loss is the other player's gain. In a matrix game, we have an $m \times n$ *payoff matrix*, a *row player*, and a *column player*. In each round of the game, the row player chooses a row of the payoff matrix and the column player chooses a column of the payoff matrix. These choices are then cross-indexed to find the payoff for the round. *In this book, the payoffs in the matrix are always listed as winnings for the row player*; winnings for the column player appear as negative entries in the payoff matrix. Hence, the row player wishes to maximize the payoff and the column player wishes to minimize the payoff. By an *optimal strategy* for a player of a matrix game, we mean a strategy whereby a player can maximize his winnings or minimize his losses, assuming that the other player will have perfect knowledge of this strategy and also play so as to maximize his winnings or minimize his losses subject to this strategy. In other words, an optimal strategy for a player of a matrix game assumes an omniscient opponent. This is a crucial assumption and will be used repeatedly.

The procedure used to simplify the matrix game of Example 1 is called *domination*.

Domination in a Matrix Game

Whenever one row of a payoff matrix is term-by-term less than or equal to another row, delete the smaller row from the game (since the row player is trying to maximize the outcome). Whenever one column of a payoff matrix is term-by-term greater than or equal to another column, delete the larger column from the game (since the column player is trying to minimize the outcome). Continue deleting rows and/or columns until no row or column "dominates" another.

§2. Linear Programming Formulation of Matrix Games

The purpose of this section is to formulate the determination of the optimal strategies of a matrix game as dual noncanonical linear programming problems to which the methods of 4§6 can be applied. Such a formulation depends on a careful analysis which we begin now.

Definition 2. Let $A = [a_{ij}]_{m \times n}$ be an $m \times n$ matrix game. A *mixed (or probabilistic) strategy for the row player* is a column vector

$$P = \begin{bmatrix} p_1 \\ p_2 \\ \vdots \\ p_m \end{bmatrix}$$

such that $p_i \geq 0$ for all i and

$$\sum_{i=1}^{m} p_i = 1.$$

A *mixed (or probabilistic) strategy for the column player* is a row vector

$$Q = [q_1 \quad q_2 \quad \cdots \quad q_n]$$

such that $q_j \geq 0$ for all j and

$$\sum_{j=1}^{n} q_j = 1.$$

Any mixed strategy containing an entry of 1 (whence all of the other entries are necessarily 0) is said to be a *pure strategy*.

The interpretation of the mixed strategy for the row player is that, if the row player uses strategy P, he will choose row i of the matrix with probability p_i. Similarly, the interpretation of the mixed strategy for the column player is that, if the column player uses strategy Q, he will choose column j of the matrix with probability q_j. If a player uses a pure strategy, he will constantly choose the same row or column, namely the row or column corresponding to the probability 1.

Note that neither of the optimal strategies of the players in the game of Example 1 will be a pure strategy. To see this, recall the payoff matrix for the game of Example 1:

$$\begin{array}{cc} & \begin{array}{cc} \text{"ODD"} \\ \text{PLAYER'S} \\ \text{CHOICE} \\ 1 \quad\quad 2 \end{array} \\ \begin{array}{c} \text{"EVEN"} \quad 2 \\ \text{PLAYER'S} \\ \text{CHOICE} \quad 3 \end{array} & \begin{bmatrix} -3 & 4 \\ 2 & -3 \end{bmatrix} \end{array}$$

Now put yourself in the position of one of the players, say the "even" player. Would you ever play a pure strategy? If you constantly choose the first row of the matrix, the "odd" player is going to constantly choose the first column of the matrix (remember that the "odd" player knows your strategy!) and you will lose \$3 per round of the game. Likewise, if you constantly choose the second row of the matrix, the "odd" player is going to constantly choose the second column of the matrix and you will again lose \$3 per round of the game. Certainly the "even" player can do better than this! Similar reasoning applies to the wisdom of the column player using a pure strategy. In fact, similar reasoning applies to *any* strategy that is predictable. In general, any player who can predict with certainty what his opponent will do in a matrix game has a decided advantage. Hence the optimal strategies of both players in the game above will be mixed strategies. Each row and column of the matrix will be assigned a probability— the players will then choose their rows or columns consistent with these probabilities. Our goal is to determine the optimal assignment of probabilities to the rows and columns of this matrix game and, more generally, an arbitrary matrix game.

Let $A = [a_{ij}]_{m \times n}$ be an $m \times n$ matrix game. Assume, for the moment, that the column player always chooses column j of the matrix, i.e., the column player is using the pure strategy

$$Q = [0 \quad \cdots \quad 0 \quad 1 \quad 0 \quad \cdots \quad 0].$$
$$\uparrow$$
$$j$$

If the row player uses mixed strategy

$$P = \begin{bmatrix} p_1 \\ p_2 \\ \vdots \\ p_m \end{bmatrix},$$

then the expected value of his winnings, denoted $E_j(P)$, is

$$E_j(P) = p_1 a_{1j} + p_2 a_{2j} + \cdots + p_m a_{mj}$$

by elementary probability theory. Now the row player's optimal strategy would assure that the expected value of his winnings is maximal *no matter what column the column player chooses*. Stated a bit differently, the row player's optimal strategy would assure that his minimum expected winnings are as large as possible. Hence, the optimal strategy for the row player is to choose strategy P such that

$$\min_{1 \le j \le n} E_j(P) \text{ is maximal.}$$

Similarly, assume, for the moment, that the row player always chooses row i of the matrix, i.e., the row player is using the pure strategy

$$P = \begin{bmatrix} 0 \\ \vdots \\ 0 \\ 1 \\ 0 \\ \vdots \\ 0 \end{bmatrix} \leftarrow i$$

If the column player uses mixed strategy

$$Q = [q_1 \quad q_2 \quad \cdots \quad q_n],$$

then the expected value of his losses (remember that matrix game entries are in terms of winnings for the row player!), denoted $F_i(Q)$, is

$$F_i(Q) = q_1 a_{i1} + q_2 a_{i2} + \cdots + q_n a_{in}$$

by elementary probability theory. Now the column player's optimal strategy would assure that the expected value of his losses is minimal *no matter what row the row player chooses.* Stated a bit differently, the column player's optimal strategy would assure that his maximum expected losses are as small as possible. Hence, the optimal strategy for the column player is to choose strategy Q such that

$$\max_{1 \le i \le m} F_i(Q) \text{ is minimal.}$$

The expected winnings of the row player per round of the game provided that both players play their optimal strategies is

$$u = \max_{P} \min_{1 \le j \le n} E_j(P).$$

The expected losses of the column player per round of the game provided that both players play their optimal strategies is

$$v = \min_{Q} \max_{1 \le i \le m} F_i(Q).$$

Notice the "duality" present in the optimal strategies above. It is perhaps not surprising then that these strategies are obtained for a given matrix game by solving dual linear programming problems. Since the optimal strategy for the row player is essentially a maximization problem and the optimal strategy for the column player is essentially a minimization problem, one might expect that the row player's optimal strategy appears as the maximization problem of the tableau and that the column player's optimal strategy appears as the dual minimization problem. In fact, exactly the opposite is true as we see now.

Theorem 3. *Let* $A = [a_{ij}]_{m \times n}$ *be an* $m \times n$ *matrix game. Then the mixed strategies*

$$P = \begin{bmatrix} p_1 \\ p_2 \\ \vdots \\ p_m \end{bmatrix}$$

and

$$Q = [q_1 \quad q_2 \quad \cdots \quad q_n]$$

obtained from the solution of the dual noncanonical linear programming problems

$\widehat{v}$	q_1	q_2	$\cdots$	q_n	-1	
$\widehat{u}$	0	-1	-1 $\cdots$	-1	-1	$= -0$
P_1	-1				0	$= -t_1$
P_2	-1				0	$= -t_2$
$\vdots$	$\vdots$		A		$\vdots$	$\vdots$
P_m	-1				0	$= -t_m$
-1	-1	0	0 $\cdots$	0	0	$= f$
	$= 0$	$= s_1$	$= s_2 \cdots$	$= s_n$	$= g$	

are optimal for the row and column player respectively. The dual noncanonical tableau above is called the game tableau *for A.*

PROOF. We show that the maximization problem of the game tableau yields the optimal strategy for the column player; the proof that the minimization problem yields the optimal strategy for the row player is similar. The first equation of the maximization problem is

$$\sum_{j=1}^{n} q_j = 1;$$

along with $q_j \geq 0$ for all j, we have that

$$Q = [q_1 \quad q_2 \quad \cdots \quad q_n]$$

is a mixed strategy. The next m equations of the maximization problem are

$$-v + F_i(Q) = -t_i, \quad i = 1, 2, \ldots, m;$$

in non-slack form, these m equations become the inequalities

$$F_i(Q) \leq v, \quad i = 1, 2, \ldots, m.$$

Finally, the last equation of the maximization problem says to maximize $f = -v$ or, equivalently, to minimize v. Hence, the maximization problem of the game tableau finds the mixed strategy Q so that the maximum value of $F_i(Q)$, $i = 1, 2, \ldots, m$, is minimal; this is precisely the optimal strategy for the column player. $\qquad\square$

Theorem 3 gives us a procedure for solving a matrix game—having reduced the determination of optimal strategies to dual noncanonical linear programming problems, we simply apply the techniques and theory of Chapter 2, Chapter 3, and Chapter 4 to solve the problem. Notice that Theorem 3 does *not* guarantee the existence of a pair of optimal solutions for the dual noncanonical linear programming problems arising from a matrix game. (For example, isn't it possible that dual problems arising from a matrix game could display one of the combinations of infeasibility and unboundedness as given in (ii)–(iv) of the duality theorem in Chapter 4? If so, what does each combination say about the matrix game itself or about the strategies of the players involved?) Theorem 3 only implements the analysis undertaken prior to its statement and assumes that this analysis makes mathematical "sense." This matter will be reconciled completely in §3. Notice, however, that if a pair of optimal solutions for the dual noncanonical linear programming problems of Theorem 3 exists, then $f = g$ at these solutions whence $u = v$ since $f = -v$ and $g = -u$. This value $u = v$ will be important in §3.

A few additional remarks are in order. Always use domination to reduce a given matrix game as far as possible before forming the game tableau. This reduction does not affect the optimal strategies of the players and it is desirable to have as small a game tableau as possible. Also, note that to transform the noncanonical game tableau into canonical form, we must pivot v down to the east and 0 up to the north in the maximization problem and pivot u down to the south and 0 up to the west in the minimization problem. Unfortunately, this can not be accomplished in a single pivot since 0 is not an acceptable pivot entry. However, we can obtain a maximum basic feasible canonical maximization problem in only two pivots if the pivots are chosen carefully:

(1) Find the maximum entry in each column of the matrix game A.
(2) Choose the minimum of these maximum entries, say it is the entry a_{ij} of A.
(3) Pivot on * and ** (in either order) as given below:

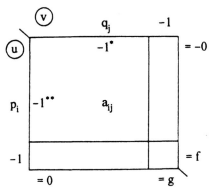

Check that you have a maximum basic feasible tableau after pivoting on * and ** as above. If not, an error has been made—locate it before continuing!

§3. The Von Neumann Minimax Theorem

As stated before, Theorem 3 of §2 assumes implicitly that it makes mathematical "sense" to speak of optimal strategies for players in a matrix game. But isn't it possible that the dual noncanonical linear programming problems of Theorem 3 arising from a matrix game could display one of the combinations of infeasibility and unboundedness as given in (ii)–(iv) of the duality theorem in Chapter 4? And, if so, what does each combination say about the matrix game itself or about the strategies of the players involved?

Fortunately, an important theorem of game theory called the *von Neumann minimax theorem* (in honor of John von Neumann who was a pioneer in the field of game theory) rules out the possibility of a game tableau ever displaying pathological behavior. The von Neumann minimax theorem is an existence theorem; it assures the existence of optimal strategies for both players of a matrix game. Theorem 3 of §2, on the other hand, gives a procedure whereby these optimal strategies are constructed while implicitly assuming the existence of such strategies. The statement of the von Neumann minimax theorem is given without proof (see, for example, [W1] for a proof).

Theorem 4 (Von Neumann Minimax Theorem). *Let $A = [a_{ij}]_{m \times n}$ be an $m \times n$ matrix game. Then there exist optimal mixed strategies P^* and Q^* for the row player and the column player respectively. Furthermore,*

$$\min_{1 \le j \le n} E_j(P^*) = \max_P \min_{1 \le j \le n} E_j(P) = \min_Q \max_{1 \le i \le m} F_i(Q) = \max_{1 \le i \le m} F_i(Q^*);$$

$$\underset{u}{\uparrow} \qquad\qquad \underset{v}{\uparrow}$$

this common value is said to be the von Neumann value *of the game.*

The von Neumann value of a matrix game is the expected winnings of the row player and the expected losses of the column player per round of the game provided that both players play their optimal strategies. A positive von Neumann value hence indicates that the game favors the row player, a negative von Neumann value indicates that the game favors the column player, and a von Neumann value of 0 indicates that the game is fair.

§4. The Example Revisited

We now solve the matrix game in Example 1 of §1.

EXAMPLE 1 (Continued). Recall the matrix game from §1:

$$
\begin{array}{cc}
 & \text{"ODD"} \\
 & \text{PLAYER'S} \\
 & \text{CHOICE} \\
\end{array}
$$

		1	2
"EVEN"	2	$\begin{bmatrix} -3 \end{bmatrix}$	4
PLAYER'S CHOICE	3	2	-3

$$\begin{array}{cc}
 & \text{"ODD" PLAYER'S CHOICE} \\
 & \begin{array}{cc} 1 & 2 \end{array} \\
\begin{array}{c} \text{"EVEN"} \\ \text{PLAYER'S} \\ \text{CHOICE} \end{array} \begin{array}{c} 2 \\ \\ 3 \end{array} & \begin{bmatrix} -3 & 4 \\ 2 & -3 \end{bmatrix}
\end{array}$$

According to Theorem 3, we must solve the dual noncanonical linear programming problems

v	q_1	q_2	-1	
u	0 -1^{*}	-1	-1	$= -0$
p_1	-1 -3	4	0	$= -t_1$
p_2	-1^{**} 2	-3	0	$= -t_2$
-1	-1 0	0	0	$= f$
	$= 0$ $= s_1$	$= s_2$	$= g$	

The pivots * and ** (in either order) yield a maximum basic feasible tableau as discussed in §2. In fact, the entire solution of these dual linear programming problems can be found in Example 20 of Chapter 4. Note that the notation used there is slightly different from the notation used here. In any event, the optimal solutions (with the notation changed from Example 20 to coincide with the notation of the game tableau above) are

$$t_2 = t_1 = 0, \quad q_1 = 7/12, \quad q_2 = 5/12, \quad \max f = 1/12,$$
$$\min v = \min - f = - \max f = - 1/12,$$
$$s_1 = s_2 = 0, \quad p_2 = 7/12, \quad p_1 = 5/12, \quad \min g = 1/12,$$
$$\max u = \max - g = - \min g = - 1/12.$$

This game favors the "odd" player since the von Neumann value of the game is negative ($u = v = - 1/12$); on the average, the "odd" player will win $1/12 ($\approx$ 8¢) per round of the game provided that both players play their optimal strategies. (Note that it is impossible for the "odd" player to win $1/12 in any single round of the game. Remember that the von Neumann value of a game is an expected value, i.e., a value which measures the benefit of the game to one of the players *after many rounds of the game.* For example, after 1200 rounds of the game, we would expect that the "odd" player would be winning approximately ($1/12)(1200) = $100.) The optimal strategy for the "even" player is given by

$$P* = \begin{bmatrix} p_1 \\ p_2 \end{bmatrix} = \begin{bmatrix} 5/12 \\ 7/12 \end{bmatrix},$$

i.e., the "even" player should choose the first row of the matrix (choose the number 2) with probability $p_1 = 5/12$ and choose the second row of the matrix (choose the number 3) with probability $p_2 = 7/12$. The "even" player should never choose the number 1. The optimal strategy for the "odd" player is given by

$$Q* = [q_1 \quad q_2] = [7/12 \quad 5/12],$$

i.e., the "odd" player should choose the first column of the matrix (choose the number 1) with probability $q_1 = 7/12$ and choose the second column of the matrix (choose the number 2) with probability $q_2 = 5/12$. The "odd" player should never choose the number 3. All of this information is summarized below:

"odd"
player

	choice	1	2
		prob. 7/12	5/12
"even"	2	5/12 $\begin{bmatrix} -3 \end{bmatrix}$	4
player	3	7/12 $\begin{bmatrix} 2 \end{bmatrix}$	-3

$$\begin{array}{c} \text{prob. } 7/12 \quad 5/12 \\ \begin{bmatrix} -3 & 4 \\ 2 & -3 \end{bmatrix} \end{array} \quad u = v = -1/12$$

Did you guess back in §1 that the "odd" player was favored in this game? Are you impressed with the power of the dual noncanonical tableau in solving matrix games?

§5. Two More Examples

We conclude our discussion of matrix games with two more examples. Both of these examples are simplified "poker-like" card games and, as such, differ from the game of §1 in two important respects:

(i) the games involve cards dealt from a deck of cards; the players have no control over the cards dealt—they can only react to the cards that they receive;

(ii) the games are multiphase games, i.e., one player makes a decision in the game (phase 1) and then, dependent upon what that player does, the other player makes a decision in the game (phase 2) etc.

These games also serve as a nice introduction to more general matrix games that are included in more complete discussions of game theory (see, for example, [O1]). Without further ado, let's deal the cards!

EXAMPLE 5. There are two players, say player I and player II, and a deck of three playing cards, a jack (J), a queen (Q), and a king (K). The ranking of these cards, from lowest to highest, is J, Q, and K; the suits of these cards are irrelevant. Each player antes a quarter and is then dealt a single card face down. Each player looks at his card. Player I now has two options:

FOLD—Player I loses his ante to player II
BET—Player I adds a dime to the pot.

If player I bets, player II has two options:

FOLD—Player II loses his ante to player I
SEE—Player II adds a dime to the pot.

In the event that player II sees, both cards are revealed and the high hand wins the pot. The cards are then returned to the deck.

Given this game, which player (if any) has the advantage? What is the von Neumann value of this game? What is the optimal strategy for each player?

We work toward the payoff matrix for this game. A choice for player I in any round of the game is a reaction to the card dealt, i.e., a decision on whether to fold (F) or bet (B) given a J, Q, or K. One choice for player I would be to fold no matter what card he receives—we denote such a strategy by FFF (fold on J, fold on Q, fold on K). (Is this a wise strategy?) Another choice for player I would be to fold if he receives a J or Q, and bet if he receives a K—such a strategy is denoted by FFB (fold on J, fold on Q, bet on K). Continuing in such a manner, we obtain eight choices for player I in any round of the game:

Choice for player I:

FFF   FFB   FBF   BFF   FBB   BFB   BBF   BBB

In each choice, the first F or B is the decision on what to do if a J is dealt, the second F or B is the decision on what to do if a Q is dealt, and the third F or B is the decision on what to do if a K is dealt. Note again that the players have no control over the cards dealt—this is left entirely to chance. The players can only react to the cards that they receive.

Similarly, a choice for player II in any round of the game is a decision on whether to fold (F) or see (S) given a J, Q, or K *provided player I bets*. Hence:

Choices for player II:

FFF   FFS   FSF   SFF   FSS   SFS   SSF   SSS

As before, the first F or S is the decision on what to do if a J is dealt, the second F or S is the decision on what to do if a Q is dealt, and the third F or S is the decision on what to do if a K is dealt.

We are now ready to compute entries of the payoff matrix. This payoff matrix tabulates the result of the interaction of any two choices from the two players; hence, it will be an 8×8 matrix. Also, since the game depends on chance, the entries of the payoff matrix are the expected values of each interaction. Furthermore, all entries will be in terms of winnings for player I, our row player. We illustrate with the actual computation of a matrix entry.

Assume that player I plays strategy FBB and that player II plays strategy SFS. There are six possible two card hands that could be dealt from the three card deck, each occurring with equal probability (1/6). Now, given each of these hands, we can compute the outcome of the round provided that the aforementioned strategies are played:

Player I plays FBB, player II plays SFS

	I II	I II	I II	I II	I II	I II
Hand dealt:	JQ	JK	QJ	QK	KJ	KQ
Probability:	1/6	1/6	1/6	1/6	1/6	1/6
Outcome: (Winnings for player I)	−25	−25	35	−35	35	25

For example, if player I is dealt a J (as in the hands J Q and J K), player I folds and hence player II wins player I's ante of 25¢. If player I is dealt a Q (as in the hands Q J and Q K), player I bets and adds 10¢ to the pot. Player II sees in either case by adding 10¢ to the pot; player II loses 25¢ + 10¢ = 35¢ to player I if player II has a J and player II wins 25¢ + 10¢ = 35¢ from player I if player II has a K. Finally, if player I is dealt a K (as in the hands K J and K Q), player I bets and is assured of winning. Player I wins 25¢ + 10¢ = 35¢ from player II if player II has a J (since player II sees on a J) and player I wins player II's ante of 25¢ if player II has a Q (since player II folds on a Q). Now the expected value of the interaction of FBB and SFS is the sum of the products of the probabilities and outcomes:

$$E(\text{FBB}, \text{SFS}) = 1/6(-25) + 1/6(-25) + 1/6(35) + 1/6(-35)$$
$$+ 1/6(35) + 1/6(25)$$
$$= 1/6(-25 - 25 + 35 - 35 + 35 + 25)$$
$$= 5/3.$$

Hence, the FBB, SFS entry of the payoff matrix is 5/3. Since the payoff matrix is an 8×8 matrix, we must perform computations similar to that above 63 more times. Although it is not suggested that one actually do this in its entirety, one should verify at least a few of the entries of the payoff matrix below:

		FFF	FFS	FSF	SFF	FSS	SFS	SSF	SSS
	FFF	-25	-25	-25	-25	-25	-25	-25	-25
	FFB	$-25/3$	$-25/3$	$-20/3$	$-20/3$	$-20/3$	$-20/3$	-5	-5
	FBF	$-25/3$	$-55/3$	$-25/3$	$-20/3$	$-55/3$	$-50/3$	$-20/3$	$-50/3$
I	BFF	$-25/3$	$-55/3$	$-55/3$	$-25/3$	$-85/3$	$-55/3$	$-55/3$	$-85/3$
	FBB	$25/3$	$-5/3$	10	$35/3$	0	$5/3$	$40/3$	$10/3$
	BFB	$25/3$	$-5/3$	0	10	-10	0	$5/3$	$-25/3$
	BBF	$25/3$	$-35/3$	$-5/3$	10	$-65/3$	-10	0	-20
	BBB	25	5	$50/3$	$85/3$	$-10/3$	$25/3$	20	0

The top of the matrix is labeled **II**.

Fortunately, the matrix above reduces considerably by domination. The first, second, third, fourth, sixth, and seventh rows can be deleted upon comparison with (for example) the fifth row. Then the first, third, fourth, sixth, seventh, and eighth columns can be deleted upon comparison with the fifth column. Hence, the payoff matrix above reduces by domination to

		FFS	FSS
I	FBB	$-5/3$	0
	BBB	5	$-10/3$

with top label **II**.

We now apply our linear programming techniques to the reduced payoff matrix:

Ⓥ

		q_1	q_2	-1	
ⓤ	0	-1	-1^*	-1	$=-0$
p_1	-1^{**}	$-5/3$	0	0	$=-t_1$
p_2	-1	5	$-10/3$	0	$=-t_2$
-1	-1	0	0	0	$=f$
	$=0$	$=s_1$	$=s_2$	$=g$	

pivot on *

Ⓥ

		q_1	0	-1	
s_2	0	1	-1	1	$=-q_2$
p_1	-1^{**}	$-5/3$	0	0	$=-t_1$
p_2	-1	$25/3$	$-10/3$	$10/3$	$=-t_2$
-1	-1	0	0	0	$=f$
	$=0$	$=s_1$	$=$ⓤ	$=g$	

pivot on **

	t_1	q_1	-1	
s_2	0	1	1	$=-q_2$
0	-1	$5/3$	0	$=$Ⓥ
p_2	-1	10^*	$10/3$	$=-t_2$
-1	-1	$5/3$	0	$=f$
	$=p_1$	$=s_1$	$=g$	

simplex algorithm

(Note: In game tableaus, the filed equations for u and v need not be recorded; u and v can be obtained from f and g since $f = -v$ and $g = -u$.)

	t_1	t_2	-1	
s_2	$1/10$	$-1/10$	$2/3$	$=-q_2$
s_1	$-1/10$	$1/10$	$1/3$	$=-q_1$
-1	$-5/6$	$-1/6$	$-5/9$	$=f$
	$=p_1$	$=p_2$	$=g$	

The basic solutions of the final tableau above are optimal:

$$t_1 = t_2 = 0, q_2 = 2/3, q_1 = 1/3, \max f = 5/9,$$
$$\min v = \min -f = -\max f = -5/9,$$

$$s_2 = s_1 = 0, p_1 = 5/6, p_2 = 1/6, \min g = 5/9,$$
$$\max u = \max - g = -\min g = -5/9.$$

The von Neumann value of this game is $-5/9$, i.e., this game favors player II who will win, on the average, $5/9$¢ per round of the game provided that both players play their optimal strategies. These optimal strategies are summarized below:

II

	choice	FFS	FSS
		prob. 1/3	2/3
I	FBB	5/6 $\begin{bmatrix} -5/3 \end{bmatrix}$	$\begin{bmatrix} 0 \end{bmatrix}$
	BBB	1/6 $\begin{bmatrix} 5 \end{bmatrix}$	$\begin{bmatrix} -10/3 \end{bmatrix}$

$u = v = -5/9$

In other words, it is optimal for player I to bet with a J (i.e., bluff) with probability $1/6$ and always bet with a Q or K; it is optimal for player II to always fold with a J, fold with a Q with probability $1/3$, and always see with a K.

EXAMPLE 6. There are two players, say player I and player II, and a standard 52-card deck of playing cards. The black suits (i.e., spades (♠'s) and clubs (♣'s)) rank higher than the red suits (i.e., hearts (♥'s) and diamonds (♦'s)); the denominations of these cards are irrelevant. Each player antes $\$x$ ($x \geq 0$) and is then dealt a single card face down. Each player looks at his card. Player I now has two options:

PASS—Both cards are revealed and the high hand wins the pot (if the hands are equal, the pot is divided equally)

BET—Player I adds $\$y$ ($y > 0$) to the pot.

If player I bets, player II has two options:

FOLD—Player II loses his ante to player I

SEE—Player II adds $\$y$ to the pot.

In the event that player II sees, both cards are revealed and the high hand wins the pot (if the hands are equal, the pot is divided equally). The cards are then returned to the deck.

Given this game, which player (if any) has the advantage? What is the von Neumann value of this game? What is the optimal strategy for each player?

This game is similar to the game of Example 5. The choices for both players appear below:

Choices for player I:

PP   PB   BP   BB

Choices for player II:

$$FF \quad FS \quad SF \quad SS$$

In each choice, the first letter represents the decision on what to do if a black card (denoted b) is dealt and the second letter represents the decision on what to do if a red card (denoted r) is dealt. Under the assumption that all hands are equally likely,* the entries of the payoff matrix are now computed as in Example 5. We illustrate with an example.

	Player I plays BP,	player II	plays FS
	I II	I II	I II	I II
Hand dealt:	b b	b r	r b	r r
Probability:	1/4	1/4	1/4	1/4
Outcome: (Winnings for player I)	x	$x + y$	$-x$	0

$$E(BP, FS) = 1/4(x) + 1/4(x + y) + 1/4(-x) + 1/4(0)$$
$$= 1/4(x + (x + y) - x)$$
$$= (x + y)/4.$$

The payoff matrix is

$$
\begin{array}{c}
 \\
\text{I} \quad
\begin{array}{c} PP \\ PB \\ BP \\ BB \end{array}
\end{array}
\begin{array}{c}
\text{II} \\
\begin{array}{cccc}
FF & FS & SF & SS \\
\left[\begin{array}{cccc}
0 & 0 & 0 & 0 \\
3x/4 & x/2 & (x-y)/4 & -y/4 \\
x/4 & (x+y)/4 & 0 & y/4 \\
x & (3x+y)/4 & (x-y)/4 & 0
\end{array}\right]
\end{array}
\end{array}
$$

(Verify a few of the entries above before continuing!)

The payoff matrix above reduces by domination. Before we illustrate this reduction, it is possible to make an educated guess as to which player is probably favored by this game by inspecting this matrix. Notice that the first row of the payoff matrix consists entirely of zeros. Hence player I can force at least a fair game by constantly choosing strategy PP, i.e., passing no matter what color card is dealt to him. Given this pure strategy, the expected winnings of player I per round of the game (or, equivalently, the expected losses of player II per round of the game) is 0 no matter what strategy player II uses, i.e., the game is fair. But the pure strategy of choosing PP for player I may not be optimal, i.e., there may be a pure or mixed strategy for player I whereby player I can achieve an expected winnings per round of the game that is greater

*All hands in this game are *not* equally likely. The probability of the players getting cards of different colors is slightly higher than the probability of the players getting cards of the same color. (See Exercise 5.) We assume equal likelihood of the hands for computational convenience.

than 0. Hence, this card game probably favors player I. Our forthcoming analysis will corroborate this fact. In addition, however, we will obtain the exact expected winnings for player I per round of the game (the von Neumann value of the game) and the optimal strategy for each player.

We now apply domination to our payoff matrix. The first row can be deleted upon comparison with the third row and the second row can be deleted upon comparison with the fourth row. Then the first and second columns can be deleted upon comparison with the third column leaving

$$
\begin{array}{c}
\text{II} \\
\begin{array}{cc}
\text{SF} & \text{SS}
\end{array} \\
\text{I}\quad
\begin{array}{c}
\text{BP} \\
\text{BB}
\end{array}
\begin{bmatrix}
0 & y/4 \\
(x-y)/4 & 0
\end{bmatrix}
\end{array}
$$

We now consider two cases.

Case I. $x \leq y$. Domination reduces the payoff matrix even further. The second row can be deleted upon comparison with the first row and then the second column can be deleted upon comparison with the first column to obtain

$$
\begin{array}{c}
\text{II} \\
\text{SF} \\
\text{I}\quad \text{BP}\quad [0]
\end{array}
$$

Here, the von Neumann value of the game is 0, i.e., the game is fair. The optimal strategies for the players are pure strategies, namely BP for player I and SF for player II. In other words, it is optimal for player I to always bet with a black card and always pass with a red card; it is optimal for player II to always see with a black card and always fold with a red card.

Case II. $x > y$. We apply our linear programming techniques to the 2×2 payoff matrix above:

v	q_1	q_2	-1	
u 　 0	-1	$-1^{\bullet}$	-1	$= -0$
p_1 　 $-1^{\bullet\bullet}$	0	$y/4$	0	$= -t_1$
p_2 　 -1	$(x-y)/4$	0	0	$= -t_2$
-1 　 -1	0	0	0	$= f$
$= 0$	$= s_1$	$= s_2$	$= g$	

pivot
on
*

(Note: The maximum entry in the first column of the payoff matrix is $(x - y)/4$; the maximum entry in the second column of the payoff matrix is $y/4$. But which of $(x - y)/4$ and $y/4$ is minimal? This depends on how much larger x is than y. The choice of $y/4$ as minimal works in general for Case II (as does the choice of $(x - y)/4$; see Exercise 6) and we use $y/4$.)

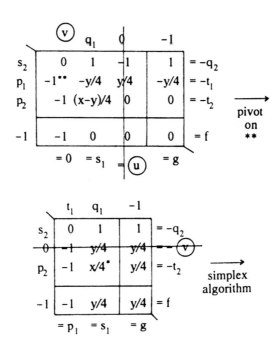

(Note: The tableau above is canonical and maximum basic feasible. Since $x > y > 0$, we have $x > 0$; since $(y/4)/(x/4) < 1$, our pivot choice by the simplex algorithm is $x/4$.)

	t_1	t_2	-1	
s_2	$4/x$	$-4/x$	$(x-y)/x$	$= -q_2$
s_1	$-4/x$	$4/x$	y/x	$= -q_1$
-1	$(y-x)/x$	$-y/x$	$y(x-y)/(4x)$	$= f$
	$= p_1$	$= p_2$	$= g$	

The basic solutions of the final tableau above are optimal:

$$t_1 = t_2 = 0, q_2 = (x - y)/x, q_1 = y/x, \max f = y(y - x)/(4x),$$
$$\min v = y(x - y)/(4x),$$
$$s_2 = s_1 = 0, p_1 = (x - y)/x, p_2 = y/x, \min g = y(y - x)/(4x),$$
$$\max u = y(x - y)/(4x).$$

The von Neumann value of the game is $y(x - y)/(4x)$; since $x > y > 0$, we have $y(x - y)/(4x) > 0$ and hence the game favors player I who will win, on the average, $\$y(x - y)/(4x)$ per round of the game provided both players play their optimal strategies. These optimal strategies are summarized below:

II

	choice		SF	SS
		prob.	y/x	(x-y)/x
I	BP	(x-y)/x	0	y/4
	BB	y/x	(x-y)/4	0

$$u = v = y(x-y)/(4x)$$

In other words, it is optimal for player I to always bet with a black card and bet with probability y/x with a red card; it is optimal for player II to always see with a black card and see with probability $(x - y)/x$ with a red card.

§6. Concluding Remarks

Game theory is a dynamic and ever-widening field. While a rigorous and complete treatment of the subject would require a firm foundation in advanced calculus (at least), we have attempted in the preceding sections to introduce the subject through the concept of a two-person zero-sum matrix game. The solution procedure for such games illustrates quite graphically the power of linear programming (in particular, the dual noncanonical tableau) in the analysis of games. More advanced discussions of game-theoretic topics may be found in [O1].

EXERCISES

1. Find the von Neumann value and the optimal strategy for each player in each of the matrix games below.

a.
$$\text{II}$$
$$I \begin{bmatrix} 2 & 1 & 4 & 2 \\ 1 & 2 & 1 & 1 \\ -2 & 6 & 3 & -2 \\ 3 & -3 & 5 & 1 \\ 1 & 2 & 2 & 1 \end{bmatrix}$$

b.
$$\text{II}$$
$$I \begin{bmatrix} -1 & 0 & 2 & -2 & 0 \\ 1 & -2 & -4 & 2 & 2 \\ 0 & -1 & 1 & 1 & -1 \\ 0 & 5 & 4 & 2 & 0 \end{bmatrix}$$

c.
$$\text{II}$$
$$I \begin{bmatrix} 1 & -3 & 1 & 0 & 1 \\ -3 & -2 & -1 & 0 & 1 \\ 1 & -1 & 1 & 1 & -1 \\ -2 & -1 & 0 & 1 & 2 \\ 1 & -1 & -1 & -1 & 1 \end{bmatrix}$$

d.   II

$$\begin{matrix} & & \\ I & \begin{bmatrix} -1 & 1 & -1 & 2 \\ -1 & -1 & 1 & 1 \\ 0 & 1 & 1 & -1 \end{bmatrix} \end{matrix}$$

2. Find the von Neumann value and the optimal strategy for each player in each of the games below.

   a. Player I and player II each have a penny and a nickel. They each choose one of their coins and display them simultaneously. If the coins are the same, player I wins the sum of the coins from player II; if the coins are different, player II wins a nickel from player I.

   b. Player I has the two of spades (2♠) and the three of hearts (3♥) from a deck of playing cards and player II has the three of spades (3♠) and the four of hearts (4♥). They each choose one of their cards and display them simultaneously. If the colors are the same, player I wins; if the colors are different, player II wins. If player I plays the 2♠, the payoff consists of the difference of the numbers on the cards played in dollars; if player I plays the 3♥, the payoff consists of the sum of the numbers on the cards played in dollars.

   c. (The excerpt below is from *The Purloined Letter* by Edgar Allan Poe.)

   "I knew one [student] about eight years of age, whose success at guessing in the game of 'even and odd' attracted universal admiration. This game is simple, and is played with marbles. One player holds in his hand a number of these toys, and demands of another whether that number is even or odd. If the guess is right, the guesser wins one; if wrong, he loses one. The boy to whom I allude won all the marbles of the school. Of course he had some principle of guessing; and this lay in mere observation and admeasurement of the astuteness of his opponents. For example, an arrant simpleton is his opponent, and, holding up his closed hand, asks, 'are they even or odd?' Our schoolboy replies, 'odd,' and loses; but upon the second trial he wins, for he then says to himself, 'the simpleton had them even upon the first trial, and his amount of cunning is just sufficient to make him have them odd upon the second; I will therefore guess odd;'—he guesses odd, and wins. Now, with a simpleton a degree above the first, he would have reasoned thus: 'This fellow finds that in the first instance I guessed odd, and, in the second, he will propose to himself, upon the first impulse, a simple variation from even to odd, as did the first simpleton; but then a second thought will suggest that this is too simple a variation, and finally he will decide upon putting it even as before. I will therefore guess even;'—he guesses even, and wins. Now this mode of reasoning in the schoolboy, whom his fellows termed 'lucky,'—what, in its last analysis, is it?".

3. Consider the game below:

   Player I and player II each have two pennies. Each player holds 0, 1, or 2 pennies in his left hand and the remainder of the pennies (2, 1, or 0 respectively) in his right hand. Each player reveals both hands simultaneously. If the number of coins in one of player I's hands is greater than the number of coins in the respective hand of player II, player I wins the difference in pennies; otherwise, no money is exchanged.

   a. Which player is favored in the game? (No work is required here!)

   b. Find the von Neumann value and the optimal strategy for each player in the game. If any player has infinitely many optimal strategies, find all optimal strategies.

  c. If player II owed $100 to player I, approximately how many rounds of the game would have to be played, on the average, to cancel the debt?

  d. Assume that player II is allowed three pennies. Repeat parts a, b, and c for this new game.

  e. Assume that player II is allowed four pennies. Find the von Neumann value of this new game. (No work is required here—be clever!)

4. Find the von Neumann value of the matrix game below:

$$
I\begin{array}{c} \\ \\ \\ \\ \\ \\ \\ \\ \end{array}
\begin{bmatrix}
-75 & -75 & -75 & -75 & -75 & -75 & -75 & -75 \\
-25 & -25 & -20 & -20 & -20 & -20 & -15 & -15 \\
-25 & -55 & -25 & -20 & -55 & -50 & -20 & -50 \\
-25 & -55 & -55 & -25 & -85 & -55 & -55 & -85 \\
25 & -5 & 30 & 35 & 0 & 5 & 40 & 10 \\
25 & -5 & 0 & 30 & -30 & 0 & 5 & -25 \\
25 & -35 & -5 & 30 & -65 & -30 & 0 & -60 \\
75 & 15 & 50 & 85 & -10 & 25 & 60 & 0
\end{bmatrix}
$$

$$\text{II}$$

[Hint: Compare the matrix above to the matrix of Example 5.]
[Note: The method motivated in this exercise can be used generally to convert fractional entries of matrix games to integers.]

5. Find the actual probability of occurrence of each of the hands in Example 6, thus proving that the hands are *not* equally likely.

6. Show that the choice of $(x - y)/4$ as minimal works in general for Case II of Example 6.

7. Find the von Neumann value and the optimal strategy for each player in each of the multiphase games below.

  a. Player I and player II each secretly toss a coin. Heads ranks higher than tails. Each player looks at his coin. Player I now has two options:

    PASS—Both coins are revealed and the high coin wins. If player I has the high coin, he wins $2 from player II; if player II has the high coin, he wins $4 from player I. If both coins are the same, no money is exchanged.

    BID—Player II has two options:
      FOLD—Player I wins $4 from player II
      SEE—Both coins are revealed and the high coin wins $12. If both coins are the same, no money is exchanged.

  b. Player I and player II are each dealt a single card face down from a deck of three playing cards, a jack (J), a queen (Q), and a king (K). The ranking of these cards, from lowest to highest, is J, Q, and K; the suits of these cards are irrelevant. Each player looks at his card. Player I now has two options:

PASS—Both cards are revealed and the high card wins. If player I has the high card, he wins $2 from player II; if player II has the high card, he wins $3 from player I.

BET—Player I puts $1 in the pot.

If player I bets, player II has two options:

PASS—Player II adds $3 to the pot and player I adds $1 to the pot. Both cards are revealed and the high hand wins the pot.

SEE—Player II puts $1 in the pot.

In the event that player II sees, both cards are revealed and the high hand wins the pot. The cards are then returned to the deck.

c. Player I and player II each ante $5. Each is then dealt a single card face down from a standard 52-card deck of playing cards. The black suits (i.e., spades (♠'s) and clubs (♣'s)) rank higher than the red suits (i.e., hearts (♥'s) and diamonds (♦'s)); the denominations of these cards are irrelevant. Each player looks at his card. Player I now has two options:

PASS—Both cards are revealed and the high hand wins the pot (if the hands are equal, the pot is divided equally)

BET—Player I adds $1 to the pot.

If player I bets, player II has three options:

FOLD—Player II loses his ante to player I

SEE—Player II adds $1 to the pot, both cards are revealed, and the high hand wins the pot (if the hands are equal, the pot is divided equally)

RAISE—Player II adds $2 to the pot.

If player II raises, player I has two options:

FOLD—Player I loses his ante and bet to player II

SEE—Player I adds $1 to the pot, both cards are revealed, and the high hand wins the pot (if the hands are equal, the pot is divided equally).

The cards are then returned to the deck.

[Note: Assume equal likelihood of the hands for computational convenience (but see Exercise 5 above!).]

8. Assume that the ante is $1 (instead of $5) in the game of Exercise 7c above. Prove that this new game is fair. [Hint: It suffices to show that *one* row and *one* column of the payoff matrix consists entirely of zeros. (Why?)]

9. Let $x, y \in \mathbf{R}$ and consider the matrix game below:

$$
\begin{array}{c}
 \quad \text{II} \\
\text{I} \quad \begin{bmatrix} x & 0 \\ 0 & y \end{bmatrix}
\end{array}
$$

a. Determine a necessary and sufficient condition for the matrix game above to reduce by domination to a single entry.

b. Given the condition of part a, find the von Neumann value and the optimal strategy for each player in the matrix game above. [Hint: There are two cases.]

10. Let x, y, $z \in \mathbf{R}$. Find the von Neumann value and the optimal strategy for each player in the matrix game below:

$$
\begin{array}{c}
 \quad \text{II} \\
I \quad \begin{bmatrix} x & x \\ y & z \end{bmatrix}
\end{array}
$$

[Hint: Consider several cases and reduce by domination.]

11. a. Let $x > 0$. Find the von Neumann value and the optimal strategy for each player in the matrix game below:

$$
\begin{array}{c}
 \qquad \text{II} \\
I \begin{bmatrix} -(x+2) & x+1 \\ x+1 & -x \end{bmatrix}
\end{array}
$$

b. Assume now that x can be any real number. For what values of x does the matrix game above reduce by domination to a single entry?

12. Prove that the minimization problem of the game tableau in Theorem 3 yields the optimal strategy for the row player.

CHAPTER 6

Transportation and Assignment Problems

§0. Introduction

Transportation and assignment problems are traditional examples of linear programming problems. Although these problems are solvable by using the techniques of Chapters 2–4 directly, the solution procedure is cumbersome; hence, we develop much more efficient algorithms for handling these problems. In the case of transportation problems, the algorithm is essentially a disguised form of the dual simplex algorithm of 4§2. Assignment problems, which are special cases of transportation problems, pose difficulties for the transportation algorithm and require the development of an algorithm which takes advantage of the simpler nature of these problems.

§1. An Example; The Balanced Transportation Problem

We begin with a typical example of a transportation problem.

EXAMPLE 1. A manufacturer of widgits owns three warehouses and sells to three markets. The supply of each warehouse, the demand of each market, and the shipping cost per ton of widgits from each warehouse to each market are as follows:

warehouse supplies

	Market 1	Market 2	Market 3	
Warehouse 1	$2/ton	$1/ton	$2/ton	40 tons
Warehouse 2	$9/ton	$4/ton	$7/ton	60 tons
Warehouse 3	$1/ton	$2/ton	$9/ton	10 tons
market demands $\longrightarrow$	40 tons	50 tons	20 tons	110 tons $\longleftarrow$ total demand

total supply

How should the manufacturer ship the widgits so as to minimize total transportation cost?

The problem can be solved by using the techniques of Chapters 2–4 directly. For $i, j = 1, 2, 3$, let

$x_{ij} = $ # of tons of widgits shipped from warehouse i to market j.

Then the objective is to minimize the total transportation cost, i.e.,

Minimize $C(x_{11}, x_{12}, x_{13}, x_{21}, x_{22}, x_{23}, x_{31}, x_{32}, x_{33})$
$$= 2x_{11} + x_{12} + 2x_{13} + 9x_{21} + 4x_{22} + 7x_{23} + x_{31} + 2x_{32} + 9x_{33}.$$

What are the constraints? Note that the total supply of the three warehouses is 110 tons and that the total demand of the three markets is 110 tons. Hence, in order to satisfy the demand of the markets, each warehouse will have to ship precisely its current supply of widgits. Furthermore, the amount of widgits sent to any market by the three warehouses must equal the demand of that market. Hence we obtain six equality constraints for our transportation problem:

$$x_{11} + x_{12} + x_{13} = 40 \quad \text{(Warehouse 1 supply constraint)}$$
$$x_{21} + x_{22} + x_{23} = 60 \quad \text{(Warehouse 2 supply constraint)}$$
$$x_{31} + x_{32} + x_{33} = 10 \quad \text{(Warehouse 3 supply constraint)}$$
$$x_{11} + x_{21} + x_{31} = 40 \quad \text{(Market 1 demand constraint)}$$
$$x_{12} + x_{22} + x_{32} = 50 \quad \text{(Market 2 demand constraint)}$$
$$x_{13} + x_{23} + x_{33} = 20 \quad \text{(Market 3 demand constraint)}.$$

Finally, we impose nonnegativity constraints on the x_{ij}'s:

$$x_{11}, x_{12}, x_{13}, x_{21}, x_{22}, x_{23}, x_{31}, x_{32}, x_{33} \geqq 0.$$

The initial Tucker tableau for the solution of this problem via the techniques of Chapters 2–4 is

x_{11}	1	0	0	1	0	0	2
x_{12}	1	0	0	0	1	0	1
x_{13}	1	0	0	0	0	1	2
x_{21}	0	1	0	1	0	0	9
x_{22}	0	1	0	0	1	0	4
x_{23}	0	1	0	0	0	1	7
x_{31}	0	0	1	1	0	0	1
x_{32}	0	0	1	0	1	0	2
x_{33}	0	0	1	0	0	1	9
-1	40	60	10	40	50	20	0
	$=0$	$=0$	$=0$	$=0$	$=0$	$=0$	$=C$

WOW! A relatively small transportation problem with three warehouses and three markets has expanded into a 10×7 Tucker tableau! Although we could use the techniques of Chapters 2--4 to solve this problem, we will opt instead for a more direct algorithm which operates on a smaller tableau. We leave Example 1 until its solution with this algorithm in §4.

Example 1 above is an example of a balanced transportation problem. We now state the general balanced transportation problem. A manufacturer of a certain good owns m warehouses $W_1, W_2,..., W_m$ and sells to n markets $M_1, M_2,..., M_n$. Let $s_i, i = 1, 2,..., m$, be the supply of W_i, let $d_j, j = 1, 2,..., n$, be the demand of M_j, and let c_{ij} be the unit shipping cost from W_i to M_j. If x_{ij} is the number of units of the good to be shipped from W_i to M_j, then the general balanced transportation problem is

Minimize $\quad C = \sum_{i=1}^{m} \sum_{j=1}^{n} c_{ij} x_{ij}$

subject to $\quad \sum_{j=1}^{n} x_{ij} = s_i, \quad i = 1, 2,..., m \left.\right\}$ Warehouse constraints

$\qquad \sum_{i=1}^{m} x_{ij} = d_j, \quad j = 1, 2,..., n \left.\right\}$ Market constraints

$\qquad x_{ij} \geqq 0, \quad \forall i, j.$

Here, total supply is equal to total demand:

$$\text{total supply} = \sum_{i=1}^{m} s_i = \sum_{i=1}^{m} \left(\sum_{j=1}^{n} x_{ij} \right) = \sum_{i=1}^{m} \sum_{j=1}^{n} x_{ij}$$

$$= \sum_{j=1}^{n} \left(\sum_{i=1}^{m} x_{ij} \right) = \sum_{j=1}^{n} d_j = \text{total demand};$$

it is, in this sense, that the transportation problem is said to be *balanced*. (Unbalanced transportation problems will be discussed in §5.) The relevant *balanced transportation tableau* is given by

$$
\begin{array}{c|cccc|c}
 & M_1 & M_2 & \cdots & M_n & \\
\hline
W_1 & c_{11} & c_{12} & \cdots & c_{1n} & s_1 \\
W_2 & c_{21} & c_{22} & \cdots & c_{2n} & s_2 \\
\vdots & \vdots & \vdots & & \vdots & \vdots \\
W_m & c_{m1} & c_{m2} & \cdots & c_{mn} & s_m \\
\hline
 & d_1 & d_2 & \cdots & d_n & \\
\end{array}
$$

$$\sum_{i=1}^{m} s_i = \sum_{j=1}^{n} d_j$$

The entries of the transportation tableau are called *cells*. An extremely important remark is in order here. The transportation tableau above is *not* a Tucker tableau. In fact, the algorithm to be developed essentially translates the steps of the dual simplex algorithm of 4§2 (which operates on a Tucker tableau) into the language of transportation problems; in so doing, we will obtain a disguised form of the dual simplex algorithm which operates directly on the transportation tableau rather than on the much larger Tucker tableau. The next two sections give this algorithm. Although no proofs are given, comments are provided to enable the reader to see the correspondence between the steps of the two algorithms. For further discussions of the relationships between the transportation algorithm and simplex algorithm techniques, see [L2].

§2. The Vogel Advanced-Start Method (VAM)

The Vogel Advanced-Start Method (VAM), named after W.R. Vogel ([R1]), implements the reduction of the minimum Tucker tableau of a transportation problem to minimum basic feasible form. This algorithm would hence correspond to the transformation of the Tucker tableau to canonical form and the subsequent application of steps (1)–(6) of the dual simplex algorithm of 4§2. We should remark here that VAM is not the only algorithm that implements this reduction. Other methods include, for example, the minimum-entry method and the northwest-corner method (see Exercise 6). In fact, the use of VAM in large transportation problems can be quite cumbersome. But VAM is usually considered to be superior for smaller transportation problems and is especially suitable for hand computations since it generally results in a feasible solution that is closer to being optimal than the other procedures.

VAM

(0) Given: An initial balanced transportation tableau.

(1) Compute the difference of the two smallest entries in every row and column of the tableau and write this difference opposite the row or column. (If there is only one entry in any row or column, write that entry.)

(2) Choose the largest difference and use the smallest cost in the corresponding row or column to empty a warehouse or completely fill a market demand. (If there is a tie for the largest difference, use the smallest entry in the corresponding rows and/or columns. If there is a tie for the smallest entry, use any such entry.) Circle the cost used and write above the circle the amount of goods shipped by that route. Reduce the supply and demand in the row and column containing the cost used.

(3) Delete the row or column corresponding to the emptied warehouse or fully supplied market; if both happen simultaneously, delete the row unless that row is the only row remaining in which case delete the column.

(4) If all tableau entries are deleted, STOP; otherwise, go to (1).

We now apply VAM to Example 1 of §1.

EXAMPLE 1 (Continued). The parenthetical numbers below correspond to the steps of VAM.

(0)

$$
\begin{array}{c|ccc|c}
 & M_1 & M_2 & M_3 & \\
\hline
W_1 & 2 & 1 & 2 & 40 \\
W_2 & 9 & 4 & 7 & 60 \\
W_3 & 1 & 2 & 9 & 10 \\
\hline
 & 40 & 50 & 20 & 110
\end{array}
$$

The W_i's and the M_j's will be suppressed computationally.

(1)

(2) The largest difference in the tableau above is 5 corresponding to the third column. Hence we use the smallest cost in the third column, namely 2, to empty a warehouse or completely fill a market demand. 2 denotes the unit cost of shipping widgits from W_1 to M_3; since M_3 only needs 20 tons of the possible 40 tons in W_1, we ship 20 tons of widgits from W_1 to M_3 and

therefore fulfill the demand of M_3. We then adjust the supply of W_1 and the demand of M_3 accordingly, i.e., after such a shipment, the current supply of W_1 is $40 - 20 = 20$ and the current demand of M_3 is $20 - 20 = 0$. The entire transaction is recorded as follows:

	1	1	5	
1	2	1	(2)²⁰	4̶0̶ 20
3	9	4	7	60
1	1	2	9	10
	40	50	2̶0̶ 0	

What is the rationale behind the choice of the largest difference and the subsequent choice of the smallest cost in the corresponding row or column? The largest difference at any stage of VAM is a measure of the "regret" we would have for not using the smallest cost possible in the row or column of this difference. Referring to the tableau above, if we do not take advantage of the 2 in the third column, then, because of the larger difference, we will eventually have to use a much larger cost to fulfill the demand of M_3. Hence we ship as many tons of widgits as we can via the cost of 2 in the hope of avoiding the much larger costs in the same column.

(3) M_3 has been fully supplied in step (2) above; hence we delete the third column of the tableau:

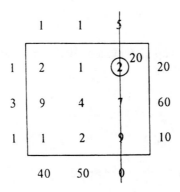

Note that we have successfully avoided using the high costs of 7 and 9 in the third column!

(4) All tableau entries have not been deleted so we go to step (1).

(1)

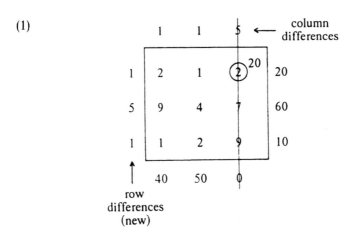

(2) The largest difference in the tableau above is 5 corresponding to the second row. Hence we use the smallest cost in the second row, namely 4, to ship as many tons of widgits as we can from W_2 to M_2—this amount is 50 tons (fulfilling the demand of M_2). The supply of W_2 is adjusted to $60 - 50 = 10$ and the demand of M_2 is adjusted to $50 - 50 = 0$;

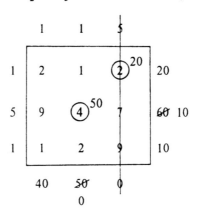

(3) M_2 has been fully supplied in step (2) above; hence we delete the second column of the tableau:

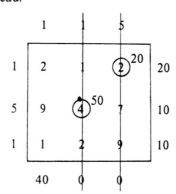

(4) All tableau entries have not been deleted so we go to step (1).

(1)

	1	1	5	
2	2	1	②^{20}	20
9	9	④^{50}	7	10
1	1	2	9	10
	40	0	0	

(Remember: If a row or column contains only one entry, write that entry when computing differences.)

(2) The largest difference in the tableau above is 9 corresponding to the second row. Hence we use the smallest cost in the second row, namely 9, to ship as many tons of widgits as we can from W_2 to M_1—this amount is 10 tons (emptying W_2). The supply of W_2 and the demand of M_1 are adjusted accordingly:

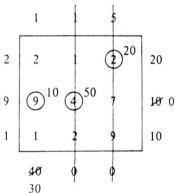

(3) W_2 has been emptied in step (2) above; hence we delete the second row of the tableau:

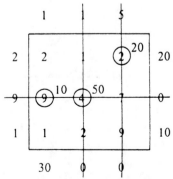

(4) All tableau entries have not been deleted so we go to step (1).

(1)

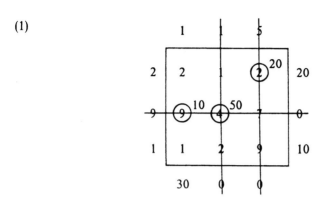

(2) Provide your own justification for the tableau below:

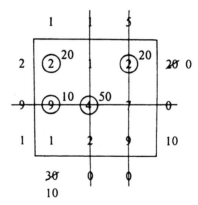

(3)

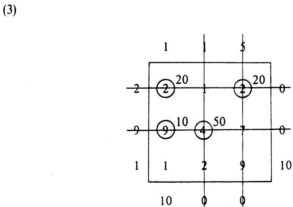

(4) Go to step (1).

(1)

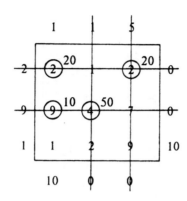

(2)

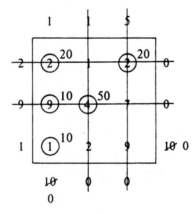

(3) A warehouse has been emptied and a market has been fully supplied simultaneously in step (2) above. Although it really does not matter at this point whether we delete the row or column (since all tableau entries will have been deleted in any event and VAM will terminate in step (4)), we delete the column in accordance with step (3) as stated previously:

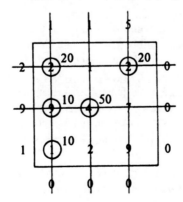

(4) All tableau entries have been deleted—STOP.

Our transportation tableau after VAM is

$(2)^{20}$	1	$(2)^{20}$	40
$(9)^{10}$	$(4)^{50}$	7	60
$(1)^{10}$	2	9	10
40	50	20	

Note that the solution obtained by VAM is a feasible solution. To see this, check that the total number of tons of widgits shipped from each warehouse is equal to the total supply of that warehouse and that the total number of tons of widgits shipped to each market is equal to the total demand of that market. This feasible solution is given by

$$x_{11} = 20, \quad x_{12} = 0, \quad x_{13} = 20,$$
$$x_{21} = 10, \quad x_{22} = 50, \quad x_{23} = 0,$$
$$x_{31} = 10, \quad x_{32} = 0, \quad x_{33} = 0$$

with corresponding total transportation cost

$$C = \$2(20) + \$2(20) + \$9(10) + \$4(50) + \$1(10) = \$380.$$

Is such a solution optimal? We postpone the answer to this question until the next section. The interested reader may wish to attempt the construction of a feasible solution having lower total transportation cost than $380.

Definition 2. A feasible solution of a balanced transportation problem is said to be a *basic feasible solution* if at most $m + n - 1$ of the x_{ij}'s are positive where m is the number of warehouses and n is the number of markets.

Not surprisingly, the notion of Definition 2 above is completely analogous to the concept of a basic feasible solution of a Tucker tableau. VAM produced a basic feasible solution from the tableau of Example 1 of §1. Exactly five of the x_{ij}'s are positive (namely $x_{11}, x_{13}, x_{21}, x_{22}$ and x_{31}) and $m + n - 1 = 3 + 3 - 1 = 5$. Note though that basic feasible solutions in transportation tableaus need not have exactly $m + n - 1$ positive x_{ij}'s as in this example—the requirement is *at most* $m + n - 1$ positive x_{ij}'s. Does VAM always produce a basic feasible solution from a balanced transportation tableau? YES!

Theorem 3. *VAM produces a basic feasible solution for any balanced transportation problem. Furthermore, the basic feasible solution corresponds to exactly*

$m + n - 1$ *distinguished (circled) cells of the transportation tableau where m is the number of warehouses and n is the number of markets. These distinguished cells are said to constitute a* basis *for the basic feasible solution.*

Note particularly the "furthermore" in Theorem 3 above. VAM will always terminate with exactly $m + n - 1$ circled cells where m is the number of warehouses and n is the number of markets. This is crucial! Chaos may result later if you do not check for this immediately after using VAM. Theorem 3 does *not* say that exactly $m + n - 1$ of the x_{ij}'s will be positive—even though exactly $m + n - 1$ of the cells will be circled (and all noncircled cells will have x_{ij}-value 0), it is possible for one (or more) circled cells to have x_{ij}-value 0. This phenomenon did not happen in Example 1 above but will be illustrated later.

§3. The Transportation Algorithm

Definition 4. Let T be the tableau of a balanced transportation problem. A *cycle C* in T is a subset of cells of T such that each row and each column of T contains exactly zero or two cells of C.

EXAMPLE 5. In each tableau T below, the circled cells form a cycle C in T.

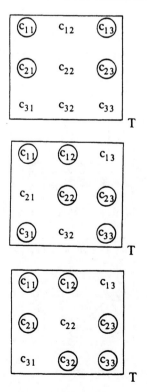

By connecting the cells of a cycle using horizontal and vertical movement only, we may visualize cycles in transportation tableaus as usual graph-theoretic cycles. Never use diagonal movement in this regard (even though it may yield a graph-theoretic cycle). The reason for disallowing diagonal movement is investigated in Exercise 7.

EXAMPLE 6. The cycles of the tableaus in Example 5 above may be visualized as

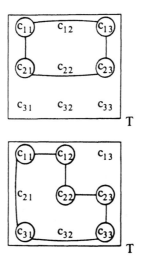

and

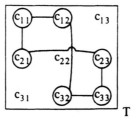

respectively. The cycle in the final tableau above should *not* be visualized as

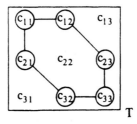

since diagonal movement is used here.

We now give the transportation algorithm, the disguised form of the dual simplex algorithm which will solve balanced transportation problems.

The Transportation Algorithm

(0) Given: An initial balanced transportation tableau.

(1) Apply VAM to obtain a basic feasible solution and a corresponding basis (§2).

(2) Let $b_1 = 0$. Determine $a_1, a_2, \ldots, a_m, b_2, b_3, \ldots, b_n$ uniquely such that $a_i + b_j = c_{ij}$ for all basis cells c_{ij}.

(3) Replace each cell c_{ij} by $c_{ij} - a_i - b_j$; these are the new cells c_{ij}.

(4) If $c_{ij} \geq 0$ for all i and j, STOP; replace all cells with their original costs from (0); the basic feasible solution given by the current basis cells is optimal. Otherwise, continue.

(5) Choose $c_{ij} < 0$. (Usually, the most appropriate choice is the most negative c_{ij}, but see Exercise 8.) Label this cell as a "getter" cell (+). (By convention, this cell is distinguished by squaring it instead of circling it.) Find the unique cycle C in the tableau determined by this (squared) cell and basis cells. Label the cells in C alternately as "giver" cells (−) and "getter" cells (+). Choose the "giver" cell associated with the smallest amount of goods. (If there is a tie among certain "giver" cells for the smallest amount of goods, choose any such cell.)

(6) Add the squared cell of (5) to the basis, i.e., circle it in a new tableau. Remove the chosen "giver" cell of (5) from the basis, i.e., do not circle it in a new tableau. Add the amount of goods given up by this "giver" cell to all amounts of goods of "getter" cells in C; subtract the amount of goods given up by this "giver" cell from all amounts of goods of "giver" cells in C. Go to (2).

Before we illustrate the transportation algorithm, we make two remarks. First of all, balanced transportation problems, by their very nature, are never infeasible or unbounded. VAM produces an initial feasible solution ruling out infeasibility; the constraints force the x_{ij}'s to have finite upper bounds ruling out unboundedness. Secondly, recall that VAM applied to any balanced transportation problem results in exactly $m + n - 1$ basis cells. If this basic feasible solution is not optimal, steps (5) and (6) then determine a new basis for a new basic feasible solution—one of the old basis cells leaves the basis (namely the "giver" cell associated with the smallest amount of goods) and a new cell enters the basis (namely the squared cell). If all cells are replaced with their original costs, this new basic feasible solution generally has lower total transportation cost than the original VAM basic feasible solution. (In any event, this new basic feasible solution will not have greater transportation cost than the original VAM basic feasible solution. Occasionally, the cost of the new solution will equal the cost of the old solution (remember cycling in 2§8?); more on this later.) If this new basic feasible solution is not optimal, then a second "sweep" through the transportation algorithm will be necessary to try to improve the solution further by determining another new basis for another new basic feasible solution. This process of constructing basic feasible solutions which successively improve the objective function is completely analogous to the procedure used by the simplex algorithm and usually terminates with an optimal solution.

We now illustrate the transportation algorithm with the solution of Example 1.

EXAMPLE 1 (Continued). The parenthetical numbers below correspond to the steps of the transportation algorithm.

(0), (1) These steps have already been performed in §2. The tableau obtained by VAM is

$$
\begin{array}{|ccc|c}
\hline
②^{20} \quad 1 & ②^{20} & & 40 \\
⑨^{10} \quad ④^{50} & 7 & & 60 \\
①^{10} \quad 2 & 9 & & 10 \\
\hline
\end{array}
$$

$$40 \qquad 50 \qquad 20$$

Since the warehouse supplies and market demands are no longer needed, we suppress these quantities hereafter.

(2) Given $b_1 = 0$, we wish to find $a_1, a_2, a_3, b_2,$ and b_3 uniquely such that $a_i + b_j = c_{ij}$ for all basis cells c_{ij}.

$$
\begin{array}{c}
\quad b_1(=0) \quad b_2 \quad b_3 \\[4pt]
\begin{array}{c}
a_1 \\[18pt]
a_2 \\[18pt]
a_3
\end{array}
\begin{array}{|ccc|}
\hline
②^{20} \quad 1 & ②^{20} \\
⑨^{10} \quad ④^{50} & 7 \\
①^{10} \quad 2 & 9 \\
\hline
\end{array}
\end{array}
$$

Now

$$
\begin{aligned}
a_1 + b_1 &= c_{11} = 2 \;\Rightarrow\; a_1 = 2 \\
a_2 + b_1 &= c_{21} = 9 \;\Rightarrow\; a_2 = 9 \\
a_3 + b_1 &= c_{31} = 1 \;\Rightarrow\; a_3 = 1 \\
a_2 + b_2 &= c_{22} = 4 \;\Rightarrow\; b_2 = -5 \\
a_1 + b_3 &= c_{13} = 2 \;\Rightarrow\; b_3 = 0.
\end{aligned}
$$

Hence we have

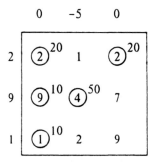

(3) Every cell c_{ij} gets replaced by a new cost, namely the old cost less the a_i indexing the row of the cost less the b_j indexing the column of the cost. Note that all basis cells will necessarily have cost 0 after this replacement; for basis cells, the a_i's and b_j's satisfy $a_i + b_j = c_{ij}$ forcing $c_{ij} - a_i - b_j = 0$ for these cells. The new cells are given below:

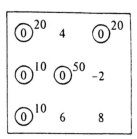

(4) Since $c_{23} < 0$, we continue with the transportation algorithm.

(5)

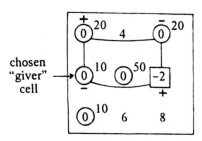

Note that the unique cycle must involve the squared cell but, in general, will not involve all of the current basis cells. Answer the following questions before continuing:

(i) Why does the cycle above not involve the basis cell $\textcircled{0}^{\,50}$ as in

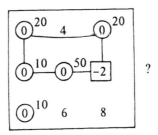

(Hint: Look at Definition 4.)

(ii) Which cell above will enter the basis in step (6)?

(iii) Which cell above will leave the basis in step (6)?

(6)

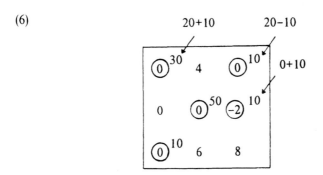

Here, c_{23} (the squared cell of step (5)) has entered the basis and c_{21} (the chosen "giver" cell of step (5)) has left the basis. In addition, goods have been redistributed around the cycle of step (5)—the "getter" cells c_{11} and c_{23} have increased their amounts by 10 and the "giver" cells c_{13} and c_{21} have decreased their amounts by 10. Inasmuch as c_{21} leaves the basis, we do not record the superscripted 0 amount of goods here. Go to step (2).

(2)

	(b_1)	(b_2)	(b_3)
	0	2	0
(a_1) 0	$⓪^{30}$ 4	$⓪^{10}$
(a_2) -2	0	$⓪^{50}$ (-2) 10
(a_3) 0	$⓪^{10}$ 6 8

(3)

$\text{\textcircled{0}}^{30}$	2	$\text{\textcircled{0}}^{10}$
2	$\text{\textcircled{0}}^{50}$	$\text{\textcircled{0}}^{10}$
$\text{\textcircled{0}}^{10}$	4	8

(4) Since $c_{ij} \geq 0$ for all i and j, we STOP. Replacing all cells with their original costs from step (0), we obtain

$\text{\textcircled{2}}^{30}$	1	$\text{\textcircled{2}}^{10}$
9	$\text{\textcircled{4}}^{50}$	$\text{\textcircled{7}}^{10}$
$\text{\textcircled{1}}^{10}$	2	9

and corresponding optimal solution

$$x_{11} = 30, \ x_{12} = 0, \ x_{13} = 10,$$
$$x_{21} = 0, \ x_{22} = 50, \ x_{23} = 10,$$
$$x_{31} = 10, \ x_{32} = 0, \ x_{33} = 0,$$

$$\min C = \$2(30) + \$2(10) + \$4(50) + \$7(10) + \$1(10) = \$360.$$

§4. Another Example

EXAMPLE 7. Solve the transportation problem below:

	M_1	M_2	M_3	M_4	
W_1	5	12	8	50	26
W_2	11	4	10	8	20
W_3	14	50	1	9	30
	15	20	26	15	

The parenthetical numbers below correspond to the steps of the transportation algorithm.

(0) Total supply is equal to total demand (76 in each case).

(1)

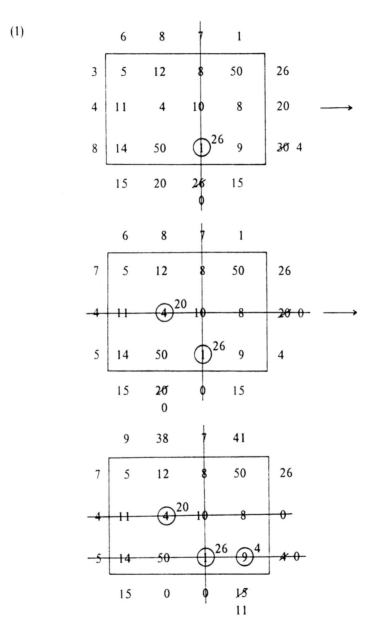

We pause here for a moment. In the first tableau above, 8 is the largest difference; since 8 corresponds to a row and a column, the smallest cost among the entries of both the row and the column is chosen in accordance with step (2) of VAM. In the second tableau above, a warehouse was emptied and a market was fully supplied simultaneously. The row was deleted in accordance with step (3) of VAM. In the third and last tableau above, three of the deleted cells have been circled and three cells remain; since VAM results in exactly $m + n - 1 = 3 + 4 - 1 = 6$ circled cells for this problem by Theorem 3, we know that the final basic feasible solution obtained by VAM must be

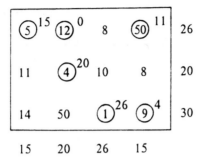

⑤^{15}	⑫^{0}	8	㊿^{11}	26
11	④^{20}	10	8	20
14	50	①^{26}	⑨^{4}	30
15	20	26	15	

It is crucial that the superscripted 0 on the cost of $c_{12} = 12$ be recorded as we will see later in the transportation algorithm. This is the phenomenon alluded to at the end of §2.

(2)

	0	7	37	45
5	⑤^{15}	⑫^{0}	8	㊿^{11}
−3	11	④^{20}	10	8
−36	14	50	①^{26}	⑨^{4}

(3)

⓪^{15}	⓪^{0}	−34	⓪^{11}
14	⓪^{20}	−24	−34
50	79	⓪^{26}	⓪^{4}

(4) Since there are several negative c_{ij}'s, we continue with the transportation algorithm.

(5)

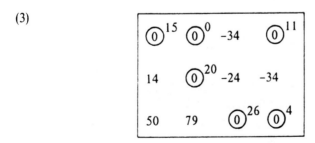

chosen "giver" cell

⓪^{15}	⓪$^{+0}$	−34	⓪$^{-11}$
14	⓪^{20}	−24	−34
50	79	⓪^{26}	⓪^{4}

Note that there are three choices for a negative c_{ij} here. Our choice corresponds to the most negative c_{ij} but, more importantly, emphasizes the importance of including the superscripted 0 cell as a basis cell. The ambitious reader is invited to solve the problem by using the other two choices. (See also Exercise 8.)

(6)

$(0)^{15}$	$(0)^{11}$	-34	0
14	$(0)^{9}$	-24	$(-34)^{11}$
50	79	$(0)^{26}$	$(0)^{4}$

Go to step (2).

(2)

	0	0	−34	−34
0	$(0)^{15}$	$(0)^{11}$	-34	0
0	14	$(0)^{9}$	-24	$(-34)^{11}$
34	50	79	$(0)^{26}$	$(0)^{4}$

(3)

$(0)^{15}$	$(0)^{11}$	0	34
14	$(0)^{9}$	10	$(0)^{11}$
16	45	$(0)^{26}$	$(0)^{4}$

(4) Since $c_{ij} \geq 0$ for all i and j, we STOP. Replacing all cells with their original costs, we obtain

$(5)^{15}$	$(12)^{11}$	8	50
11	$(4)^{9}$	10	$(8)^{11}$
14	50	$(1)^{26}$	$(9)^{4}$

and corresponding optimal solution

$$x_{11} = 15, \ x_{12} = 11, \ x_{13} = x_{14} = 0,$$
$$x_{21} = 0, \ x_{22} = 9, \ x_{23} = 0, \ x_{24} = 11,$$
$$x_{31} = x_{32} = 0, \ x_{33} = 26, \ x_{34} = 4,$$

$$\min C = 5(15) + 12(11) + 4(9) + 8(11) + 1(26) + 9(4) = 393.$$

We conclude this section with some general remarks on transportation problems. Sometimes, transportation problems are such that no desirable routes exist between certain warehouses and certain markets. For example, a certain warehouse and market may be separated by a steep mountain or wide river making travel from warehouse to market difficult. Such routes can usually be eliminated from active consideration by placing very high transportation costs on those routes. The costs of 50 in Example 7 accomplished exactly this. Even though one of the 50's was involved in the VAM basic feasible solution, none of the 50's were involved in the optimal solution. Similarly, if one wishes to force certain routes between warehouses and markets to be used, one can place very low transportation costs on these routes. In fact, even negative costs could be placed on particular routes; negative costs can be viewed as subsidy payments from the markets to the warehouses for using routes that are advantageous to the markets.

§5. Unbalanced Transportation Problems

In this section, we consider transportation problems with tableaus as follows:

	M_1	M_2	$\cdots$	M_n	
W_1	c_{11}	c_{12}	$\cdots$	c_{1n}	s_1
W_2	c_{21}	c_{22}	$\cdots$	c_{2n}	s_2
$\vdots$	$\vdots$	$\vdots$		$\vdots$	$\vdots$
W_m	c_{m1}	c_{m2}	$\cdots$	c_{mn}	s_m
	d_1	d_2	$\cdots$	d_n	

$$\sum_{i=1}^{m} s_i \neq \sum_{j=1}^{n} d_j$$

Such transportation problems are said to be *unbalanced*. We consider two cases.

Case I. $\sum_{i=1}^{m} s_i < \sum_{j=1}^{n} d_j$.

Here, the current demand of the markets exceeds the current supply of the warehouses. This is a rationing problem where goods must be allocated among the markets. We introduce a fictitious warehouse W_{m+1} with supply

s_{m+1} such that

$$\sum_{i=1}^{m+1} s_i = \sum_{j=1}^{n} d_j,$$

i.e., the $m + 1^{st}$ warehouse supplies the excess demand. This creates a balanced transportation problem. When a market receives goods from the fictitious warehouse, it doesn't really receive any goods at all. The transportation cost of such non-shipment will be assumed negligible compared to other transportation costs and assigned a value of 0. (In reality, the assigned cost would reflect, for example, loss in sales as well as costs associated with expediting the shipment of the goods from another source.)

Case II. $\sum_{i=1}^{m} s_i > \sum_{j=1}^{n} d_j.$

Here, the current supply of the warehouses exceeds the current demand of the markets. This is usually the case in well-managed inventory situations. We introduce a fictitious market M_{n+1} with demand d_{n+1} such that

$$\sum_{i=1}^{m} s_i = \sum_{j=1}^{n+1} d_j,$$

i.e., the $n + 1^{st}$ market demands the excess inventory. This creates a balanced transportation problem. When a warehouse is instructed to ship goods to the fictitious market, it "ships to itself", i.e., it retains the goods. The transportation cost of such self-shipment will be assumed negligible compared to other transportation costs and assigned a value of 0. (In reality, the assigned cost would include, for example, spoilage costs (if the good is perishable) and storage costs.)

We illustrate unbalanced transportation problems with two examples.

EXAMPLE 8. Solve the transportation problem below:

	M_1	M_2	M_3	
W_1	2	1	2	40
W_2	9	4	7	60
W_3	1	2	9	10
	50	60	30	

Note that the transportation problem is unbalanced since

$$110 = \sum_{i=1}^{3} s_i < \sum_{j=1}^{3} d_j = 140.$$

Always check this—the transportation algorithm only works with balanced transportation problems! Since demand exceeds supply (Case I), we add a fictitious warehouse W_4 (with associated transportation costs of 0) to supply the excess demand of 30:

$$
\begin{array}{c|ccc|c}
 & M_1 & M_2 & M_3 & \\
\hline
W_1 & 2 & 1 & 2 & 40 \\
W_2 & 9 & 4 & 7 & 60 \\
W_3 & 1 & 2 & 9 & 10 \\
W_4 & 0 & 0 & 0 & 30 \\
\hline
 & 50 & 60 & 30 &
\end{array}
$$

The transportation algorithm is now applied to this balanced transportation problem. As an exercise, verify that **VAM** yields the basic feasible solution

and that such a shipping schedule is optimal. (You owe it to yourself to perform this verification. If you are observant, you will notice some strange behavior. Although this behavior does not usually occur with transportation problems, it will occur repeatedly with assignment problems in §6 and is the primary reason behind the development of a new algorithm for such problems.) In this optimal solution, notice that M_3 does not receive any goods since it receives all of its 30 units from the fictitious warehouse W_4. Notice also that Example 8 is precisely Example 1 (solved in §3) where each market is assumed to require 10 more units of the good than indicated. Of the two problems, we would expect a lower total shipping cost in Example 8 since the use of higher cost transportation routes can probably be lessened or avoided by not fully satisfying certain markets along these routes. This is indeed the case—the total transportation cost in Example 1 was 360 as compared to the total transportation cost of 330 in Example 8.

EXAMPLE 9. Solve the transportation problem below:

$$
\begin{array}{c|ccc|c}
 & M_1 & M_2 & M_3 & \\
\hline
W_1 & 2 & 1 & 2 & 50 \\
W_2 & 9 & 4 & 7 & 70 \\
W_3 & 1 & 2 & 9 & 20 \\
\hline
 & 40 & 50 & 20 &
\end{array}
$$

Note that the transportation problem is unbalanced since

$$140 = \sum_{i=1}^{3} s_i > \sum_{i=1}^{3} d_j = 110.$$

Again, always check this—the transportation algorithm only works with balanced transportation problems! Since supply exceeds demand (Case II), we add a fictitious fourth market M_4 (with associated transportation costs of 0) to demand the excess inventory of 30:

$$
\begin{array}{c|cccc|c}
 & M_1 & M_2 & M_3 & M_4 & \\
\hline
W_1 & 2 & 1 & 2 & 0 & 50 \\
W_2 & 9 & 4 & 7 & 0 & 70 \\
W_3 & 1 & 2 & 9 & 0 & 20 \\
\hline
 & 40 & 50 & 20 & 30 &
\end{array}
$$

The transportation algorithm is now applied to this balanced transportation tableau. As an exercise, verify that VAM yields the basic feasible solution

$$
\begin{array}{|cccc|c}
\hline
\textcircled{2}^{20} & \textcircled{1}^{10} & \textcircled{2}^{20} & 0 & 50 \\
9 & \textcircled{4}^{40} & 7 & \textcircled{0}^{30} & 70 \\
\textcircled{1}^{20} & 2 & 9 & 0 & 20 \\
\hline
40 & 50 & 20 & 30 &
\end{array}
$$

and that such a shipping schedule is optimal. In this optimal solution, notice that W_2 retains 30 units of the good since it has been instructed to ship 30 units to the fictitious fourth market M_4. Notice also that Example 9 is precisely Example 1 (solved in §3) where each warehouse is assumed to have 10 more units of the good than indicated. Of the two problems, we would expect a lower total shipping cost in Example 9 since lower cost transportation routes can probably be used more effectively. This is indeed the case—the total transportation cost in Example 1 was 360 as compared to the total transportation cost of 270 in Example 9.

§6. The Assignment Problem

The assignment problem is a special type of transportation problem. We will consider only balanced assignment problems in this section; the treatment of unbalanced assignment problems is analogous to the treatment of unbalanced transportation problems and is investigated in Exercise 13. The general *balanced assignment problem* is the general balanced transportation problem in which $m = n$ and $s_i = d_j = 1$, $i, j = 1, 2, \ldots, n$, i.e.,

$$\text{Minimize} \quad C = \sum_{i=1}^{n} \sum_{j=1}^{n} c_{ij} x_{ij}$$

$$\text{subject to} \quad \sum_{j=1}^{n} x_{ij} = 1, i = 1, 2, \ldots, n$$

$$\sum_{i=1}^{n} x_{ij} = 1, j = 1, 2, \ldots, n$$

$$x_{ij} \geq 0, \forall i, j.$$

From the statement of the general assignment problem above, it can be proven (but is by no means obvious) that each x_{ij} is either 0 or 1 in any optimal solution. We will not provide such a proof here (see, for example, [L2] for a proof).

In balanced assignment problems, i indexes a set of n persons and j indexes a set of n jobs; c_{ij} is the cost of assigning person i to job j. It is desired to assign each person to exactly one job and each job to exactly one person so that the total cost of assignment is minimized. Here,

$$x_{ij} = \begin{cases} 1, & \text{if person } i \text{ is assigned to job } j \\ 0, & \text{otherwise.} \end{cases}$$

Now, since the balanced assignment problem is a special case of the balanced transportation problem, we should be able to use the transportation algorithm to solve balanced assignment problems. However, due to the notoriously degenerate nature of balanced assignment problems, the transportation algorithm becomes inefficient and tedious to use. We illustrate with an example.

EXAMPLE 10. Solve the assignment problem below by using the transportation algorithm.

(jobs)

	J_1	J_2	J_3	
P_1	8	7	10	1
P_2	7	7	8	1
P_3	8	5	7	1
	1	1	1	

(persons)

(Can you solve this problem by inspection?)

The parenthetical numbers below correspond to the step of the transportation algorithm.

(0) The assignment problem is balanced ($m = n = 3$).

(1)

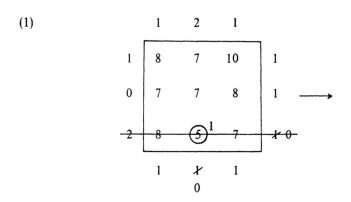

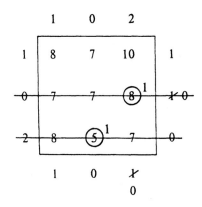

Since VAM results in exactly $m + n - 1 = 3 + 3 - 1 = 5$ circled cells, the VAM basic feasible solution is

⑧¹	⑦⁰	⑩⁰	1
7	7	⑧¹	1
8	⑤¹	7	1
1	1	1	

(2)

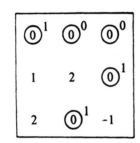

(3)

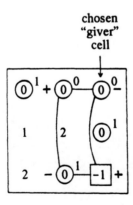

(4) $c_{33} < 0$; continue.

(5)

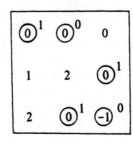

(6)

Go to step (2). (In the meantime, ponder this question: Did the distribution of 0 goods around the cycle really change anything?)

(2)

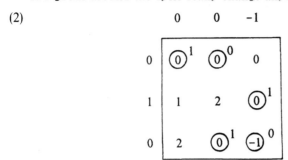

                    0   0   −1

0   ⓪¹   ⓪⁰   0

1   1   2   ⓪¹

0   2   ⓪¹   ⊝¹⁰ (−1)⁰

(3)

⓪¹   ⓪⁰   1

0   1   ⓪¹

2   ⓪¹   ⓪⁰

(4) STOP; replacing all cells with their original costs from step (0), we obtain

⑧¹   ⑦⁰   10

7   7   ⑧¹

8   ⑤¹   ⑦⁰

and corresponding optimal solution

$$x_{11} = 1,\ x_{12} = x_{13} = 0,$$
$$x_{21} = x_{22} = 0,\ x_{23} = 1,$$
$$x_{31} = 0,\ x_{32} = 1,\ x_{33} = 0,$$
$$\min C = 8 + 8 + 5 = 21.$$

Now, you may ask, what was so inefficient about that? Well, exactly this— the VAM basic feasible solution has a cost of 21 (verify this!) and is hence also an optimal solution. Look at all of the extra work that we did! An efficient algorithm would have recognized the optimality of the VAM basic feasible solution immediately and halted; the transportation algorithm, on the other hand, failed to recognize this optimality. This happens quite frequently when applying the transportation algorithm to assignment problems and was alluded to in §3. In fact, the transportation algorithm applied to assignment problems may cycle (remember 2§8?) without ever reaching an optimal solution! The culprit in both cases is the large number of superscripted 0's in the VAM basic feasible solution of an assignment problem. (There are exactly two in Example 10.) In fact, Exercise 17 shows that, in an $n \times n$ assignment problem, exactly $n - 1$ of the basis cells will have superscripted 0's. This large number of superscripted 0's in assignment problems is referred to as *degeneracy*. Degeneracy causes behavior as in step (6) above where 0 goods are distributed around a cycle causing no change in assignments or total assignment cost. The algorithm recommended for assignment problems is the Hungarian algorithm which we develop now. This algorithm takes advantage of the simpler nature of assignment problems as compared to transportation problems.

Definition 11. Let T be the tableau of a balanced assignment problem. A *permutation set of zeros Z* is a subset of zero cells of T such that every row and every column of T contains exactly one zero cell of T.

EXAMPLE 12.

$$
\begin{array}{ccc}
1 & 0 & 0^* \\
0^* & 1 & 0 \\
1 & 0^* & 1
\end{array}
$$
T

The cells distinguished by superscripted asterisks form a permutation set of zeros in T above (in fact, this permutation set of zeros in T is unique).

$$
\begin{array}{ccc}
1 & 0^* & 1 \\
0^* & 1 & 0^* \\
1 & 0 & 1
\end{array}
$$
T

The cells distinguished by superscripted asterisks do not form a permutation set of zeros in T above (in fact, there is no permutation set of zeros in T above).

$$
\begin{array}{ccc}
0^* & 0 & 1 \\
0 & 0^* & 0 \\
1 & 0 & 0^*
\end{array}
$$
T

The cells distinguished by superscripted asterisks form a permutation set of zeros in T above. (Find two other permutation sets of zeros in T above.)

We now give the Hungarian algorithm. This algorithm was developed in 1955 by H.W. Kuhn ([K2]) and is so named because it was based on the work of two Hungarian mathematicians, König and Egerváry. Several comments on certain steps of the algorithm will be made after the complete statement of the algorithm.

The Hungarian Algorithm

(0) Given: An initial balanced ($n \times n$) assignment tableau.
(1) Convert all c_{ij}'s to nonnegative integers if necessary by application of one or both of the following steps:
  (i) (Nonnegativity) If $c_{ij} < 0$ for some i and j, compute

$$k_1 = \max_{i,j} \{|c_{ij}|:c_{ij} < 0\},$$

  and add k_1 to every entry of the tableau.
  (ii) (Integrality) If $c_{ij} \notin \mathbf{Z}$ and $c_{ij} \in \mathbf{Q}$ for some i and j, form the set

$$S = \{c_{ij} = p_{ij}/q_{ij} : c_{ij} \notin \mathbf{Z}, c_{ij} \in \mathbf{Q}, p_{ij}, q_{ij} \in \mathbf{Z}, q_{ij} > 0\},$$

  and compute

$$k_2 = \mathrm{lcm}\, \{q_{ij} : c_{ij} = p_{ij}/q_{ij} \in S\}.$$

  (Here, lcm denotes the least common multiple.) Multiply every entry of the tableau by k_2.
(2) Subtract the smallest entry in each row from every entry of the row to obtain a new tableau. Subtract the smallest entry in each column of the new tableau from every entry of the column to obtain (what will be called) the *reduced tableau.*
(3) Draw a minimum number k of horizontal and/or vertical lines (extending the length and width of the tableau respectively) to cover all zero entries of the reduced tableau.
(4) If $k = n$, STOP; a permutation set of zeros can be found among the zero entries of the reduced tableau; the optimal solution corresponds to this permutation set of zeros when all cells are replaced with their original entries from (0). If $k < n$, choose the smallest uncovered entry. Subtract this entry from all uncovered entries (including itself) and add this entry to all covered entries corresponding to intersections of horizontal and vertical lines (all other covered entries remain unchanged), hence obtaining a new reduced tableau. Go to (3).

Several comments are in order. The following numbers correspond to the steps of the Hungarian algorithm.

(1) (i) In other words, this step says that if there are negative entries in the tableau, then choose the most negative entry, take its absolute value (called k_1), and add this quantity to every entry of the tableau.

(1) (ii) In other words, this step says that if there are nonintegral rational entries in the tableau, then write each such entry as a quotient of integers with positive denominator, find the least common multiple of these denominators (called k_2), and multiply every entry of the tableau by this quantity. This step clears all rational numbers of their denominators. What if there are irrational entries in the tableau? It is reasonable to assume that irrational c_{ij}'s do not occur in assignment problems. After all, the c_{ij}'s represent costs and irrational costs are not usually appropriate in practical situations. (When is the last time you paid $\$\pi$ for something?) Furthermore, any irrational entries could be approximated within any positive degree of accuracy by rational numbers if necessary.

(1) The optimal assignment plan is unaffected by the conversion to nonnegative integers since the same positive quantity is added to or multiplied with every entry.

(3) The crucial word in this step is *minimum*. Incorrect answers usually result if the zero entries are covered with more horizontal and/or vertical lines than necessary. Note that the minimum number k must satisfy $k \leq n$ (one could delete all entries of the tableau by drawing, for example, n horizontal lines!).

We now illustrate the Hungarian algorithm with several examples.

EXAMPLE 13. Illustrate step (1) (ii) of the Hungarian algorithm by converting the assignment tableau below to nonnegative integers.

	J_1	J_2	J_3	
P_1	0.5	2	1	1
P_2	1.2	1/6	7	1
P_3	5/9	0	3.14	1
	1	1	1	

We first write all rational numbers in the tableau as quotients of integers with positive denominators. In the tableau below, all fractions have been reduced. Although this is not necessary, it will result in a smaller value of k_2.

1/2	2	1
6/5	1/6	7
5/9	0	157/50

Then $k_2 = \mathrm{lcm}\ \{2, 5, 6, 9, 50\} = 450$; multiplying every entry of the tableau above by $k_2 = 450$, we obtain

$$\begin{array}{|ccc|}
\hline
225 & 900 & 450 \\
540 & 75 & 3150 \\
250 & 0 & 1413 \\
\hline
\end{array}$$

as desired.

EXAMPLE 14. Solve the assignment problem of Example 10 below by using the Hungarian algorithm.

$$
\begin{array}{c c c c c}
 & J_1 & J_2 & J_3 & \\
P_1 & 8 & 7 & 10 & 1 \\
P_2 & 7 & 7 & 8 & 1 \\
P_3 & 8 & 5 & 7 & 1 \\
 & 1 & 1 & 1 &
\end{array}
$$

The parenthetical numbers below correspond to the steps of the Hungarian algorithm.

(0) The initial tableau is balanced. Note that the supplies and demands are really unnecessary in an assignment tableau (each supply and demand is 1!). Hereafter, all supplies and demands will be suppressed in assignment problems.

(1) Each c_{ij} is a nonnegative integer already!

(2)

$$\begin{array}{|ccc|}
\hline
8 & 7 & 10 \\
7 & 7 & 8 \\
8 & 5 & 7 \\
\hline
\end{array} \longrightarrow$$

$$\begin{array}{|ccc|}
\hline
1 & 0 & 3 \\
0 & 0 & 1 \\
3 & 0 & 2 \\
\hline
\end{array} \longrightarrow$$

$$\begin{array}{|ccc|}
\hline
1 & 0 & 2 \\
0 & 0 & 0 \\
3 & 0 & 1 \\
\hline
\end{array}$$

reduced tableau

(3)

(The minimum k is 2 here.)

(4) $2 = k < n = 3$:

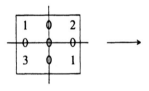

reduced tableau

Go to step (3).

(3)

(The minimum k is 3 here.)

(4) $k = n = 3$; hence, a permutation set of zeros can be found among the zero entries of the reduced tableau. In fact, there are two such permutation sets of zeros in the tableau, denoted by * and ** below:

$$
\begin{array}{ccc}
0^{*} & 0^{**} & 1 \\
0^{**} & 1 & 0^{*} \\
2 & 0^{*} & 0^{**}
\end{array}
$$

Replacing all cells with their original entries, we obtain

8$^{\bullet}$	7$^{\bullet\bullet}$	10
7$^{\bullet\bullet}$	7	8$^{\bullet}$
8	5$^{\bullet}$	7$^{\bullet\bullet}$

and corresponding optimal solutions

$$*: \begin{cases} x_{11} = x_{23} = x_{32} = 1, \text{ all other } x_{ij}\text{'s } 0, \\ \min C = 8 + 8 + 5 = 21 \end{cases}$$

$$**: \begin{cases} x_{12} = x_{21} = x_{33} = 1, \text{ all other } x_{ij}\text{'s } 0, \\ \min C = 7 + 7 + 7 = 21. \end{cases}$$

Remember that $x_{ij} = 1$ in assignment problems is to be interpreted as meaning that person i gets assigned to job j. Write out the optimal assignment plans of * and ** above in words.

EXAMPLE 15. A company wishes to assign five of its workers to five different jobs (one worker to each job and vice versa). The rating of each worker with respect to each job on a scale of 0 to 10 (10 being a high rating) is given by the following table:

(jobs)

(workers)		J_1	J_2	J_3	J_4	J_5
	W_1	5	4	2	8	5
	W_2	7	6	4	6	9
	W_3	5	5	3	3	2
	W_4	4	3	5	5	4
	W_5	3	6	4	10	2

If the company wishes to maximize the total rating of the assignment, find the optimal assignment plan and the corresponding maximum total rating.

There is a slight difficulty here. The problem as stated above is a maximization problem. But the Hungarian algorithm solves assignment problems which are minimization problems! The difficulty is eliminated by transforming the maximization problem into an equivalent minimization problem to which the Hungarian algorithm can be applied. This is easy—maximizing the assignment of the given tableau is equivalent to minimizing the assignment of the tableau consisting of the negatives of the given tableau entries. As long as we are careful to interpret the optimal solutions in terms of the entries of the given tableau, the Hungarian algorithm is "fooled" into solving a maximization assignment problem. Hence, we begin with the altered tableau

-5	-4	-2	-8	-5
-7	-6	-4	-6	-9
-5	-5	-3	-3	-2
-4	-3	-5	-5	-4
-3	-6	-4	-10	-2

The Hungarian algorithm is now applied to this tableau. The parenthetical numbers below correspond to the steps of the algorithm.

(0) The tableau above is balanced. (One need only check that there is the same number of workers as jobs!)

(1) (i) $k_1 = |-10| = 10$:

-5	-4	-2	-8	-5
-7	-6	-4	-6	-9
-5	-5	-3	-3	-2
-4	-3	-5	-5	-4
-3	-6	-4	-10	-2

$\longrightarrow$

5	6	8	2	5
3	4	6	4	1
5	5	7	7	8
6	7	5	5	6
7	4	6	0	8

(2)

5	6	8	2	5
3	4	6	4	1
5	5	7	7	8
6	7	5	5	6
7	4	6	0	8

$\longrightarrow$

3	4	6	0	3
2	3	5	3	0
0	0	2	2	3
1	2	0	0	1
7	4	6	0	8

reduced tableau

Note that no reduction in the columns is necessary above since every column contains a 0 after reduction in the rows.

(3)

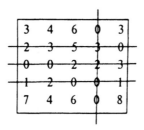

(The minimum k is 4 here. We note that the covering of the zeros with four horizontal and/or vertical lines above is not unique. The interested reader is invited to find the other covering and proceed from this covering to the optimal solution.)

(4) $4 = k < n = 5$:

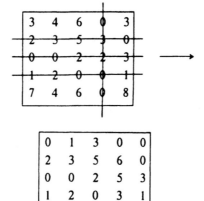

0	1	3	0	0
2	3	5	6	0
0	0	2	5	3
1	2	0	3	1
4	1	3	0	5

reduced tableau

Go to step (3).

(3)

0	1	3	0	0
2	3	5	6	0
0	0	2	5	3
1	2	0	3	1
4	1	3	0	5

(The minimum k is 5 here.)

(4) $k = n = 5$; hence, a permutation set of zeros can be found among the zero entries of the reduced tableau. The unique such permutation set of zeros (verify the uniqueness!) is given below:

$$
\begin{array}{ccccc}
0^{\bullet} & 1 & 3 & 0 & 0 \\
2 & 3 & 5 & 6 & 0^{\bullet} \\
0 & 0^{\bullet} & 2 & 5 & 3 \\
1 & \bar{2} & 0^{\bullet} & 3 & 1 \\
4 & 1 & 3 & 0^{\bullet} & 5
\end{array}
$$

Replacing all cells with their original entries in the statement of the problem, we obtain

$$
\begin{array}{ccccc}
5^{\bullet} & 4 & 2 & 8 & 5 \\
7 & 6 & 4 & 6 & 9^{\bullet} \\
4 & 5^{\bullet} & 3 & 3 & 2 \\
5 & 3 & 5^{\bullet} & 5 & 4 \\
3 & 6 & 4 & 10^{\bullet} & 2
\end{array}
$$

and corresponding optimal solution

$$x_{11} = x_{25} = x_{32} = x_{43} = x_{54} = 1, \text{ all other } x_{ij}\text{'s } 0,$$
$$\text{maximum rating} = 5 + 9 + 5 + 5 + 10 = 34.$$

§7. Concluding Remarks

There is no denying the importance of transportation and assignment problems as a class of problems that arise quite frequently in a variety of real-world applications. We wish to emphasize a more subtle and mathematical importance, namely that transportation and assignment problems highlight limitations of the linear programming solution procedures of Chapters 2–4, forcing the development of new algorithms. Even though the solution procedures of Chapters 2–4 will usually solve transportation and assignment problems, the size of the initial Tucker tableaus and the specialized nature of the problems suggest that perhaps alternate and easier algorithms exist. The intent and goal, then, is to develop new specialized algorithms for these specialized problems. In the case of transportation problems, which are special types of noncanonical linear programming problems, the new algorithm is essentially a mimic of a known algorithm, unrecognizable as such since it operates on a structurally different (and smaller!) tableau. In the case of assignment problems, which are special cases of transportation problems, yet another new (but related) algorithm is developed. Since specialized algorithms are usually dependent upon a given problem structure, such algorithms would generally not be valid for problems not possessing the required structure. (For example, the Hungarian algorithm is *not* valid for transportation problems in general and the transportation algorithm is *not* valid for noncanonical linear programming problems in general.) The development and analysis of effective algorithms is crucial in all areas of mathematics; at this point, the reader is hopefully impressed with such development and analysis as it pertains to linear programming.

EXERCISES

1. Solve each of the transportation problems below.

a.

7	2	4	10
10	5	9	20
7	3	5	30

20   10   30

b.

4	5	5
3	2	7
6	3	9
7	5	4

14   11

c.

3	2	1	30
2	5	9	75

40   30   50

d.

12	10	8	28
8	9	11	62

20   38   22

e.

8	2	3	7	42
9	4	5	6	17
7	1	6	5	17

9   14   24   29

f.

3	8	5	5
2	7	3	14
4	4	2	8
6	5	8	7
8	10	18	

g.

6	5	4	10
3	7	2	16
5	10	8	10
4	6	3	12
10	7	6	

h.

5	9	10	6	4
10	7	5	4	5
4	5	5	4	2
6	5	7	5	3
3	4	4	3	

i.

10	20	15	6	0	15
26	30	30	20	16	10
28	29	25	13	8	15
15	20	25	5	5	16
9	15	9	15	8	

2. Solve the transportation problem below where x denotes a prohibitively high cost.

6	9	−1	20
3	9	11	15
9	1	x	20
x	6	7	15
20	20	30	

3. It is shown in [G2] that a transportation problem has a unique optimal solution if and only if all nonbasis cells at the point of termination of the transportation algorithm are strictly positive (not zero).

   a. Which of the transportation problems in Exercise 1 above have unique optimal solutions?

   b. Find an alternate optimal solution for each transportation problem in Exercise 1 above that does not have a unique optimal solution.

4. Let $i \in \mathbf{Z}$, $0 \le i \le 30$. Show that there exists an optimal solution to the problem of Example 8 for which M_1 is not supplied i units of the good and M_3 is not supplied $30 - i$ units of the good.

5. Formulate Exercise 9b from Chapter 2 as a transportation problem and solve.
    [Hint: The "warehouses" are new towels, dirty towels from day 1, and dirty towels
    from day 2.]

6. Two alternate methods for obtaining initial basic feasible solutions in transpor-
    tation problems are given by the algorithms below.

The Minimum-Entry Method

(0) Given: An initial balanced transportation tableau.
(1) Use the smallest cost in the tableau to empty a warehouse or completely fill a
    market demand. (If there is a tie for the smallest entry, use any such entry.)
    Circle the cost used and write above the circle the amount of goods shipped by
    that route. Reduce the supply and demand in the row and column containing
    the cost used.
(2) Delete the row or column corresponding to the emptied warehouse or fully
    supplied market; if both happen simultaneously, delete the row unless that row
    is the only row remaining in which case delete the column.
(3) If all tableau entries are deleted, STOP; otherwise go to (1).

The Northwest-Corner Method

(0) Given: An initial balanced transportation tableau.
(1) Use the northwest-most cost in the tableau to empty a warehouse or
    completely fill a market demand. (The northwest-most cost is that cost in the
    top left position of the tableau.) Circle the cost used and write above the circle
    the amount of goods shipped by that route. Reduce the supply and demand in
    the row and column containing the cost used.
(2) Delete the row or column corresponding to the emptied warehouse or fully
    supplied market; if both happen simultaneously, delete the row unless that row
    is the only row remaining in which case delete the column.
(3) If all tableau entries are deleted, STOP; otherwise go to (1).

a. Apply the minimum-entry method and the northwest-corner method to
    Exercise 1a above. Compare the basic feasible solutions so obtained with the
    VAM basic feasible solution.
b. Apply the minimum-entry method and the northwest-corner method to
    Exercise 1b above. Compare the basic feasible solutions so obtained with the
    VAM basic feasible solution.

7. Assume that a transportation problem has the VAM basic feasible solution below
    (the costs are irrelevant):

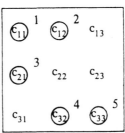

Furthermore, assume that the transportation algorithm determines that the squared cell below should enter the basis:

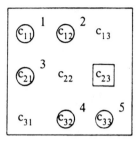

a. Prove that the visualization of the cycle as

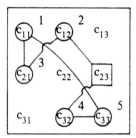

and the subsequent application of steps (5) and (6) of the transportation algorithm would *not* result in a new basic feasible solution for the problem.

b. Would the visualization of the cycle as

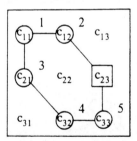

result in a new basic feasible solution for the problem? [After answering this question, consult the answers section in the back of this book for an important note.]

8. An anticycling rule for the transportation algorithm is given below.

Transportation Algorithm Anticycling Rule

Whenever there is more than one possible choice of negative c_{ij} in step (5) of the transportation algorithm, choose the northwest-most negative c_{ij}, i.e., choose the negative c_{ij} with minimal i and, if more than one such c_{ij} has minimal i, choose the c_{ij} among those cells with minimal j.

Solve Example 7 by using the transportation algorithm with the anticycling rule above.

9. Consider the assignment problem below:

$$
\begin{array}{ccc}
2 & 1 & 2 \\
9 & 4 & 7 \\
1 & 2 & 9
\end{array}
$$

   a. Solve the problem by using the transportation algorithm.
   b. Solve the problem by using the Hungarian algorithm.
   c. Which algorithm is preferable here?

10. Solve each of the assignment problems below.

   a.
   $$
   \begin{array}{ccc}
   38 & 21 & 34 \\
   41 & 14 & 36 \\
   28 & 20 & 25
   \end{array}
   $$

   b.
   $$
   \begin{array}{cccc}
   2 & 3 & 2 & 4 \\
   5 & 8 & 4 & 3 \\
   5 & 9 & 5 & 2 \\
   7 & 6 & 7 & 4
   \end{array}
   $$

   c.
   $$
   \begin{array}{cccc}
   4 & 6 & 5 & 10 \\
   10 & 9 & 7 & 13 \\
   7 & 11 & 8 & 13 \\
   12 & 13 & 12 & 17
   \end{array}
   $$

   d.
   $$
   \begin{array}{ccccc}
   8 & 6 & 3 & 5 & 10 \\
   2 & 4 & 3 & 5 & 4 \\
   5 & 7 & 5 & 4 & 3 \\
   6 & 9 & 2 & 4 & 2 \\
   4 & 6 & 5 & 3 & 6
   \end{array}
   $$

11. The optimal assignment in the assignment problem below is not unique. Find *all* optimal assignments.

$$
\begin{array}{c|ccccc}
1 & 6 & 2 & 7 & 5 \\
2 & 4 & 3 & 6 & 5 \\
3 & 6 & 4 & 8 & 6 \\
4 & 5 & 4 & 7 & 7 \\
5 & 8 & 6 & 9 & 6
\end{array}
$$

12. Solve the assignment problem below where x denotes a prohibitively high cost.

$$\begin{bmatrix} 6 & 8 & -1 & x \\ 3 & 8 & 6 & 4 \\ 7 & 1 & x & -1 \\ x & 6 & 7 & 2 \end{bmatrix}$$

13. Balance each of the unbalanced assignment problems below by using the techniques of §5 and then use the Hungarian algorithm to solve the problems. Interpret each of the optimal assignment plans in words.

a.
$$\begin{bmatrix} 9 & 7 & 8 & 6 & 8 \\ 10 & 8 & 7 & 9 & 6 \\ 9 & 6 & 9 & 7 & 8 \\ 8 & 9 & 10 & 7 & 6 \end{bmatrix}$$

b.
$$\begin{bmatrix} 10 & 6 & 8 & 8 \\ 9 & 8 & 10 & 7 \\ 8 & 9 & 7 & 6 \\ 9 & 7 & 9 & 9 \\ 8 & 10 & 8 & 10 \end{bmatrix}$$

14. A company wishes to assign six of its workers to six different jobs (one worker to each job and vice versa). The rating of each worker with respect to each job on a scale of 0 to 10 (10 being a high rating) is given by the following table:

(jobs)

	J_1	J_2	J_3	J_4	J_5	J_6
W_1	8	9	6	3	7	5
W_2	4	3	9	7	5	6
W_3	7	3	2	1	9	7
W_4	4	6	5	4	8	5
W_5	7	6	1	2	8	7
W_6	4	4	5	4	5	7

(workers)

If the company wishes to maximize the total rating of the assignment, find the optimal assignment plan and the corresponding maximum total rating.

15. A group of five men and five women live on an island. The amount of happiness that the ith man and the jth woman derive by spending a fraction x_{ij} of their lives together is $c_{ij}x_{ij}$ where c_{ij} is given in the table below:

(women)

		1	2	3	4	5
	1	4	2	4	5	2
	2	4	5	4	1	3
(men)	3	4	4	3	3	5
	4	2	2	6	4	5
	5	3	5	7	5	2

Find the living arrangements that maximize the total happiness of the islanders.

16. Label the following statement TRUE or FALSE. If the statement is FALSE, provide a counterexample.

    The Hungarian algorithm applied to an assignment problem terminates after at most two occurrences of step (3).

17. Let T be an $n \times n$ assignment tableau. Prove that VAM applied to T results in exactly $n - 1$ distinguished (circled) cells with x_{ij}-value 0.

18. Consider the diagram below. (Such a diagram will be called a weighted directed network in Chapter 7.)

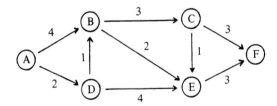

Interpret the arrows as one-way routes between the lettered nodes and interpret the numbers as the distances between these nodes. Formulate and solve an assignment problem for which the optimal solution will yield the shortest distance from node A to node F as well as the actual route from node A to node F which achieves this shortest distance.

CHAPTER 7

Network-Flow Problems

§0. Introduction

Our final application of linear programming occurs in the graph-theoretic domain. In fact, we will see that the transportation and assignment problems of the previous chapter can be reformulated as a certain type of network-flow problem. In view of this, network-flow problems encompass a wide range of linear programming problems. As with the transportation and assignment problems, the network-flow problems of this chapter are solvable by using the techniques of Chapter 2–4 directly. We, however, opt for easier and more direct graph-theoretic algorithms, one of which has its roots in duality theory.

§1. Graph-Theoretic Preliminaries

This section develops the notation and terminology used in the remainder of the chapter.

Definition 1. A *directed network* (or *directed graph*) $N = [V, E]$ is a finite nonempty set V of elements called *vertices* and a set E of ordered pairs of distinct elements of V called *edges*. N is said to be *capacitated* if, to each edge $(v_i, v_j) \in E$, there corresponds a real number $c_{ij} \geq 0$ called its *capacity*. A *flow* in a capacitated directed network is an assignment of a real number x_{ij} to each edge $(v_i, v_j) \in E$ such that $0 \leq x_{ij} \leq c_{ij}$.

EXAMPLE 2. An example of a capacitated directed network is given below:

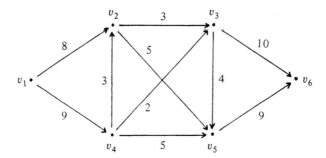

Note that vertices are represented as points and that edges are represented as directed lines between these points. The sets V and E for the directed network above are

$$V = \{v_1, v_2, v_3, v_4, v_5, v_6\}$$
$$E = \{(v_1, v_2), (v_1, v_4), (v_2, v_3), (v_2, v_5), (v_3, v_5),$$
$$(v_3, v_6), (v_4, v_2), (v_4, v_3), (v_4, v_5), (v_5, v_6)\}.$$

Edges only occur between distinct elements of V by definition; hence loops such as (v, v), i.e.,

are not permitted. The capacity c_{ij} of each edge (v_i, v_j) is also given. We now produce a flow in the capacitated directed network above by assigning numbers x_{ij} (distinguished by circles) to the edges subject to $0 \leq x_{ij} \leq c_{ij}$:

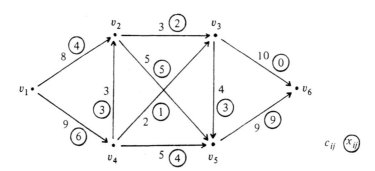

We can imagine the capacitated directed network and flow above as a picture of any one of a number of real-life situations—for example, a system of oil pipelines, a display of railroads between cities, or a network of communication cables.

Definition 3. Let $N = [V, E]$ be a capacitated directed network with a given flow. If $v_j \in V$, then the *net input flow at vertex* v_j, denoted $\varphi(v_j)$, is

$$\varphi(v_j) = \sum_i x_{ij} - \sum_i x_{ji}.$$

If $\varphi(v_j) < 0$, then v_j is said to be a *source*; if $\varphi(v_j) > 0$, then v_j is said to be a *sink*; if $\varphi(v_j) = 0$, then v_j is said to be an *intermediate vertex*.

In other words, the net input flow at a vertex is the sum of all flow numbers on edges into the vertex minus the sum of all flow numbers on edges out of the vertex.

EXAMPLE 4. Consider the capacitated directed network and given flow of Example 2:

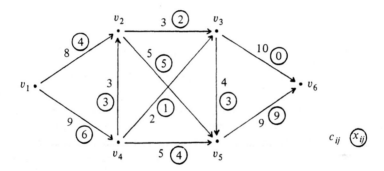

What is $\varphi(v_4)$? The sum of all flow numbers on edges into v_4 (namely x_{14}) is 6 and the sum of all flow numbers on edges out of v_4 (namely $x_{42} + x_{43} + x_{45}$) is $3 + 1 + 4 = 8$; hence

$$\varphi(v_4) = \sum_i x_{i4} - \sum_i x_{4i} = 6 - 8 = -2$$

and v_4 is a source. Similar computations for the other vertices yield the following table (verify!):

i	$\varphi(v_i)$	Type of vertex
1	-10	source
2	0	intermediate vertex
3	0	intermediate vertex
4	-2	source
5	3	sink
6	9	sink

In Example 4 above, we notice that what comes out of the sources (namely

$10 + 2 = 12$ net units of flow—this value is negative in the table because φ is net *input* flow) goes into the sinks $(3 + 9 = 12)$. Such a fact is true in general and is termed *conservation of flow*.

Theorem 5 (Conservation of Flow). *Any flow in a capacitated directed network* $N = [V, E]$ *satisfies*

$$\sum_j \varphi(v_j) = 0.$$

PROOF.
$$\sum_j \varphi(v_j) = \sum_j \left(\sum_i x_{ij} - \sum_i x_{ji} \right) \quad \text{(by Definition 3)}$$

$$= \sum_j \sum_i x_{ij} - \sum_j \sum_i x_{ji}.$$

Now every flow number of the network is represented exactly once in each of the double summations above (albeit in a different order) and hence

$$\sum_j \varphi(v_j) = 0$$

as desired.   □

We conclude this section with an important discussion. The claim is this: Any flow in a capacitated directed network can be transformed into a flow having a unique source and a unique sink by augmenting the structure of the network; furthermore, this augmentation can be implemented so that there are no edges into the source and no edges out of the sink. The augmentation procedure in general is simple. Vertices representing the desired unique source and desired unique sink are added to the network. Edges from the desired unique source to each of the previous sources and edges from each of the previous sinks to the desired unique sink are then added to the network. Each of these added edges is assumed to have infinite capacity. The flow numbers assigned to the added edges are finally computed so that the previous sources and sinks become intermediate vertices. All of this is illustrated for the network and flow of Example 2 below:

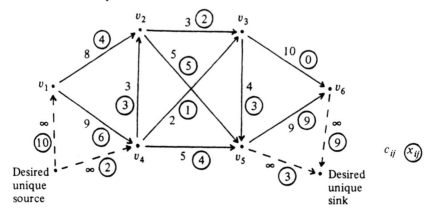

Make sure that you see that the flow above has all the properties expressed in the claim.

Now assume, for the moment, that we are given a capacitated directed network and that we specify certain vertices of the network as sources and sinks. The network-flow problems in the forthcoming sections are concerned with asking different questions about the collection of flows through the network having these specified sources and sinks. In view of the above discussion, we can augment the structure of the network and ask equivalent questions about the collection of flows through the augmented network having a unique source, a unique sink, no edges into the source, and no edges out of the sink. Hence, in what follows, *we restrict our attention to flows having a unique specified source and a unique specified sink as well as the edge properties as above.* Due to the augmentation process described previously, this restriction is without loss of generality and hence is really no restriction at all. The unique specified source and unique specified sink in such a network are denoted v_s and v_d respectively (s for source and d for sink (drain) if you will).

§2. The Maximal-Flow Network Problem

Given a capacitated directed network with unique fixed source and unique fixed sink, no edges into the source, and no edges out of the sink, our first network problem is to find the maximal flow through the network. Note, first of all, that what comes out of the source (namely $-\varphi(v_s)$ since $\varphi(v_s)$ is net *input* flow) must go into the sink by conservation of flow. Hence

$$-\varphi(v_s) = \varphi(v_d);$$

this is the quantity to be maximized:

Maximize $\quad f = -\varphi(v_s) = \varphi(v_d) = \sum_i x_{id} - \sum_i x_{di}$

$$= \sum_i x_{id} \quad (\sum_i x_{di} = 0 \text{ since there are no}$$
$$\text{edges out of } v_d \text{ by assumption}).$$

Now there are two constraints. The first constraint says that every vertex except the source and the sink should be an intermediate vertex; the second constraint says that the flow numbers should be nonnegative and not exceed the given capacities of the edges:

$$\varphi(v_j) = \sum_i x_{ij} - \sum_i x_{ji} = 0, \forall v_j \in V, j \neq s, d$$
$$0 \leq x_{ij} \leq c_{ij}, \forall i,j.$$

Definition 6. Let $N = [V, E]$ be a capacitated directed network with unique fixed source and unique fixed sink, no edges into the source, and no edges out of the sink. The *maximal-flow network problem* is (as above)

Maximize $\quad f = \sum_i x_{id}$

subject to $\quad \sum_i x_{ij} - \sum_i x_{ji} = 0, \forall v_j \in V, j \neq s, d \qquad\qquad$ (1)

$$0 \leqq x_{ij} \leqq c_{ij}, \forall i, j.$$

Note that the zero flow (i.e., $x_{ij} = 0$ for all i and j) is a feasible solution to (1). Also, the x_{ij}'s have finite upper bounds since $x_{ij} \leqq c_{ij}$ for all i and j. Hence the maximal-flow network problem is never infeasible or unbounded. Not surprisingly, the maximal-flow network problem can be solved by using the techniques of Chapters 2–4. We illustrate the setup of such a problem with an example.

EXAMPLE 7. If the maximal-flow network problem below is to be solved by the techniques of Chapters 2–4, find the initial Tucker tableau for the solution.

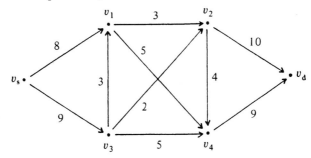

The desired tableau is

x_{s1}	x_{s3}	x_{12}	x_{14}	x_{24}	x_{31}	x_{32}	x_{34}	x_{2d}	x_{4d}	-1	
1	0	-1	-1	0	1	0	0	0	0	0	$= -0$
0	0	1	0	-1	0	1	0	-1	0	0	$= -0$
0	1	0	0	0	-1	-1	-1	0	0	0	$= -0$
0	0	0	1	1	0	0	1	0	-1	0	$= -0$
1	0	0	0	0	0	0	0	0	0	8	$= -t_{s1}$
0	1	0	0	0	0	0	0	0	0	9	$= -t_{s3}$
0	0	1	0	0	0	0	0	0	0	3	$= -t_{12}$
0	0	0	1	0	0	0	0	0	0	5	$= -t_{14}$
0	0	0	0	1	0	0	0	0	0	4	$= -t_{24}$
0	0	0	0	0	1	0	0	0	0	3	$= -t_{31}$
0	0	0	0	0	0	1	0	0	0	2	$= -t_{32}$
0	0	0	0	0	0	0	1	0	0	5	$= -t_{34}$
0	0	0	0	0	0	0	0	1	0	10	$= -t_{2d}$
0	0	0	0	0	0	0	0	0	1	9	$= -t_{4d}$
0	0	0	0	0	0	0	0	1	1	0	$= f$

WOW! The first four rows of the tableau record the intermediate vertex constraints for v_1, v_2, v_3, and v_4 respectively while the next ten rows of the tableau record the upper capacity restrictions $x_{ij} \leq c_{ij}$ for all i and j. The final row of the tableau records (of course) the objective function. Verify these facts!

Do we really want to solve general maximal-flow network problems using the techniques of Chapters 2–4 on Tucker tableaus such as that of Example 7? To say the very least, such an approach appears to be a rather unwieldy procedure. We therefore opt instead for a more direct graph-theoretic algorithm. This algorithm relies heavily on duality; it is this reliance that is emphasized in the next section where we actually derive the algorithm theoretically.

We conclude this section with a brief discussion of the dual problem of the maximal-flow network problem. The dual minimization linear programming problem to the maximal-flow network problem (1) is

$$\text{Minimize} \quad g = \sum_{(v_i, v_j) \in E} c_{ij} y_{ij}$$

$$\begin{aligned}
\text{subject to} \quad & \mu_j + y_{sj} \geq 0, \forall (v_s, v_j) \in E \\
& -\mu_i + \mu_j + y_{ij} \geq 0, \forall (v_i, v_j) \in E, i \neq s, j \neq d \\
& -\mu_i + y_{id} \geq 1, \forall (v_i, v_d) \in E \\
& y_{ij} \geq 0, \forall (v_i, v_j) \in E.
\end{aligned} \quad (2)$$

This fact is motivated further in Exercise 6; the interested reader is immediately referred there. If we put $\mu_s = 0$ and $\mu_d = -1$, (2) simplifies:

$$\text{Minimize} \quad g = \sum_{(v_i, v_j) \in E} c_{ij} y_{ij}$$

$$\begin{aligned}
\text{subject to} \quad & -\mu_i + \mu_j + y_{ij} \geq 0, \forall (v_i, v_j) \in E \\
& y_{ij} \geq 0, \forall (v_i, v_j) \in E \\
& \mu_s = 0, \mu_d = -1.
\end{aligned} \quad (3)$$

To see this, note that $i = s$ in the first constraint of (3) yields the first constraint of (2) and that $j = d$ in the first constraint of (3) yields the third constraint of (2); the first constraint of (3) is identical to the second constraint of (2) for all other $(v_i, v_j) \in E$. This simplified minimization problem is intimately connected to the concept of a cut to be discussed in the next section; in fact, the minimum cut shares a strong relationship with the desired maximal flow (as might be expected since they are dual problems), ultimately leading to the maximal-flow algorithm.

§3. The Max-Flow Min-Cut Theorem; The Maximal-Flow Algorithm

Definition 8. Let $N = [V, E]$ be a capacitated directed network with unique fixed source and unique fixed sink, no edges into the source, and no edges out of the sink. A *cut* $C = (V_1, V_2)$ in N is a partition of all elements of V into two disjoint subsets V_1 and V_2 such that $v_s \in V_1$ and $v_d \in V_2$. The *cut-set* of the cut $C = (V_1, V_2)$ is the set

$$\{(v_i, v_j) \in E: v_i \in V_1, v_j \in V_2\}.$$

The *capacity* of the cut $C = (V_1, V_2)$, denoted $c(V_1, V_2)$, is

$$c(V_1, V_2) = \sum_{v_i \in V_1, v_j \in V_2} c_{ij}.$$

EXAMPLE 9. Consider the capacitated directed network N below:

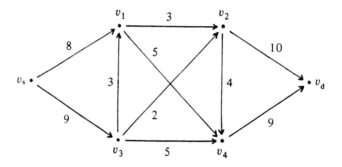

Then

$$C = (V_1 = \{v_s, v_1, v_3\}, V_2 = \{v_2, v_4, v_d\})$$

is a cut in N. The cut-set of C consists of all edges in E having initial vertex in V_1 and terminal vertex in V_2. Hence the cut-set of C is

$$\{(v_1, v_2), (v_1, v_4), (v_3, v_2), (v_3, v_4)\}.$$

The capacity of C is the sum of the capacities of the edges in the cut-set:

$$c(V_1, V_2) = \sum_{v_i \in V_1, v_j \in V_2} c_{ij} = 3 + 5 + 2 + 5 = 15.$$

The cut C, its cut-set, and its capacity may be diagrammed as follows:

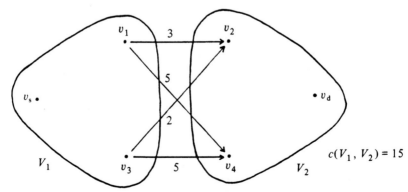

Another cut in N, its cut-set, and its capacity are diagrammed below:

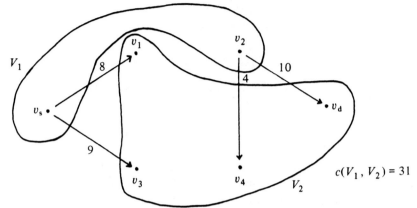

Note that the edges (v_1, v_2) and (v_3, v_2) are *not* cut-set edges since their initial vertices are in V_2 (not V_1) and their terminal vertices are in V_1 (not V_2).

We note immediately from Example 9 above that the capacities of cuts in a given capacitated directed network may vary greatly. These capacities relate to the minimization problem (3) of §2 as follows. Given a cut $C = (V_1, V_2)$ in a capacitated directed network, put $\mu_i = 0$ if $v_i \in V_1$ and $\mu_j = -1$ if $v_j \in V_2$. (Note, in particular, that $\mu_s = 0$ and $\mu_d = -1$ in accordance with (3).) For every edge (v_i, v_j) of the cut-set of C, put $y_{ij} = 1$; otherwise, put $y_{ij} = 0$. Then these values give a feasible solution to (3) and the value of the objective function g is the capacity of C. Conversely, given a capacitated directed network and any feasible solution to (3) with μ-values equal to 0 or -1 and y-values determined by $y_{ij} = \max \{0, \mu_i - \mu_j\}$ (so that $-\mu_i + \mu_j + y_{ij} \geq 0$ and so that y_{ij} is equal to 0 or 1; see Exercise 7), put $v_i \in V_1$ if $\mu_i = 0$ and $v_j \in V_2$ if $\mu_j = -1$. Then $C = (V_1, V_2)$ is a cut in the network and the edge (v_i, v_j) is in the cut-set of C if and only if $y_{ij} = 1$. Hence all cuts in a capacitated directed network are mathematically modeled by (3). We illustrate with an example.

EXAMPLE 10. Consider the first cut diagrammed in Example 9:

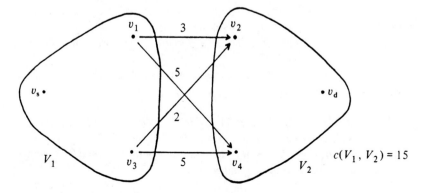

Then

$$\mu_s - \mu_1 - \mu_3 = 0$$
$$\mu_2 = \mu_4 = \mu_d = -1$$
$$y_{12} = y_{14} = y_{32} = y_{34} = 1$$
$$y_{s1} = y_{s3} = y_{24} = y_{2d} = y_{31} = y_{4d} = 0.$$

One can now easily check that all constraints of (3) are satisfied (check this!). Furthermore,

$$g = \sum_{(v_i,v_j)\in E} c_{ij}y_{ij} = c_{12} + c_{14} + c_{32} + c_{34} = 3 + 5 + 2 + 5 = 15$$

as desired. Conversely, consider the capacitated directed network N of Example 9; we wish to construct a feasible solution to (3) with μ-values equal to 0 or -1 and y-values equal to 0 or 1. Let

$$\mu_s = \mu_2 = 0$$
$$\mu_1 = \mu_3 = \mu_4 = \mu_d = -1$$

(for example). Then

$$y_{s1} = \max\{0, \mu_s - \mu_1\} \Rightarrow y_{s1} = 1$$
$$y_{s3} = \max\{0, \mu_s - \mu_3\} \Rightarrow y_{s3} = 1$$
$$y_{12} = \max\{0, \mu_1 - \mu_2\} \Rightarrow y_{12} = 0$$
$$y_{14} = \max\{0, \mu_1 - \mu_4\} \Rightarrow y_{14} = 0$$
$$y_{24} = \max\{0, \mu_2 - \mu_4\} \Rightarrow y_{24} = 1$$
$$y_{2d} = \max\{0, \mu_2 - \mu_d\} \Rightarrow y_{2d} = 1$$
$$y_{31} = \max\{0, \mu_3 - \mu_1\} \Rightarrow y_{31} = 0$$
$$y_{32} = \max\{0, \mu_3 - \mu_2\} \Rightarrow y_{32} = 0$$
$$y_{34} = \max\{0, \mu_3 - \mu_4\} \Rightarrow y_{34} = 0$$
$$y_{4d} = \max\{0, \mu_4 - \mu_d\} \Rightarrow y_{4d} = 0$$

and the μ's and the y's form a feasible solution to (3). The cut in N given by this feasible solution is $C = (V_1, V_2)$ where $V_1 = \{v_s, v_2\}$ (from the μ's equal to 0) and $V_2 = \{v_1, v_3, v_4, v_d\}$ (from the μ's equal to 1); since the edge (v_i, v_j) is in the cut-set of C if and only if $y_{ij} = 1$, the cut-set of C is $\{(v_s, v_1),(v_s, v_3),(v_2, v_4),(v_2, v_d)\}$. Note that the cut just produced is the second cut diagrammed in Example 9.

We are interested primarily in the minimum possible cut capacity in a given network for the following reason.

Theorem 11 (Max-Flow Min-Cut Theorem). *Let $N = [V, E]$ be a capacitated directed network with unique fixed source and unique fixed sink, no edges into the source, and no edges out of the sink. Then the value of the maximal flow from v_s to v_d is equal to the minimal cut capacity in N.*

Theorem 11 is perhaps the single most important result in elementary graph theory. Notice the blatant display of duality here! If we accept the fact that the dual minimization problem of the maximal-flow problem mathematically models the concept of cuts in networks (see Example 10), then this theorem simply says that $f = g$ at the optimal solutions to the maximal-flow network problem (objective function f) and minimal-cut network problem (objective function g), something we know already from Chapter 4. We, however, will provide a completely new graph-theoretic proof of this theorem since such a proof is the basis for a graph-theoretic algorithm for solving maximal-flow network problems. This proof also illustrates again the importance of duality as a theoretical tool in linear programming. We first give a definition.

Definition 12. Let $N = [V, E]$ be a capacitated directed network with unique fixed source and unique fixed sink, no edges into the source, and no edges out of the sink. A finite nonempty set P of ordered pairs of elements of V of the form

$$P = \{(v_0, v_1), (v_1, v_2), \ldots, (v_{n-1}, v_n)\}$$

is said to be an α-*path* in N from v_0 to v_n if

(i) the vertices $v_0, v_1, \ldots, v_n$ are distinct and
(ii) $(v_i, v_j) \in P$ implies that $(v_i, v_j) \in E$ or $(v_j, v_i) \in E$.

If $(v_i, v_j) \in P$ and $(v_i, v_j) \in E$, then (v_i, v_j) is said to be a *forward edge* of P in N; if $(v_i, v_j) \in P$ and $(v_j, v_i) \in E$, then (v_i, v_j) is said to be a *backward edge* of P in N.

EXAMPLE 13. Consider the capacitated directed network N below:

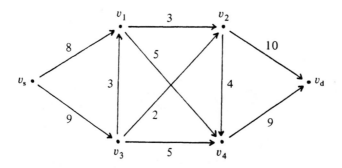

Then

$$P = \{(v_s, v_3), (v_3, v_4), (v_4, v_2), (v_2, v_d)\}$$

is an α-path in N from v_s to v_d. $(v_s, v_3), (v_3, v_4)$, and (v_2, v_d) are forward edges of P in N since they respect the direction of the original edges of N; (v_4, v_2) is a backward edge of P in N since it traverses an original edge of N in the opposite direction.

In the proof of the max-flow min-cut theorem, we will have occasion to refer to the objective function and constraints of the maximal-flow network problem (1). We recall that this problem is given by

$$\text{Maximize} \quad f = \sum_i x_{id} \tag{1.1}$$

$$\text{subject to} \quad \sum_i x_{ij} - \sum_i x_{ji} = 0, \forall v_j \in V, j \neq s, d \tag{1.2}$$

$$0 \leq x_{ij} \leq c_{ij}, \forall i, j. \tag{1.3}$$

We now present the proof of the max-flow min-cut theorem.

PROOF (of Theorem 11). The proof consists of two parts. In the first part, we show that the value of the maximal flow is less than or equal to the minimal cut capacity. In the second part, we then show that a cut exists whose capacity is equal to the value of the maximal flow. These two parts are sufficient to prove the theorem.

Part 1. Consider any feasible flow in N with flow numbers x_{ij} and flow value f and let $C = (V_1, V_2)$ be any cut in N. Now

$$f = \left(\sum_{v_j \in V_2, j \neq d} 0 \right) + f$$

$$= \sum_{v_j \in V_2, j \neq d} \left(\sum_i x_{ij} - \sum_i x_{ji} \right) + \sum_i x_{id} \quad \text{(by (1.2) and (1.1) respectively)}$$

$$= \sum_{v_j \in V_2, j \neq d} \left(\sum_i x_{ij} - \sum_i x_{ji} \right) + \sum_i x_{id} - \sum_i x_{di}$$

$$= \sum_{v_j \in V_2} \left(\sum_i x_{ij} - \sum_i x_{ji} \right)$$

$$= \sum_{v_j \in V_2} \left[\left(\sum_{v_i \in V_1} x_{ij} + \sum_{v_i \in V_2} x_{ij} \right) - \left(\sum_{v_i \in V_1} x_{ji} + \sum_{v_i \in V_2} x_{ji} \right) \right]$$

$$= \sum_{v_i \in V_1, v_j \in V_2} x_{ij} + \sum_{v_i \in V_2, v_j \in V_2} x_{ij} - \sum_{v_i \in V_1, v_j \in V_2} x_{ji} - \sum_{v_i \in V_2, v_j \in V_2} x_{ji}$$

$$= \sum_{v_i \in V_1, v_j \in V_2} x_{ij} - \sum_{v_i \in V_1, v_j \in V_2} x_{ji} + \sum_{v_i \in V_2, v_j \in V_2} x_{ij} - \sum_{v_i \in V_2, v_j \in V_2} x_{ji}$$

$$= \sum_{v_i \in V_1, v_j \in V_2} x_{ij} - \sum_{v_i \in V_1, v_j \in V_2} x_{ji}, \quad \text{(the last two } \sum\text{'s above cancel since } i \text{ and } j \text{ range over the same set)}$$

i.e.,

$$f = \sum_{v_i \in V_1, v_j \in V_2} x_{ij} - \sum_{v_i \in V_1, v_j \in V_2} x_{ji}. \tag{4}$$

Then

$$f \underset{(4)}{=} \sum_{v_i \in V_1, v_j \in V_2} x_{ij} - \sum_{v_i \in V_1, v_j \in V_2} x_{ji} \leq \sum_{v_i \in V_1, v_j \in V_2} x_{ij}$$

$$\underset{(1.3)}{\leq} \sum_{v_i \in V_1, v_j \in V_2} c_{ij} = c(V_1, V_2),$$

i.e. $f \leqq c(V_1, V_2)$. Since the feasible flow value f and the cut $C = (V_1, V_2)$ were arbitrary, we have

$$\max f \leqq \min c(V_1, V_2). \tag{5}$$

Part 2. Since the maximal-flow network problem is never infeasible or unbounded, a maximal flow exists; let the value of this maximal flow be f' corresponding to flow numbers x'_{ij}. We now construct two disjoint subsets V'_1 and V'_2 of V as follows:

Construct V'_1 by putting v_s into V'_1 and then by putting v_j into V'_1 if and only if

(i) $v_i \in V'_1$, $(v_i, v_j) \in E$, and $x'_{ij} < c_{ij}$ or
(ii) $v_i \in V'_1$, $(v_j, v_i) \in E$, and $x'_{ji} > 0$.

After V'_1 has been constructed, put $V'_2 = V - V'_1$.

We wish to show that (V'_1, V'_2) is a cut in N. It suffices to show that $v_d \in V'_2$. Assume, by way of contradiction, that $v_d \notin V'_2$, i.e., $v_d \in V'_1$. Then v_d was put into V'_1 by virtue of a sequence of steps (i) and (ii) above. In other words, there exists an α-path P in N from v_s to v_d such that, for every forward edge (v_i, v_j) of P, we have

(i) $c_{ij} - x'_{ij} > 0$

and, for every backward edge (v_i, v_j) of P, we have

(ii) $x'_{ji} > 0$.

Define

$$q = \min \left\{ \begin{array}{cc} \min_{\substack{(v_i, v_j) \\ \text{a fwd.} \\ \text{edge} \\ \text{of } P}} \{c_{ij} - x'_{ij}\}, & \min_{\substack{(v_i, v_j) \\ \text{a bwd.} \\ \text{edge} \\ \text{of } P}} x'_{ji} \end{array} \right\} > 0.$$

Define a new flow in N by adding q to the flow numbers on all forward edges of P in N and by subtracting q from the flow numbers on all backward edges of P in N. This new flow has value $f' + q$, contradicting the maximality of f'. Hence $v_d \in V'_2$ whence (V'_1, V'_2) is a cut in N. Note that we must necessarily have

(i) $x'_{ij} = c_{ij}$ if $(v_i, v_j) \in E$, $v_i \in V'_1$, and $v_j \in V'_2$ *and* $\qquad$ (6)
(ii) $x'_{ji} = 0$ if $(v_j, v_i) \in E$, $v_j \in V'_2$, and $v_i \in V'_1$ $\qquad$ (7)

by the constructions of V'_1 and V'_2. Then

$$f' \underset{(4)}{=} \sum_{v_i \in V'_1, v_j \in V'_2} x'_{ij} - \sum_{v_i \in V'_1, v_j \in V'_2} x'_{ji}$$

$$\underset{(7)}{=} \sum_{v_i \in V'_1, v_j \in V'_2} x'_{ij}$$

$$\underset{(6)}{=} \sum_{v_i \in V'_1, v_j \in V'_2} c_{ij}$$

$$= c(V'_1, V'_2),$$

i.e.,

$$f' - c(V'_1, V'_2)$$

as desired.   □

The validity of the maximal-flow algorithm comes directly from the proof of the max-flow min-cut theorem above. The idea of the maximal-flow algorithm is to begin with any feasible flow and successively increase the value of this flow to the maximal flow value by finding α-paths from v_s to v_d until no such paths exist. Each α-path increases the flow value by the quantity q of the proof above. We claim that when this procedure terminates, the maximal flow has been found. Why? Since no α-paths from v_s to v_d exist in the network, the cut (V'_1, V'_2) of the proof above can be constructed (note that it is a true cut by the proof!) and its capacity will be equal to the current flow value. (Before reading further, make sure that you see the truth of these facts; go back to the proof of the max-flow min-cut theorem if necessary for verification.) Now assume, by way of contradiction, that the current flow is not maximal. Then

$$\max f > c(V'_1, V'_2),$$

contradicting the fact that the maximal flow value is equal to the minimal cut capacity. Hence, the current flow is indeed maximal. Stated a bit differently, any time a flow value in a network agrees with a cut capacity in the same network, one simultaneously has the maximal flow and the minimal cut of the network.

We now state the maximal-flow algorithm. The algorithm is due to L.R. Ford, Jr., and D.R. Fulkerson ([F1]). The notation has been changed slightly from that used in the proof of Theorem 11.

The Maximal-Flow Algorithm

(0) Given: A capacitated directed network $N = [V, E]$ with unique fixed source and unique fixed sink, no edges into the source, and no edges out of the sink.

(1) Find an initial feasible flow in N. We may, for example, begin with the zero flow in N, i.e., $x_{ij} = 0$ for all i and j.

(2) Find an α-path P in N from v_s to v_d such that

    (i) each forward edge (v_i, v_j) of P satisfies $x_{ij} < c_{ij}$ and
    (ii) each backward edge (v_i, v_j) of P satisfies $x_{ji} > 0$.

If no such α-path exists, go to (4).

(3) Compute

$$q = \min\left\{ \min_{\substack{(v_i,v_j) \\ \text{a fwd.} \\ \text{edge} \\ \text{of } P}} \{c_{ij} - x_{ij}\}, \min_{\substack{(v_i,v_j) \\ \text{a bwd.} \\ \text{edge} \\ \text{of } P}} x_{ji} \right\} > 0.$$

Add q to the flow numbers on all forward edges of P in N and subtract q from the flow numbers on all backward edges of P in N. Go to (2).
(4) STOP; the current flow is maximal.
    (*Note*: The minimal cut (V_1, V_2) corresponding to this maximal flow by the proof of Theorem 11 is constructed as follows:
        Construct V_1 by putting v_s into V_1 and then by putting v_j into V_1 if and only if

      (i) $v_i \in V_1$, $(v_i, v_j) \in E$, and $x_{ij} < c_{ij}$ or
      (ii) $v_i \in V_1$, $(v_j, v_i) \in E$, and $x_{ji} > 0$.

    After V_1 has been constructed, put $V_2 = V - V_1$.
    Any edge $(v_i, v_j) \in E$ of the cut-set satisfies $x_{ij} = c_{ij}$ by (6); any edge $(v_j, v_i) \in E$ such that $v_j \in V_2$ and $v_i \in V_1$ satisfies $x_{ji} = 0$ by (7).)

The actual construction of the cut in the note of step (4) above is *not* necessary for producing the maximal flow of the network. However, the construction of this cut does offer the advantage of providing a check that no mistakes were made in the basic algorithm. For example, after finding the maximal flow of a network, one can check that the capacity of the constructed cut agrees with the value of this flow (validating the maximality of the flow) and that pertinent edges display the properties of (6) and (7) as remarked above. More fundamentally, the construction of the cut illuminates the presence of duality in our graph-theoretic setting and serves as a reminder of the theoretical importance of duality. We conclude this section with two examples of maximal-flow network problems.

EXAMPLE 14. Solve the maximal-flow network problem below. Display the corresponding minimal cut and cut-set as constructed in the proof of the max-flow min-cut theorem.

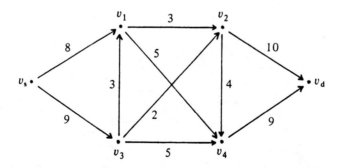

The parenthetical numbers below correspond to the steps of the maximal-flow algorithm.

(0) The given maximal-flow network problem is of the desired form.
(1) We begin with the zero flow in N:

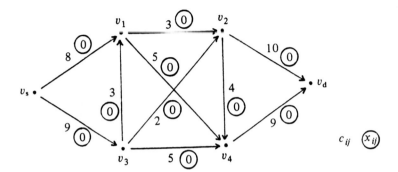

(2) Our choice for an α-path from v_s to v_d is $P = \{(v_s, v_1), (v_1, v_2), (v_2, v_d)\}$ or, more concisely, $P: v_s \rightarrow v_1 \rightarrow v_2 \rightarrow v_d$. (There are many other choices for α-paths here and hence many other ways to solve this problem; this leniency of choice for α-paths is characteristic of step (2) in general.) For this α-path, only forward edges have been used; note that $x_{ij} < c_{ij}$ for these edges (each x_{ij} is currently 0).

(3) Since no backward edges were used in the α-path of step (2) above, we have

$$q = \min_{\substack{(v_i, v_j) \\ \text{a fwd.} \\ \text{edge} \\ \text{of } P}} \{c_{ij} - x_{ij}\} = \min \{8 - 0, 3 - 0, 10 - 0\} = 3.$$

Hence 3 is added to the flow numbers on all edges of the α-path $v_s \rightarrow v_1 \rightarrow v_2 \rightarrow v_d$:

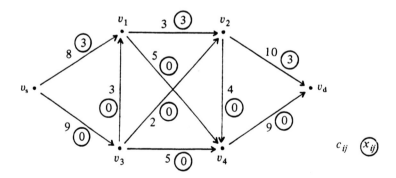

Go to step (2).

(2) We choose the α-path $P: v_s \rightarrow v_3 \rightarrow v_4 \rightarrow v_d$. For this α-path, only forward edges have been used and $x_{ij} < c_{ij}$ for these edges.

(3) $q = \min_{\substack{(v_i, v_j) \\ \text{a fwd.} \\ \text{edge} \\ \text{of } P}} \{c_{ij} - x_{ij}\} = \min \{9 - 0, 5 - 0, 9 - 0\} = 5;$

hence 5 is added to the flow numbers on all edges of the α-path $v_s \rightarrow v_3 \rightarrow v_4 \rightarrow v_d$:

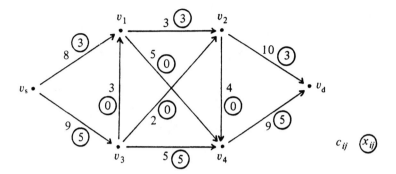

Go to step (2).

(2) We choose the α-path P: $v_s \rightarrow v_3 \rightarrow v_1 \rightarrow v_4 \rightarrow v_d$. For this α-path, only forward edges have been used and $x_{ij} < c_{ij}$ for these edges.

(3) $q = \min_{\substack{(v_i, v_j) \\ \text{a fwd.} \\ \text{edge} \\ \text{of } P}} \{c_{ij} - x_{ij}\} = \min \{9 - 5, 3 - 0, 5 - 0, 9 - 5\} = 3;$

hence 3 is added to the flow numbers on all edges of the α-path $v_s \rightarrow v_3 \rightarrow v_1 \rightarrow v_4 \rightarrow v_d$:

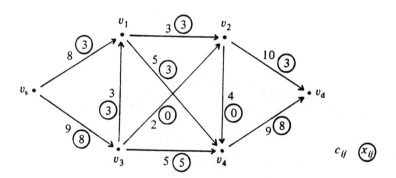

Go to step (2).

(2) We choose the α-path P: $v_s \rightarrow v_1 \rightarrow v_4 \rightarrow v_d$. For this α-path, only forward edges have been used and $x_{ij} < c_{ij}$ for these edges.

(3) $q = \min_{\substack{(v_i, v_j) \\ \text{a fwd.} \\ \text{edge} \\ \text{of } P}} \{c_{ij} - x_{ij}\} = \min \{8 - 3, 5 - 3, 9 - 8\} = 1;$

hence 1 is added to the flow numbers on all edges of the α-path $v_s \to v_1 \to v_4 \to v_d$:

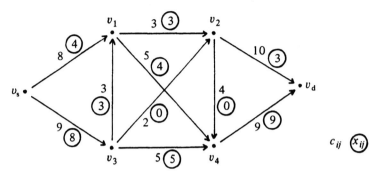

Go to step (2).

(2) We choose the α-path $P: v_s \to v_1 \to v_3 \to v_2 \to v_d$. Note that a backward edge has been used! For this α-path, $x_{ij} < c_{ij}$ for the forward edges of P and $x_{ji} > 0$ for the backward edge of P.

(3) $q = \min \left\{ \begin{array}{c} \min\limits_{\substack{(v_i,v_j) \\ \text{a fwd.} \\ \text{edge} \\ \text{of } P}} \{c_{ij} - x_{ij}\}, \min\limits_{\substack{(v_i,v_j) \\ \text{a bwd.} \\ \text{edge} \\ \text{of } P}} x_{ji} \end{array} \right\} = \min \{\min\{8-4, 2-0, 10-3\},$
$$\min\{3\}\}$$

$$= \min\{2, 3\}$$
$$= 2;$$

hence 2 is added to the flow numbers on all forward edges of P and subtracted from the flow number on the backward edge of P:

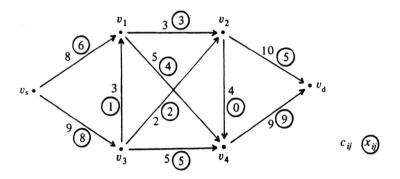

Go to step (2).

(2) There is no α-path from v_s to v_d that meets the edge criteria (i) and (ii). (Convince yourself of this!) Go to step (4).

(4) STOP; the current flow is maximal. Hence

$$\max f = \sum_i x_{id} = x_{2d} + x_{4d} = 5 + 9 = 14;$$

the x_{ij}'s appear on the final network above.

Before we construct the corresponding cut and cut-set, some remarks are in order. The succession of five α-paths made above is *not* the most efficient way to solve the problem. One could solve the problem by choosing a succession of four α-paths (see Exercise 4). In fact, it is rare that a backward edge ever has to be used in such a succession. The succession of five α-paths above was chosen precisely to illustrate the use of a backward edge. Also, while any maximal flow in the example above must have a value of 14, the corresponding flow numbers are not unique.

We now construct the corresponding minimal cut and cut-set as in the proof of Theorem 11. Put $v_s \in V_1$. Since $v_s \in V_1$, $(v_s, v_1) \in E$, and $x_{s1} = 6 < 8 = c_{s1}$, we have $v_1 \in V_1$ by (i). Similarly, since $v_1 \in V_1$, $(v_1, v_4) \in E$, and $x_{14} = 4 < 5 = c_{14}$, we have $v_4 \in V_1$ by (i). Since $v_4 \in V_1$, $(v_3, v_4) \in E$, and $x_{34} = 5 > 0$, we have $v_3 \in V_1$ by (ii). This concludes the construction of V_1; no other vertices may be admitted into V_1 by virtue of (i) or (ii). Hence, $V_1 = \{v_s, v_1, v_3, v_4\}$ and $V_2 = V - V_1 = \{v_2, v_d\}$. The cut (V_1, V_2) and its cut-set are diagrammed below:

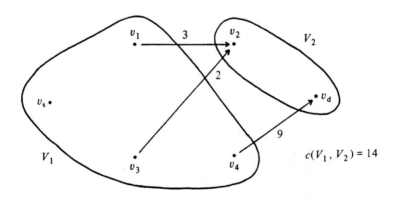

Note that the capacity of this cut agrees with the maximal flow value obtained previously. Returning to the last step (3) above, note also that every edge of the cut-set is saturated, i.e., satisfies $x_{ij} = c_{ij}$, and that every edge $(v_j, v_i) \in E$ such that $v_j \in V_2$ and $v_i \in V_1$ (there is only one such edge, namely (v_2, v_4)) satisfies $x_{ji} = 0$.

EXAMPLE 15. Solve the maximal-flow network problem below. Display the corresponding minimal cut and cut-set as constructed in the proof of the max-flow min-cut theorem.

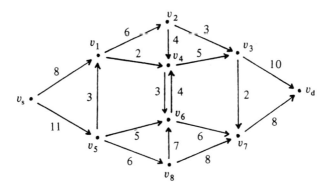

This example is purposefully sketchy. Provide all necessary details and verifications for yourself. The α-paths used to solve this problem (other choices possible!) are listed below along with the corresponding q values:

$$
\begin{aligned}
v_s \to v_1 \to v_2 \to v_3 \to v_d && (q = 3) \\
v_s \to v_5 \to v_8 \to v_7 \to v_d && (q = 6) \\
v_s \to v_1 \to v_4 \to v_3 \to v_d && (q = 2) \\
v_s \to v_5 \to v_6 \to v_7 \to v_d && (q = 2) \\
v_s \to v_5 \to v_6 \to v_4 \to v_3 \to v_d && (q = 3).
\end{aligned}
$$

Note that each α-path consists entirely of forward edges. The corresponding maximal flow is given by

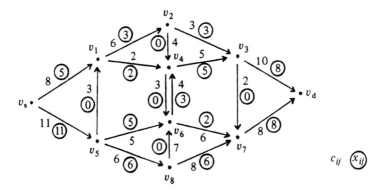

Hence, max $f = 16$. The corresponding minimal cut (V_1, V_2) and cut-set are diagrammed below:

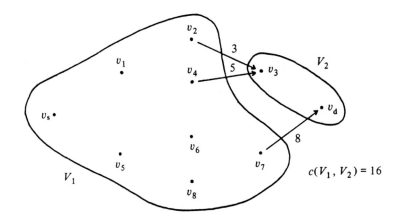

§4. The Shortest-Path Network Problem

Definition 16. Let $N = [V, E]$ be a directed network. N is said to be *weighted* if, to each edge $(v_i, v_j) \in E$, there corresponds a real number w_{ij} (not necessarily nonnegative) called its *weight*.

A weighted directed network is simply a generalization of a capacitated directed network — negative edge numbers are allowed in the former but not in the latter.

Definition 17. Let $N = [V, E]$ be a directed network. A finite nonempty set P of edges of E of the form

$$P = \{(v_0, v_1), (v_1, v_2), \ldots, (v_{n-1}, v_n)\}$$

is said to be a *path* in N from v_0 to v_n. If $v_0 = v_n$, then the path is said to be a *cycle*.

Note that paths in networks differ from α-paths in networks in two important ways: (i) paths consist of edges of E, i.e., paths must respect the direction of the edges of the original network and (ii) the vertices $v_0, v_1, \ldots, v_n$ traversed in a path need not be distinct (permitting cycling as in the path $P = \{(v_0, v_1), (v_1, v_2), (v_2, v_3), (v_3, v_1), (v_1, v_4)\}$ of the network below):

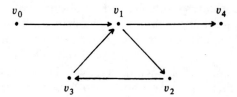

Cycles are paths that begin and end at the same vertex (as in $\{(v_1, v_2), (v_2, v_3), (v_3, v_1)\}$ above).

The intuitive formulation of the shortest-path network problem is simple. Consider a weighted directed network N and interpret the weights of the edges as distances between corresponding vertices. (You may wish to view the network as a map with the vertices representing cities and the directed edges representing one-way roads between these cities.) The shortest-path network problem is concerned with finding the path of shortest distance from one vertex, called the *derivation*, to another vertex, called the *destination*. By abuse of notation, we denote the derivation by v_s and the destination by v_d. The mathematical formulation of this problem follows.

Definition 18. Let $N = [V, E]$ be a weighted directed network with no edges into the derivation and no edges out of the destination. Furthermore, assume that no cycle in N has a net negative weight, i.e., no cycle in N consists of edges the sum of whose weights is negative. The *shortest-path network problem* is

$$\text{Minimize} \quad d = \sum_{(v_i, v_j) \in E} w_{ij} x_{ij}$$

$$\text{subject to} \quad \sum_i x_{id} = 1$$

$$\sum_i x_{ij} - \sum_i x_{ji} = 0, \quad \forall v_j \in V, \quad j \neq s, d \tag{8}$$

$$0 \leq x_{ij} \leq 1, \quad \forall i, j.$$

We now show how the intuitive formulation of the shortest-path network problem coincides with Definition 18 above. From the statement of (8) above, it can be proven (but is by no means obvious) that each x_{ij} is either 0 or 1 in any optimal solution. We will not provide such a proof here (see, for example, [D1] for a proof). The consequences of such a fact are extremely important however. Assume that we have an optimal solution to (8). Then exactly one edge into the destination v_d will have x-value equal to 1 by the first constraint—all other edges into the destination will have x-value equal to 0. The second constraint of (8) says that, if a vertex other than the derivation and the destination has an outgoing edge with x-value equal to 1, then that vertex also has an incoming edge with x-value equal to 1. By repeated application of this second constraint, we see that those edges having x-value equal to 1 will form a path through the network from the derivation to the destination—the objective function is then the minimum sum of the weights (or distances) of those edges. We should remark that the shortest-path network problem may be infeasible. For example, there is no shortest path through a network from the derivation to the destination if there is no path through the network from the derivation to the destination! If there is at least one path through the network from the derivation to the destination, then the shortest-path network problem is not infeasible. In either case, the shortest-path network problem is never unbounded.

We note that the restriction that there be no edges into the derivation v_s and no edges out of the destination v_d in a shortest-path network problem is without loss of generality. For assume that a shortest-path network problem has an edge e into v_s and that a shortest path P through the network from v_s to v_d utilizes e. Then P must exit v_s via one edge and return to v_s via e. In other words, there is a cycle in P that begins and ends at v_s. This cycle must have net zero weight. (Cycles with net negative weight in shortest-path network problems are disallowed by Definition 18. If the cycle has a net positive weight, a shorter path from v_s to v_d is obtained by eliminating the cycle from P, contradicting the minimality of P.) Hence, by eliminating the cycle from P, we obtain a path of equal value from v_s to v_d not utilizing e. Such a procedure is repeated until a shortest path is obtained utilizing no edges into v_s. A similar argument handles edges out of the destination v_d (see Exercise 11).

The shortest-path network problem (8) is solvable by using the techniques of Chapters 2–4. Not surprisingly, such an approach is cumbersome. We give instead two more direct shortest-path algorithms. The first algorithm is a standard algorithm due to Dijkstra ([D2]); unfortunately, it applies only to directed networks having nonnegative weights. The second algorithm handles the general shortest-path problem (8) and can be found in [A1]. The reader is referred to the relevant literature for further discussions of the graph-theoretic motivations behind these algorithms.

Shortest-Path Algorithm I (Dijkstra)

(0) Given: A weighted directed network $N = [V, E]$ with no edges into the derivation, no edges out of the destination, and $w_{ij} \geq 0$ for all i and j. *Note*: In what follows, l_j is to be interpreted as a "label" given to the vertex $v_j \in V$.

(1) Put $l_s = 0$. Circle this 0. If $j \neq s$, put $l_j = w_{sj}$. (If w_{sj} does not exist, put $l_j = w_{sj} = \infty$.) Put $P = \{v_s\}$ and $T = V - P$.

(2) Compute

$$l_k = \min_{v_j \in T} l_j.$$

Circle this minimum value. Put $P \leftarrow P \cup \{v_k\}$ and $T = V - P$. If $T = \varnothing$, STOP; the value of l_j is the value of the shortest path from v_s to v_j— in particular, the value of l_d is the desired value of the shortest path from v_s to v_d. Otherwise, continue.

(3) $\forall v_j \in T$, put $l_j \leftarrow \min \{l_j, l_k + w_{kj}\}$. (If w_{kj} does not exist, put $w_{kj} = \infty$.) Go to (2).

Note that Dijkstra's algorithm does not directly address the shortest-path network problem (8). On the one hand, Dijkstra's algorithm gives the values of the shortest path from the derivation to all other vertices when we are interested only in the value of the shortest path from the derivation to a particular vertex, namely the destination. In this sense, the algorithm produces more than we expect in (8). On the other hand, Dijkstra's algorithm only gives the *values* of these shortest paths; it does *not* give the shortest paths themselves. In this sense, the algorithm produces less than we expect in (8). Fortunately, the actual shortest paths are easily constructed from the labeling of the vertices during the algorithm. We illustrate with an example.

EXAMPLE 19. Solve the shortest-path network problem below by using Dijkstra's algorithm. Give both the value of the shortest path from the derivation to the destination and the shortest path itself.

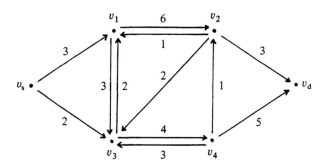

The parenthetical numbers below correspond to the steps of Dijkstra's algorithm.

(0) The given shortest-path network problem is of the desired form.

(1)

l_s	l_1	l_2	l_3	l_4	l_d	P	T
⓪	3	∞	2	∞	∞	$\{v_s\}$	$\{v_1, v_2, v_3, v_4, v_d\}$

(2) $l_k = \min_{v_j \in T} l_j = l_3 = 2;\ v_k = v_3$

l_s	l_1	l_2	l_3	l_4	l_d	P	T
⓪	3	∞	②	∞	∞	$\{v_s\}$ $\{v_s, v_3\}$	$\{v_1, v_2, v_3, v_4, v_d\}$ $\{v_1, v_2, v_4, v_d\}$

$T \neq \emptyset$, so continue.

(3) $l_1 \leftarrow \min\{l_1, l_3 + w_{31}\} = \min\{3, 2 + 2\} = 3$
$l_2 \leftarrow \min\{l_2, l_3 + w_{32}\} = \min\{\infty, 2 + \infty\} = \infty$
$l_4 \leftarrow \min\{l_4, l_3 + w_{34}\} = \min\{\infty, 2 + 4\} = 6$
$l_d \leftarrow \min\{l_d, l_3 + w_{3d}\} = \min\{\infty, 2 + \infty\} = \infty$

Hence:

l_s	l_1	l_2	l_3	l_4	l_d	P	T
⓪	3	∞	②	∞	∞	$\{v_s\}$	$\{v_1, v_2, v_3, v_4, v_d\}$
	3	∞		6	∞	$\{v_s, v_3\}$	$\{v_1, v_2, v_4, v_d\}$

Go to step (2).

(2) $l_k = \min\limits_{v_j \in T} l_j = l_1 = 3; v_k = v_1$

l_s	l_1	l_2	l_3	l_4	l_d	P	T
⓪	3	∞	②	∞	∞	$\{v_s\}$	$\{v_1, v_2, v_3, v_4, v_d\}$
	③	∞		6	∞	$\{v_s, v_3\}$	$\{v_1, v_2, v_4, v_d\}$
						$\{v_s, v_1, v_3\}$	$\{v_2, v_4, v_d\}$

$T \neq \varnothing$, so continue.

(3) $l_2 \leftarrow \min\{l_2, l_1 + w_{12}\} = \min\{\infty, 3 + 6\} = 9$

$l_4 \leftarrow \min\{l_4, l_1 + w_{14}\} = \min\{6, 3 + \infty\} = 6$

$l_d \leftarrow \min\{l_d, l_1 + w_{1d}\} = \min\{\infty, 3 + \infty\} = \infty$

Hence:

l_s	l_1	l_2	l_3	l_4	l_d	P	T
⓪	3	∞	②	∞	∞	$\{v_s\}$	$\{v_1, v_2, v_3, v_4, v_d\}$
	③	∞		6	∞	$\{v_s, v_3\}$	$\{v_1, v_2, v_4, v_d\}$
		9		6	∞	$\{v_s, v_1, v_3\}$	$\{v_2, v_4, v_d\}$

Go to step (2).

(2) $l_k = \min\limits_{v_j \in T} l_j = l_4 = 6; v_k = v_4$

l_s	l_1	l_2	l_3	l_4	l_d	P	T
⓪	3	∞	②	∞	∞	$\{v_s\}$	$\{v_1, v_2, v_3, v_4, v_d\}$
	③	∞		6	∞	$\{v_s, v_3\}$	$\{v_1, v_2, v_4, v_d\}$
		9		⑥	∞	$\{v_s, v_1, v_3\}$	$\{v_2, v_4, v_d\}$
						$\{v_s, v_1, v_3, v_4\}$	$\{v_2, v_d\}$

$T \neq \varnothing$, so continue.

(3) $l_2 \leftarrow \min\{l_2, l_4 + w_{42}\} = \min\{9, 6 + 1\} = 7$

$l_d \leftarrow \min\{l_d, l_4 + w_{4d}\} = \min\{\infty, 6 + 5\} = 11$

Hence:

l_s	l_1	l_2	l_3	l_4	l_d	P	T
⓪	3	∞	②	∞	∞	$\{v_s\}$	$\{v_1, v_2, v_3, v_4, v_d\}$
	③	∞		6	∞	$\{v_s, v_3\}$	$\{v_1, v_2, v_4, v_d\}$
		9		⑥	∞	$\{v_s, v_1, v_3\}$	$\{v_2, v_4, v_d\}$
		7			11	$\{v_s, v_1, v_3, v_4\}$	$\{v_2, v_d\}$

Go to step (2).

(2) $l_k = \min_{v_j \in T} l_j = l_2 = 7; v_k = v_2$

l_s	l_1	l_2	l_3	l_4	l_d	P	T
⓪	3	∞	②	∞	∞	$\{v_s\}$	$\{v_1, v_2, v_3, v_4, v_d\}$
	③	∞		6	∞	$\{v_s, v_3\}$	$\{v_1, v_2, v_4, v_d\}$
		9		⑥	∞	$\{v_s, v_1, v_3\}$	$\{v_2, v_4, v_d\}$
		⑦			11	$\{v_s, v_1, v_3, v_4\}$	$\{v_2, v_d\}$
						$\{v_s, v_1, v_2, v_3, v_4\}$	$\{v_d\}$

$T \neq \varnothing$, so continue.

(3) $l_d \leftarrow \min\{l_d, l_2 + w_{2d}\} = \min\{11, 7 + 3\} = 10$

Hence:

l_s	l_1	l_2	l_3	l_4	l_d	P	T
⓪	3	∞	②	∞	∞	$\{v_s\}$	$\{v_1, v_2, v_3, v_4, v_d\}$
	③	∞		6	∞	$\{v_s, v_3\}$	$\{v_1, v_2, v_4, v_d\}$
		9		⑥	∞	$\{v_s, v_1, v_3\}$	$\{v_2, v_4, v_d\}$
		⑦			11	$\{v_s, v_1, v_3, v_4\}$	$\{v_2, v_d\}$
					10	$\{v_s, v_1, v_2, v_3, v_4\}$	$\{v_d\}$

Go to step (2).

(2) $l_k = \min_{v_j \in T} l_j = l_d = 10; v_k = v_d$

l_s	l_1	l_2	l_3	l_4	l_d	P	T
⓪	3	∞	②	∞	∞	$\{v_s\}$	$\{v_1, v_2, v_3, v_4, v_d\}$
	③	∞		6	∞	$\{v_s, v_3\}$	$\{v_1, v_2, v_4, v_d\}$
		9		⑥	∞	$\{v_s, v_1, v_3\}$	$\{v_2, v_4, v_d\}$
		⑦			11	$\{v_s, v_1, v_3, v_4\}$	$\{v_2, v_d\}$
					⑩	$\{v_s, v_1, v_2, v_3, v_4\}$	$\{v_d\}$
						$\{v_s, v_1, v_2, v_3, v_4, v_d\}$	$\varnothing$

$T = \varnothing$; STOP.

The circled entry in each column above is the final label attached to each vertex. We reproduce the original network along with this labeling of the vertices:

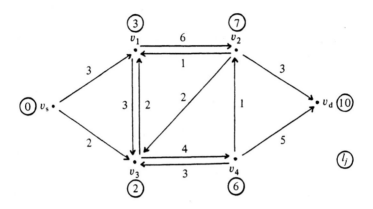

Hence, the value of the shortest path from v_s to v_d is $l_d = 10$. (Note that we also have the values of the shortest paths from v_s to all of the other vertices.) The actual shortest path is now obtained by working backward through the network from the destination to the derivation. Start at v_d. The vertex visited immediately before v_d in the shortest path must be v_2 or v_4. But the value of the shortest path from v_s to v_4 is $l_4 = 6$; if v_4 is the vertex visited before v_d in the shortest path, this would imply that the value of the shortest path from v_s to v_d is $6 + 5 = 11$ which is a contradiction. Hence v_2 is the vertex visited before v_d in the shortest path. (Note how the label $l_2 = 7$ and the weight $w_{2d} = 3$ are consistent with the label $l_d = 10$, i.e., $7 + 3 = 10$.) Now, the vertex visited immediately before v_2 in the shortest path must be v_1 or v_4. By considerations similar to those above, we find that v_4 is the desired vertex (the choice of v_4 leads to $6 + 1 = 7$ whereas the choice of v_1 leads to $3 + 6 = 9$ which is not consistent with $l_2 = 7$). The vertex visited immediately before v_4 in the shortest path must be v_3. Finally, the vertex visited immediately before v_3 must be v_s or v_1; we rule out v_1 (since $3 + 3 = 6$ is not consistent with $l_3 = 2$) and choose v_s. Hence the desired shortest path from v_s to v_d in the network above is

$$\{(v_s, v_3), (v_3, v_4), (v_4, v_2), (v_2, v_d)\}$$

or, more concisely,

$$v_s \rightarrow v_3 \rightarrow v_4 \rightarrow v_2 \rightarrow v_d.$$

The optimal solution would be recorded in the shortest-path network problem (8) as

$$x_{s3} = x_{34} = x_{42} = x_{2d} = 1, \quad \text{all other } x_{ij}\text{'s } 0,$$
$$\min d = 10.$$

The significance of the notations P and T for the sets in Dijkstra's algorithm may now be clear. At any stage of the algorithm, the vertices in P have (p)ermanent labels and the vertices in T have (t)emporary labels. Every time step (2) of the algorithm is encountered, one vertex is removed from T and placed in P, i.e., one vertex receives a permanent label. The labels on the remaining vertices in T are then revised in step (3) of the algorithm. The algorithm terminates when all vertices of the network have permanent labels, i.e., when $T = \varnothing$ (or, equivalently, $P = V$). P initially has the derivation only (since we know that the distance from the derivation to the derivation must be 0, i.e., $l_s = 0$).

The next example shows that Dijkstra's algorithm fails in general for networks containing negatively weighted edges.

EXAMPLE 20. Apply Dijkstra's algorithm to the shortest-path network problem below. Note, however, that the network has a negatively weighted edge and hence step (0) of the algorithm is violated.

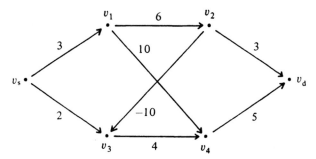

Dijkstra's algorithm (minus step (0)) yields the following (verify this!):

l_s	l_1	l_2	l_3	l_4	l_d	P	T
⓪	3	∞	②	∞	∞	$\{v_s\}$	$\{v_1, v_2, v_3, v_4, v_d\}$
	③	∞		6	∞	$\{v_s, v_3\}$	$\{v_1, v_2, v_4, v_d\}$
		9		⑥	∞	$\{v_s, v_1, v_3\}$	$\{v_2, v_4, v_d\}$
		⑨			11	$\{v_s, v_1, v_3, v_4\}$	$\{v_2, v_d\}$
					⑪	$\{v_s, v_1, v_2, v_3, v_4\}$	$\{v_d\}$
						$\{v_s, v_1, v_2, v_3, v_4, v_d\}$	$\varnothing$
							STOP

Hence the value of the shortest path from v_s to v_d in the network above according to Dijkstra's algorithm is $l_d = 11$. But the path $v_s \to v_1 \to v_2 \to v_3 \to v_4 \to v_d$ has value 8! (Which path in the network has value 11?)

Example 20 above illustrates quite vividly that Dijkstra's algorithm fails in general for networks containing negatively weighted edges. We now give an algorithm which will solve the general shortest-path network problem (8).

Shortest-Path Algorithm II

(0) Given: A weighted directed network $N = [V, E]$ with no edges into the derivation, no edges out of the destination, and such that no cycle in N has a net negative value.

   Note: In what follows, l_j is to be interpreted as a "label" given to the vertex $v_j \in V$.

(1) Put $l_s = 0$. Circle this 0. If $j \neq s$, put $l_j = w_{sj}$. (If w_{sj} does not exist, put $l_j = w_{sj} = \infty$.) Put $P = \{v_s\}$ and $T = V - P$.

(2) Compute

$$l_k = \min_{v_j \in T} l_j.$$

   Circle this minimum value. Put $P \leftarrow P \cup \{v_k\}$ and $T = V - P$. If $T = \emptyset$, STOP; the value of l_j is the value of the shortest path from v_s to v_j—in particular, the value of l_d is the desired value of the shortest path from v_s to v_d. Otherwise, continue.

(3) $\forall v_j \in V$, put $l_j \leftarrow \min \{l_j, l_k + w_{kj}\}$. (If w_{kj} does not exist, put $w_{kj} = \infty$.) For each l_j that changes during this process, put $P \leftarrow P - \{v_j\}$ and $T = V - P$. Go to (2).

   Note that the algorithm above differs from Dijkstra's algorithm only in step (3). In this step, *all* vertices of the network get revised labels. Furthermore, any time the label on a vertex v_j changes, it is removed from set P (if it is in P) and placed back in T. Hence, the set P loses some of its notational significance here—membership in P does not necessarily imply a permanent labeling since vertices in P may return to T. In fact, it is precisely this feature of the set P which makes the algorithm above more general than Dijkstra's algorithm. We now illustrate our new shortest-path algorithm with an example.

EXAMPLE 21. Apply shortest-path algorithm II to the shortest-path network problem of Example 20 below. (Recall that Dijkstra's algorithm failed for this problem.) Give both the value of the shortest path from the derivation to the destination and the shortest path itself.

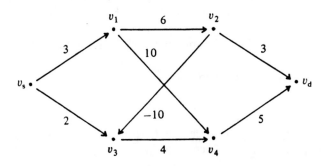

Working through the algorithm and recording information as in Example 20, we obtain

l_s	l_1	l_2	l_3	l_4	l_d	P	T
⓪	3	∞	②	∞	∞	$\{v_s\}$	$\{v_1, v_2, v_3, v_4, v_d\}$
① 0	③	∞	2	6	∞	$\{v_s, v_3\}$	$\{v_1, v_2, v_4, v_d\}$
0	3	9	2	⑥	∞	$\{v_s, v_1, v_3\}$	$\{v_2, v_4, v_d\}$
0	3	⑨	2	6	11	$\{v_s, v_1, v_3, v_4\}$	$\{v_2, v_d\}$
② 0	3	9	(−1)	6	11	$\{v_s, v_1, v_2, ⓥ_3, v_4\}$	$\{v_d\}$
0	3	9	−1	③	11	$\{v_s, v_1, v_2, v_3, ⓥ_4\}$	$\{v_d\}$
0	3	9	−1	3	⑧	$\{v_s, v_1, v_2, v_3, v_4\}$	$\{v_d\}$
						$\{v_s, v_1, v_2, v_3, v_4, v_d\}$	∅
							STOP

More detailed explanations of step (2) and step (3) of the algorithm applied to the lines marked ① and ② follow.

Line ①. (The parenthetical numbers below correspond to the steps of the algorithm.)

(2)
$$l_k = \min_{v_j \in T} l_j = l_1 = 3$$

and hence $v_k = v_1$. v_1 is added to P and removed from T (see the line following line ①). $T \neq \varnothing$ so continue.

(3) $l_s \leftarrow \min\{l_s, l_1 + w_{1s}\} = \min\{0, 3 + \infty\} = 0$

$l_1 \leftarrow \min\{l_1, l_1 + w_{11}\} = \min\{3, 3 + \infty\} = 3$

$l_2 \leftarrow \min\{l_2, l_1 + w_{12}\} = \min\{\infty, 3 + 6\} = 9$

$l_3 \leftarrow \min\{l_3, l_1 + w_{13}\} = \min\{2, 3 + \infty\} = 2$

$l_4 \leftarrow \min\{l_4, l_1 + w_{14}\} = \min\{6, 3 + 10\} = 6$

$l_d \leftarrow \min\{l_d, l_1 + w_{1d}\} = \min\{\infty, 3 + \infty\} = \infty$

(See the line following line ①.)
The only label that has changed during this process is l_2 (from ∞ to 9); hence v_2 is removed from P and placed in T. Since v_2 is not in P (and hence is already in T), this effects no change in P or T.

Line ②. (The parenthetical numbers below correspond to the steps of the algorithm.)

(2) Notice that $T = \{v_3, v_d\}$ here.

$$l_k = \min_{v_j \in T} l_j = l_3 = -1$$

and hence $v_k = v_3$. v_3 is added to P and removed from T (see the line following line ②). $T \neq \varnothing$ so continue.

(3) $l_s \leftarrow \min \{l_s, l_3 + w_{3s}\} = \min \{0, -1 + \infty\} = 0$

$\quad l_1 \leftarrow \min \{l_1, l_3 + w_{31}\} = \min \{3, -1 + \infty\} = 3$

$\quad l_2 \leftarrow \min \{l_2, l_3 + w_{32}\} = \min \{9, -1 + \infty\} = 9$

$\quad l_3 \leftarrow \min \{l_3, l_3 + w_{33}\} = \min \{-1, -1 + \infty\} = -1$

$\quad l_4 \leftarrow \min \{l_4, l_3 + w_{34}\} = \min \{6, -1 + 4\} = 3$

$\quad l_d \leftarrow \min \{l_d, l_3 + w_{3d}\} = \min \{11, -1 + \infty\} = 11$

(See the line following line ②.)

The only label that has changed during this process is l_4 (from 6 to 3); hence v_4 is removed from P and placed in T.

The last circled entry in each column of the chart above (or simply the last row of the chart above) is the final label attached to each vertex. Hence the value of the shortest path from v_s to v_d is $l_d = 8$ (not 11 as in Example 20!). By working backward through the network from the destination to the derivation, it is easy to verify that the actual shortest path is (concisely)

$$v_s \rightarrow v_1 \rightarrow v_2 \rightarrow v_3 \rightarrow v_4 \rightarrow v_d.$$

The optimal solution would be recorded in the shortest-path network problem (8) as

$$x_{s1} = x_{12} = x_{23} = x_{34} = x_{4d} = 1, \quad \text{all other } x_{ij}\text{'s } 0,$$

$$\min d = 8.$$

EXAMPLE 22. Solve the shortest-path network problem below. Give both the value of the shortest path from the derivation to the destination and the shortest path itself.

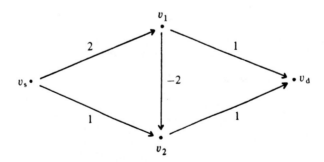

Since the given network contains a negatively weighted edge, we use shortest-path algorithm II. (The reader may wish to verify that Dijkstra's algorithm fails for this problem.) Working through the algorithm and recording information as in Example 20, we obtain

l_s	l_1	l_2	l_d	P	T
⓪	2	①	∞	$\{v_s\}$	$\{v_1, v_2, v_d\}$
0	②	1	2	$\{v_s, v_2\}$	$\{v_1, v_d\}$
0	2	⓪	2	$\{v_s, v_1, ⓥ_2\}$	$\{v_d\}$
0	2	0	①	$\{v_s, v_1, v_2\}$	$\{v_d\}$
				$\{v_s, v_1, v_2, v_d\}$	$\varnothing$
					STOP

Hence the value of the shortest path from v_s to v_d is $l_d = 1$. By working backward through the network from the destination to the derivation, it is easy to verify that the actual shortest path is (concisely)

$$v_s \to v_1 \to v_2 \to v_d.$$

The optimal solution would be recorded in the shortest-path network problem (8) as

$$x_{s1} = x_{12} = x_{2d} = 1, \text{ all other } x_{ij}\text{'s } 0,$$
$$\min d = 1.$$

One final remark is in order here. Both of the shortest-path algorithms in this section will terminate with a vertex label of ∞ if there is no path through a given network from the derivation to that vertex. Such behavior is demonstrated in Exercise 12. Consequently, the detection of an infeasible shortest-path network problem is built into both algorithms.

§5. The Minimal-Cost-Flow Network Problem

Definition 23. Let $N = [V, E]$ be a capacitated directed network with unique fixed source and unique fixed sink, no edges into the source, and no edges out of the sink. Assume that to each edge $(v_i, v_j) \in E$, there also corresponds a real number c'_{ij} to be interpreted as a cost. The *minimal-cost-flow network problem* is

$$\text{Minimize} \quad C = \sum_{(v_i, v_j) \in E} c'_{ij} x_{ij}$$

$$\text{subject to} \quad \sum_i x_{id} = F \geq 0$$

$$\sum_i x_{ij} - \sum_i x_{ji} = 0, \ \forall v_j \in V, j \neq s, d \tag{9}$$

$$0 \leq x_{ij} \leq c_{ij}, \forall i, j.$$

F is a given specified flow value.

The three constraints of (9) above say that we are interested in finding a flow of specified value F in a given capacitated directed network. But each edge of the network is also associated with a cost c'_{ij}—the goal is to produce a flow of value F having minimal total cost. Notice immediately that the minimal-cost-flow network problem may be infeasible. For example, if the flow value F exceeds the maximal flow through the network (in the sense of (1)), then there is no way to achieve such a flow much less minimize the associated cost. If F is less than or equal to the maximal flow value of the network, then the minimal-cost-flow network problem is not infeasible. In either case, the minimal-cost-flow network problem is never unbounded. The observant reader will notice something more. Compare the minimal-cost-flow network problem (9) with the shortest-path network problem (8). If we put $F = 1$ and $c_{ij} = 1$ for all i and j in (9), and if we interpret the network of (9) as a weighted directed network by using the costs c'_{ij} as weights, then (9) becomes (8). In other words, (8) is a special case of (9). (In fact, the transportation and assignment problems of Chapter 6 can be reformulated as minimal-cost-flow network problems—this connection will be studied in §6 of this chapter.) There is a good reason why we developed algorithms for the shortest-path network problem separately rather than consider the shortest-path network problem as a special case of the minimal-cost-flow network problem. In the course of the minimal-cost-flow algorithm, we will need to use a shortest-path algorithm—inasmuch as we have developed shortest-path algorithms distinctly from the minimal-cost-flow algorithm, we can use these shortest-path algorithms in the minimal-cost-flow algorithm without fear of self-reference. (Such algorithmic self-reference, termed *recursion*, is sometimes advantageous; recursive algorithms occur frequently in mathematics and are crucial in many areas of computer science.)

We now give the minimal-cost-flow algorithm. A further discussion of this algorithm may be found in [B4]. As with all of the other network-flow problems of this chapter, the minimal-cost-flow network problem (9) is solvable using the techniques of Chapters 2–4 but such an approach is ill-advised.

The Minimal-Cost-Flow Algorithm

(0) Given: A capacitated directed network $N = [V, E]$ with unique fixed source and unique fixed sink, no edges into the source, no edges out of the sink, and such that to each edge $(v_i, v_j) \in E$, there corresponds a real number c'_{ij} (in addition to the capacity c_{ij}).

(1) Let $x_{ij} = 0$ for all i and j.

(2) If
$$\varphi(v_d) = \sum_i x_{id} = F,$$

STOP; the current flow is optimal. Otherwise, continue.

(3) Form the weighted directed network $N_{\varphi(v_d)} = [V, E_{\varphi(v_d)}]$ as follows:

(i) $(v_i, v_j) \in E_{\varphi(v_d)}$ if and only if $x_{ij} < c_{ij}$; put $w_{ij} = c'_{ij}$

(ii) $(v_j, v_i) \in E_{\varphi(v_d)}$ if and only if $x_{ij} > 0$; put $w_{ji} = -c'_{ij}$.

(4) Apply a shortest-path algorithm to the network $N_{\varphi(v_d)}$ to find a shortest path from v_s to v_d. If there is no path from v_s to v_d in the network, STOP; there is no flow of value F in the network and the minimal-cost-flow network problem is infeasible. Otherwise, continue.

(5) Find the α-path P in N corresponding to the shortest path of (4). Compute

$$q = \min \left\{ \min_{\substack{(v_i, v_j) \\ \text{a fwd.} \\ \text{edge} \\ \text{of } P}} \{c_{ij} - x_{ij}\}, \min_{\substack{(v_i, v_j) \\ \text{a bwd.} \\ \text{edge} \\ \text{of } P}} x_{ji}, F - \varphi(v_d) \right\}.$$

Add q to the flow numbers on all forward edges of P in N and subtract q from the flow numbers on all backward edges of P in N. Go to (2).

Note that the minimal-cost-flow algorithm is a combination of the maximal-flow algorithm of §3 and the shortest-path algorithms of §4. The basic idea of the algorithm is easy. Step (4) applies a shortest-path algorithm to an augmented network which essentially has costs as weights. Hence the shortest path corresponds to a minimal cost path. Then step (5) determines the maximal amount of flow (q) that can be accommodated along this minimal cost path and increases the flow along the path accordingly. Such a procedure is repeated until the desired flow F is attained or the algorithm detects infeasibility. We stress that this is a simplified view of the minimal-cost-flow algorithm and that a more detailed analysis appears in [B4]. We now illustrate the algorithm with two examples.

EXAMPLE 24. Solve the minimal-cost-flow network problem below with $F = 12$. Here, the ordered pair associated to each edge is to be interpreted as (c_{ij}, c'_{ij}), i.e., the first component is the capacity of the edge and the second component is the cost of the edge.

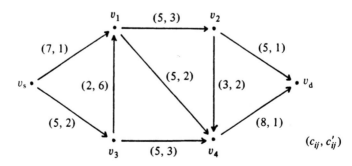

The parenthetical numbers below correspond to the steps of the minimal-cost-flow algorithm. All shortest-path algorithm implementations (in step (4) of the minimal-cost-flow algorithm) are omitted for the sake of brevity. In each occurrence of step (4), the reader should verify the resultant shortest path with a *careful* inspection of the associated network.

(0) The given minimal-cost-flow network problem is of the desired form.

(1)

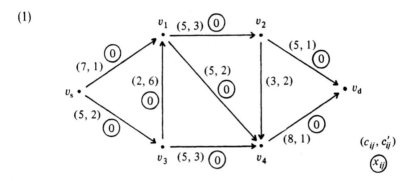

(2) $\varphi(v_d) = 0 \neq 12 = F$ so continue.
(3) $N_{\varphi(v_d)} = N_0$:

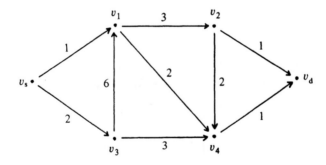

Every x_{ij} satisfies (i); no x_{ij} satisfies (ii).
(4) The shortest path in N_0 above is (concisely) $v_s \to v_1 \to v_4 \to v_d$.
(5) The α-path P in N corresponding to the shortest path in N_0 above consists of only forward edges. Hence

$$q = \min \left\{ \min_{\substack{(v_i, v_j) \\ \text{a fwd.} \\ \text{edge} \\ \text{of } P}} \{c_{ij} - x_{ij}\}, F - \varphi(v_d) \right\}$$

$$= \min \{\min \{7 - 0, 5 - 0, 8 - 0\}, 12 - 0\}$$
$$= 5.$$

Hence 5 is added to the flow numbers on all edges of the α-path $v_s \to v_1 \to v_4 \to v_d$ in N:

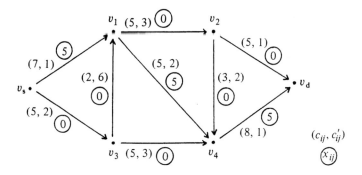

Go to step (2).
(2) $\varphi(v_d) = 5 \neq 12 = F$ so continue.
(3) $N_{\varphi(v_d)} = N_5$:

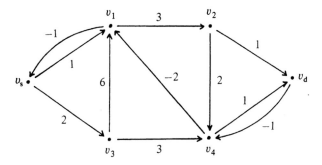

Every x_{ij} except x_{14} satisfies (i); only x_{s1}, x_{14}, and x_{4d} satisfy (ii).
(4) The shortest path in N_5 above is (concisely) $v_s \to v_1 \to v_2 \to v_d$.
(5) The α-path P in N corresponding to the shortest path in N_5 above consists of only forward edges. Hence

$$q = \min \left\{ \min_{\substack{(v_i, v_j) \\ \text{a fwd.} \\ \text{edge} \\ \text{of } P}} \{c_{ij} - x_{ij}\}, F - \varphi(v_d) \right\}$$

$$= \min \{\min \{7 - 5, 5 - 0, 5 - 0\}, 12 - 5\}$$

$$= 2.$$

Hence 2 is added to the flow numbers on all edges of the α-path $v_s \to v_1 \to v_2 \to v_d$ in N:

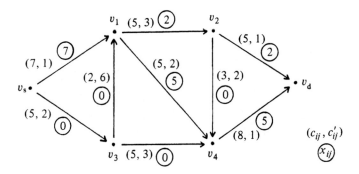

Go to step (2).

(2) $\varphi(v_d) = 7 \neq 12 = F$ so continue.

(3) $N_{\varphi(v_d)} = N_7$:

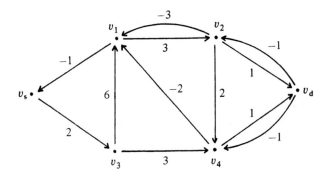

Every x_{ij} except x_{s1} and x_{14} satisfies (i); every x_{ij} except x_{s3}, x_{24}, x_{31}, and x_{34} satisfies (ii).

(4) The shortest path in N_7 above is (concisely) $v_s \to v_3 \to v_4 \to v_d$.

(5) The α-path P in N corresponding to the shortest path in N_7 above consists of only forward edges. Hence

$$q = \min \left\{ \begin{array}{l} \min_{\substack{(v_i, v_j) \\ \text{a fwd.} \\ \text{edge} \\ \text{of } P}} \{c_{ij} - x_{ij}\}, F - \varphi(v_d) \end{array} \right\}$$

$$= \min \{\min \{5 - 0, 5 - 0, 8 - 5\}, 12 - 7\}$$

$$= 3.$$

Hence 3 is added to the flow numbers on all edges of the α-path $v_s \to v_3 \to v_4 \to v_d$ in N:

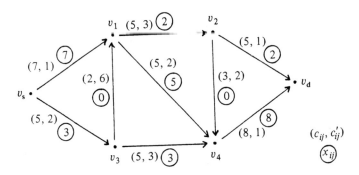

Go to step (2).
(2) $\varphi(v_d) = 10 \neq 12 = F$ so continue.
(3) $N_{\varphi(v_d)} = N_{10}$:

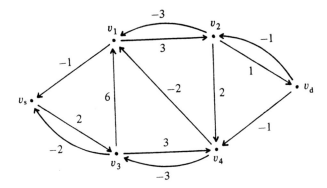

Every x_{ij} except x_{s1}, x_{14}, and x_{4d} satisfies (i); every x_{ij} except x_{24} and x_{31} satisfies (ii).
(4) The shortest path in N_{10} above is (concisely) $v_s \rightarrow v_3 \rightarrow v_4 \rightarrow v_1 \rightarrow v_2 \rightarrow v_d$.
(5) The α-path P in N corresponding to the shortest path in N_{10} above consists of forward edges and one backward edge $((v_4, v_1))$. Hence

$$q = \min \left\{ \min_{\substack{(v_i, v_j) \\ \text{a fwd.} \\ \text{edge} \\ \text{of } P}} \{c_{ij} - x_{ij}\}, \min_{\substack{(v_i, v_j) \\ \text{a bwd.} \\ \text{edge} \\ \text{of } P}} x_{ji}, F - \varphi(v_d) \right\}$$

$$= \min \{\min \{5 - 3, 5 - 3, 5 - 2, 5 - 2\}, \min \{5\}, 12 - 10\}$$

$$= 2.$$

Hence 2 is added to the flow numbers on all forward edges of the α-path $v_s \rightarrow v_3 \rightarrow v_4 \rightarrow v_1 \rightarrow v_2 \rightarrow v_d$ in N and subtracted from the flow number on the backward edge (v_4, v_1) of this α-path:

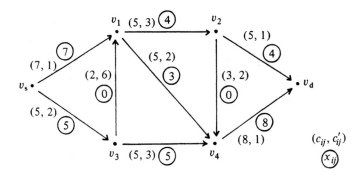

Go to step (2).

(2) $\varphi(v_d) = 12 = F$ so we STOP; the current flow is optimal. Hence

$$\min C = \sum_{(v_i,v_j)\in E} c'_{ij}x_{ij}$$

$$= c'_{s1}x_{s1} + c'_{s3}x_{s3} + c'_{12}x_{12} + c'_{14}x_{14} + c'_{24}x_{24}$$
$$+ c'_{2d}x_{2d} + c'_{31}x_{31} + c'_{34}x_{34} + c'_{4d}x_{4d}$$
$$= 1(7) + 2(5) + 3(4) + 2(3) + 2(0)$$
$$+ 1(4) + 6(0) + 3(5) + 1(8)$$
$$= 62;$$

the optimal x_{ij}'s appear on the final network above. Note that any flow of value 12 is a maximal flow in the network above since the capacities on the edges out of the source total 12; these edges are saturated (i.e., the flow numbers on these edges are equal to the edge capacities) in the minimal cost maximal flow above. Is there another maximal flow in the network above with total cost greater than 62?

EXAMPLE 25. Solve the minimal-cost-flow network problem below with $F = 9$. Here, the ordered pair associated to each edge is to be interpreted as (c_{ij}, c'_{ij}), i.e., the first component is the capacity of the edge and the second component is the cost of the edge.

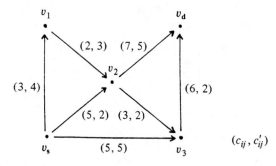

The parenthetical numbers below correspond to the steps of the minimal-cost-flow algorithm. All shortest path algorithm implementations (in step (4) of the minimal-cost-flow algorithm) are omitted for the sake of brevity. In each occurrence of step (4), the reader should verify the resultant shortest path with a *careful* inspection of the associated network.

(0) The given minimal-cost-flow network problem is of the desired form.

(1)

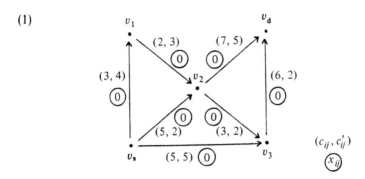

(2) $\varphi(v_d) = 0 \neq 9 = F$ so continue.
(3) $N_{\varphi(v_d)} = N_0$:

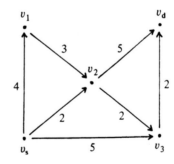

Every x_{ij} satisfies (i); no x_{ij} satisfies (ii).
(4) The shortest path in N_0 above is (concisely) $v_s \to v_2 \to v_3 \to v_d$.
(5) The α-path P in N corresponding to the shortest path in N_0 above consists of only forward edges. Hence

$$q = \min \left(\min_{\substack{(v_i, v_j) \\ \text{a fwd.} \\ \text{edge} \\ \text{of } P}} \{c_{ij} - x_{ij}\}, F - \varphi(v_d) \right)$$

$$= \min \{\min \{5 - 0, 3 - 0, 6 - 0\}, 9 - 0\}$$

$$= 3.$$

Hence 3 is added to the flow numbers on all edges of the α-path $v_s \to v_2 \to v_3 \to v_d$ in N:

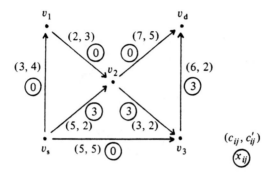

Go to step (2).

(2) $\varphi(v_d) = 3 \neq 9 = F$ so continue.

(3) $N_{\varphi(v_d)} = N_3$:

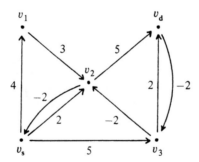

Every x_{ij} except x_{23} satisfies (i); only x_{s2}, x_{23}, and x_{3d} satisfy (ii).

(4) The shortest path in N_3 above is (concisely) $v_s \to v_2 \to v_d$ or $v_s \to v_3 \to v_d$. For definiteness, we choose $v_s \to v_2 \to v_d$.

(5) The α-path P in N corresponding to the shortest path in N_3 above consists of only forward edges. Hence

$$q = \min \left\{ \min_{\substack{(v_i, v_j) \\ \text{a fwd.} \\ \text{edge} \\ \text{of } P}} \{c_{ij} - x_{ij}\}, F - \varphi(v_d) \right\}$$

$$= \min \{\min \{5 - 3, 7 - 0\}, 9 - 3\}$$

$$= 2.$$

Hence 2 is added to the flow numbers on all edges of the α-path $v_s \to v_2 \to v_d$ in N:

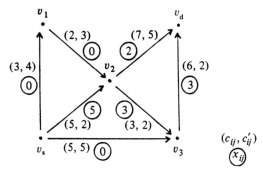

Go to step (2).

(2) $\varphi(v_d) = 5 \neq 9 = F$ so continue.

(3) $N_{\varphi(v_d)} = N_5$:

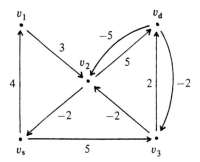

Every x_{ij} except x_{s2} and x_{23} satisfies (i); every x_{ij} except x_{s1}, x_{s3}, and x_{12} satisfies (ii).

(4) The shortest path in N_5 above is (concisely) $v_s \to v_3 \to v_d$.

(5) The α-path P in N corresponding to the shortest path in N_5 above consists of only forward edges. Hence

$$q = \min \left\{ \min_{\substack{(v_i, v_j) \\ \text{a fwd.} \\ \text{edge} \\ \text{of } P}} \{c_{ij} - x_{ij}\}, F - \varphi(v_d) \right\}$$

$$= \min \{\min \{5 - 0, 6 - 3\}, 9 - 5\}$$

$$= 3.$$

Hence 3 is added to the flow numbers on all edges of the α-path $v_s \to v_3 \to v_d$ in N:

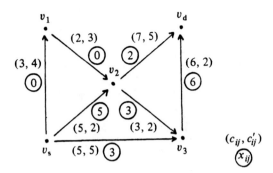

Go to step (2).

(2) $\varphi(v_\mathrm{d}) = 8 \neq 9 = F$ so continue.

(3) $N_{\varphi(v_\mathrm{d})} = N_8$:

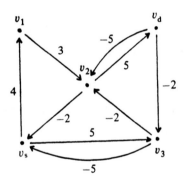

Every x_{ij} except x_{s2}, x_{23}, and x_{3d} satisfies (i); every x_{ij} except x_{s1} and x_{12} satisfies (ii).

(4) The shortest path in N_8 above is (concisely) $v_\mathrm{s} \to v_3 \to v_2 \to v_\mathrm{d}$.

(5) The α-path P in N corresponding to the shortest path in N_8 above consists of forward edges and one backward edge $((v_3, v_2))$. Hence

$$q = \min \left\{ \begin{array}{ll} \min\limits_{\substack{(v_i, v_j) \\ \text{a fwd.} \\ \text{edge} \\ \text{of } P}} \{c_{ij} - x_{ij}\}, & \min\limits_{\substack{(v_i, v_j) \\ \text{a bwd.} \\ \text{edge} \\ \text{of } P}} x_{ji}, \quad F - \varphi(v_\mathrm{d}) \end{array} \right\}$$

$$= \min \{\min \{5 - 3, 7 - 2\}, \min \{3\}, 9 - 8\}$$

$$= 1.$$

Hence 1 is added to the flow numbers on all forward edges of the α-path $v_\mathrm{s} \to v_3 \to v_2 \to v_\mathrm{d}$ in N and subtracted from the flow number on the backward edge (v_3, v_2) of this α-path:

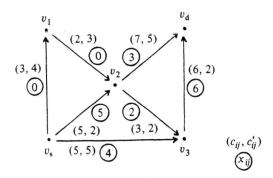

Go to step (2).

(2) $\varphi(v_d) = 9 = F$ so we STOP; the current flow is optimal. Hence

$$\min C = \sum_{(v_i, v_j) \in E} c'_{ij} x_{ij}$$

$$= c'_{s1} x_{s1} + c'_{s2} x_{s2} + c'_{s3} x_{s3} + c'_{12} x_{12} + c'_{23} x_{23} + c'_{2d} x_{2d} + c'_{3d} x_{3d}$$

$$= 4(0) + 2(5) + 5(4) + 3(0) + 2(2) + 5(3) + 2(6)$$

$$= 61;$$

the optimal x_{ij}'s appear on the final network above. Is the flow of value 9 constructed above a maximal flow in the network? Why or why not?

§6. Transportation and Assignment Problems Revisited

The transportation and assignment problems of Chapter 6 can be reformulated as minimal-cost-flow network problems. We illustrate this reformulation with an example. The reformulation of transportation and assignment problems is investigated further in Exercise 17 and Exercise 18.

EXAMPLE 26. Reformulate the (balanced) transportation problem below as a minimal-cost-flow network problem.

	M_1	M_2	M_3	
W_1	2	1	2	40
W_2	9	4	7	60
W_3	1	2	9	10
	40	50	20	

Each warehouse and each market is represented by a vertex; directed edges connect each warehouse vertex with each market vertex. Each such edge is associated with an ordered pair of real numbers. The first component of this pair is the corresponding warehouse supply; the second component of this pair is the unit shipping cost from the corresponding warehouse to the corresponding market. All of this is illustrated below:

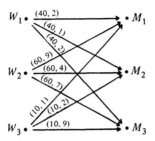

Now, to make this network into a minimal-cost-flow network problem, we need (i) a unique fixed source and a unique fixed sink with no edges into the source and no edges out of the sink and (ii) a specified flow value F. (i) is achieved by using the augmentation procedure discussed in §1. Vertices representing the unique source and the unique sink are added to the network. Then edges from the desired unique source to each of the warehouses vertices (the current "sources") and edges from each of the markets (the current "sinks") to the desired unique sink are added to the network. This augmentation is illustrated below:

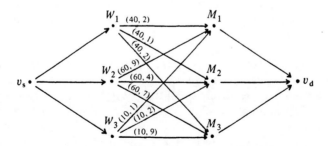

What ordered pairs of real numbers should be associated with these added edges? The second component of each pair is easy—each added edge is assumed to have zero cost. Now we examine the first components. Consider the edge (v_s, W_1). Since the first warehouse has a supply of 40, the sum of the flows on the three edges out of W_1 must be at most 40 (in fact, it must be *exactly* 40; this will be handled in a moment). Since W_1 is an intermediate vertex, the flow number on the edge into W_1 must be at most 40. Hence, the first component on the edge (v_s, W_1) is 40. Similarly, the first components on the edges (v_s, W_2) and (v_s, W_3) are 60 and 10 respectively. Consider the edge (M_1, v_d). Since the first market has a demand of 40, the sum of the flow numbers on the three edges into M_1 must be at most 40 (in fact, it must be *exactly* 40; this will be handled in a moment). Since M_1 is an intermediate vertex, the flow number on the edge out of M_1 must be at most 40. Hence, the first component on the edge (M_1, v_d) is 40. Similarly, the first components on the edges (M_2, v_d) and (M_3, v_d) are 50 and 20 respectively. Hence we have

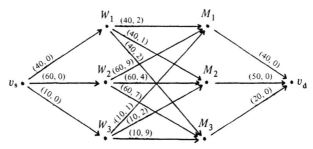

As noted parenthetically above, however, each warehouse must ship all of its current supply to exactly meet the current demand of each market since the transportation problem is balanced. We force this full shipment of current supplies by specifying a flow value of $F = 110$ which is the common value of the current supplies and demands. This value of F will guarantee that the edges out of the source are saturated (i.e., the flow numbers on these edges are equal to the edge capacities) and hence that each warehouse ships all of its current supply (since W_1, W_2, and W_3 are intermediate vertices). Similarly, this value of F will also guarantee that the edges into the sink are saturated and hence that each market receives all of its current demand. This achieves (ii) and concludes the reformulation of the given transportation problem as a minimal-cost-flow network problem.

   It is not suggested that one use the minimal-cost-flow algorithm to solve transportation and assignment problems. The complicated nature of the networks arising from relatively small transportation and assignment problems makes the minimal-cost-flow algorithm prohibitively cumbersome to use (see Exercise 17). The intent of this section is only to show the interrelationships existing between these seemingly different types of linear programming problems.

§7. Concluding Remarks

In this chapter, we have seen how the mathematical field of graph theory allows for the formulation of more direct algorithms to solve three linear programming problems, namely the maximal-flow network problem, the shortest-path network problem, and the minimal-cost-flow network problem. It should be stressed that these network problems do not form an exhaustive list of the graph-theoretic problems in linear programming. One notable omission, for example, is the longest-path network problem which is extremely useful in many applications. The algorithms commonly referred to as CPM (critical-path method) and PERT (program evaluation and review technique) arise in this domain. More complete discussions of CPM, PERT, and other network-related algorithms in linear programming may be found in [G1] and [B4].

EXERCISES

1. Consider the capacitated directed network $N = [V, E]$ and flow below:

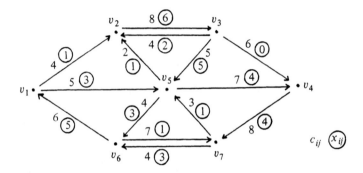

a. For each vertex $v_j \in V$, compute $\varphi(v_j)$. Verify that conservation of flow in N holds.

b. Classify each vertex $v_j \in V$ as a source, a sink, or an intermediate vertex.

c. Augment the structure of the network above to produce an equivalent flow having a unique source, a unique sink, no edges into the source, and no edges out of the sink.

2. Construct a capacitated directed network and flow having a unique source and a unique sink, but with at least one edge into the source and at least one edge out of the sink.

3. Solve each of the maximal-flow network problems below. Display each corresponding minimal cut and cut-set as constructed in the proof of the max-flow min-cut theorem.

a.

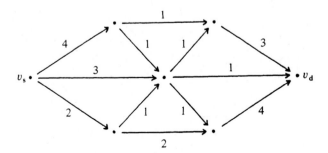

b.

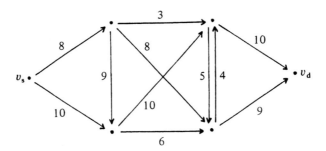

c.

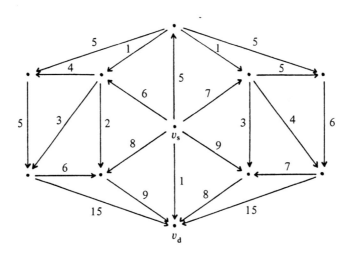

d.

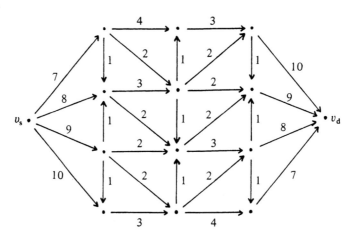

4. a. Solve the maximal-flow network problem of Example 14 with a succession of four α-paths, each using no backward edges. Display the corresponding minimal cut and cut-set as constructed in the proof of the max-flow min-cut theorem.

   b. Does there exist a succession of three α-paths that solves the maximal-flow network problem of Example 14? If so, find such a succession.

5. Consider the maximal-flow network problem below:

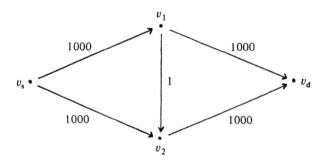

   a. What is the least number of α-paths that solves the problem? Find such a succession of α-paths.

   b. What is the greatest number of α-paths that solves the problem? Describe such a succession of α-paths.

6. Consider the Tucker tableau of Example 7. Along the west side of the tableau, put the variables (in order) $(\mu_1), (\mu_2), (\mu_3), (\mu_4)$, $y_{s1}, y_{s3}, y_{12}, y_{14}, y_{24}, y_{31}, y_{32}, y_{34}, y_{2d}$, and y_{4d}. Along the south side of the tableau, put the equal signs and variables (in order) $= u_{s1}, = u_{s3}, = u_{12}, = u_{14}, = u_{24}, u_{31}, = u_{32}, = u_{34}, = _{2d}$, and $= u_{4d}$. Show that the minimization linear programming problem so constructed takes the form of (2).

7. Let $N = [V, E]$ be a capacitated directed network with unique fixed source and unique fixed sink, no edges into the source, and no edges out of the sink. To each vertex $v_j \in V$, assign a number μ_j equal to 0 or -1. To each edge $(v_i, v_j) \in E$, assign a number y_{ij} defined by $y_{ij} = \max\{0, \mu_i - \mu_j\}$. (See the discussion immediately preceding Example 10.)

   a. Prove that $-\mu_i + \mu_j + y_{ij} \geq 0$ for all i and j.
   b. Prove that y_{ij} is equal to 0 or 1 for all i and j.
   c. Prove that at least one *optimal* solution of (3) takes the form described above. [Hint: Use the max-flow min-cut theorem.]

8. Let $N = [V, E]$ be a capacitated directed network with unique fixed source and unique fixed sink, no edges into the source, and no edges out of the sink.

   a. Prove that the flow numbers corresponding to the maximal flow in N are not necessarily unique.
   b. Let f be the maximal flow value in N corresponding to two distinct sets of flow numbers, say x_{ij} and x'_{ij}, in accordance with part a. Let $C = (V_1, V_2)$ be the minimal cut constructed in the proof of the max-flow min-cut theorem using the

flow numbers x_{ij} and let $C' = (V'_1, V'_2)$ be the minimal cut constructed in the proof of the max-flow min-cut theorem using the flow numbers x'_{ij}. Prove that $V_1 = V'_1$ and $V_2 = V'_2$.

9. Solve each of the shortest-path network problems below by using one of the shortest-path algorithms of this chapter. Use the final labels on the vertices to construct the actual shortest path(s) in the network from the derivation to the destination by working backward through the network from the destination to the derivation.

a.

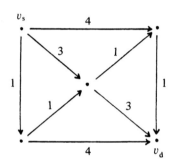

b.

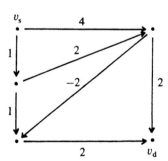

c.

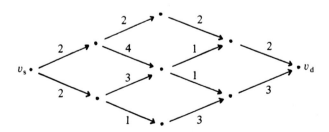

d.

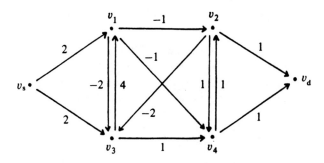

e.

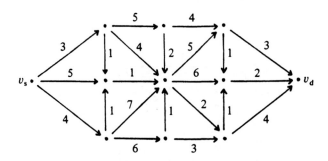

10. Change the weight on the edge (v_3, v_4) in Exercise 9d above from 1 to -1. The resulting problem is *not* a shortest-path network problem according to our definition. Why?

11. Prove that the restriction that there be no edges out of the destination in a shortest-path network problem (see Definition 18) is without loss of generality.

12. Consider the shortest-path network problem below:

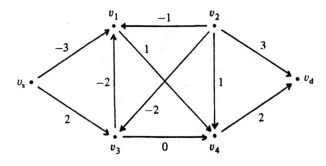

a. What will the final label on v_2 be after application of shortest-path algorithm II to the network? Why?

b. Verify your claim of part a by applying shortest-path algorithm II to the network.

13. Label each of the following statements TRUE or FALSE. If the statement is FALSE, provide a counterexample.

a. Dijkstra's algorithm fails for any shortest-path network problem in which at least one of the edges of the network is negatively weighted.

b. Let $N = [V, E]$ be a weighted directed network such that every weight is nonnegative and let $v_1, v_2, v_3 \in V$. Then the value of the shortest path from v_1 to v_3 is the sum of the values of the shortest paths from v_1 to v_2 and from v_2 to v_3.

14. Solve each of the minimal-cost-flow network problems below with $F = 8$ and $F = 10$. In each network problem, the ordered pair associated to each edge is to be interpreted as (c_{ij}, c'_{ij}), i.e., the first component is the capacity of the edge and the second component is the cost of the edge.

a.

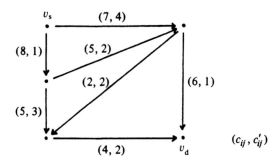

b.

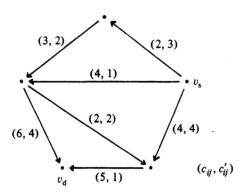

c.

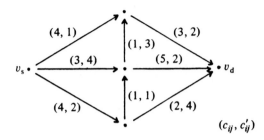

(c_{ij}, c'_{ij})

15. Find a maximal flow in the network of Example 24 that is *not* of minimal cost.

16. Find a maximal flow of minimum cost in the network of Example 25.

17. Consider the transportation problem below:

	M_1	M_2	
W_1	1	2	1
W_2	3	4	4
	2	3	

    a. Solve the problem by using the transportation algorithm.

    b. Reformulate the problem as a minimal-cost-flow network problem and solve the problem by using the minimal-cost-flow algorithm.

    c. Which algorithm is preferable here?

18. Reformulate the transportation problem below as a minimal-cost-flow network problem. Do *not* solve the network problem.

	M_1	M_2	
W_1	1	2	1
W_2	3	4	2
	3	4	

[Hint: Note that the transportation problem is unbalanced. What is a natural first step?]

Matrix Algebra

§0. Introduction

In this appendix, we summarize the elementary theory of matrices necessary for a complete understanding of Part I. This summary is intended to be rather concise; more detailed discussions of the topics here may be found in any elementary linear algebra book.

§1. Matrices

Definition 1. A rectangular array of real numbers of the form

$$\begin{bmatrix} a_{11} & a_{12} & \cdots & a_{1n} \\ a_{21} & a_{22} & \cdots & a_{2n} \\ \vdots & \vdots & & \vdots \\ a_{m1} & a_{m2} & \cdots & a_{mn} \end{bmatrix},$$

denoted $[a_{ij}]_{m \times n}$, is said to be an $m \times n$ *matrix*.

Note that an $m \times n$ matrix has m rows and n columns. The entry a_{ij} is in the ith row and the jth column of the matrix.

Definition 2. Two matrices **A** and **B** are said to be *equal*, denoted $\mathbf{A} = \mathbf{B}$, if **A** and **B** have the same size and corresponding entries are equal.

§2. Matrix Operations

Definition 3. Let $A = [a_{ij}]_{m \times n}$ and $B = [b_{ij}]_{m \times n}$. The *sum* of A and B, denoted $A + B$, is the matrix $[c_{ij}]_{m \times n}$ where $c_{ij} = a_{ij} + b_{ij}$ for all i and j.

Note that the sum of two matrices is defined if and only if the matrices have the same size.

EXAMPLE 4.

$$\begin{bmatrix} -1 & 0 & 2 \\ 3 & -2 & 1 \end{bmatrix} + \begin{bmatrix} 3 & 1 & -2 \\ 2 & -1 & 0 \end{bmatrix} = \begin{bmatrix} -1+3 & 0+1 & 2+(-2) \\ 3+2 & -2-1 & 1+0 \end{bmatrix}$$
$$= \begin{bmatrix} 2 & 1 & 0 \\ 5 & -3 & 1 \end{bmatrix}.$$

Definition 5. Let $A = [a_{ij}]_{m \times n}$ and let c be a real number. The *product* of c and A, denoted cA, is the matrix $[c_{ij}]_{m \times n}$ where $c_{ij} = ca_{ij}$ for all i and j.

EXAMPLE 6.

$$(-2)\begin{bmatrix} -1 & 0 & 2 \\ 3 & -2 & 1 \end{bmatrix} = \begin{bmatrix} (-2)(-1) & (-2)(0) & (-2)(2) \\ (-2)(3) & (-2)(-2) & (-2)(1) \end{bmatrix}$$
$$= \begin{bmatrix} 2 & 0 & -4 \\ -6 & 4 & -2 \end{bmatrix}.$$

It is customary to denote $(-1)A$ by $-A$ and to denote $A + (-B)$ by $A - B$.

Definition 7. $A = [a_{ij}]_{m \times n}$ is said to be the $m \times n$ *zero matrix*, denoted $0_{m \times n}$ (or 0 if the size is understood), if $a_{ij} = 0$ for all i and j.

Theorem 8. *Let* A, B, *and* C *be* $m \times n$ *matrices and let* c *and* d *be real numbers.*
  (i) $A + B = B + A$
  (ii) $(A + B) + C = A + (B + C)$
  (iii) $c(A + B) = cA + cB$
  (iv) $(c + d)A = cA + dA$
  (v) $(cd)A = c(dA)$
  (vi) $1A = A;\ 0A = 0$
  (vii) $A + 0 = 0 + A = A$
  (viii) $A + (-A) = (-A) + A = 0$

Definition 9. Let $A = [a_{ij}]_{m \times n}$ and $B = [b_{ij}]_{n \times k}$. The *product* of A and B, denoted AB, is the matrix $[c_{ij}]_{m \times k}$ where

$$c_{ij} = \sum_{r=1}^{n} a_{ir}b_{rj}$$

for all i and j.

Note that Definition 9 defines the product of two *matrices* while Definition 5 defines the product of a *real number* and a *matrix*. As such, the defined products are different. Note further that the product of two matrices $\mathbf{A}$ and $\mathbf{B}$ is defined if and only if the number of columns in $\mathbf{A}$ is equal to the number of rows in $\mathbf{B}$; if so, the product is a matrix having the same number of rows as $\mathbf{A}$ and the same number of columns as $\mathbf{B}$.

EXAMPLE 10. Find $\mathbf{AB}$ if

$$\mathbf{A} = [a_{ij}]_{2 \times 3} = \begin{bmatrix} -1 & 0 & 2 \\ 3 & -2 & 1 \end{bmatrix} \quad \text{and} \quad \mathbf{B} = [b_{ij}]_{3 \times 2} = \begin{bmatrix} 3 & 2 \\ 1 & -1 \\ -2 & 0 \end{bmatrix}.$$

$\mathbf{AB}$ will be a 2×2 matrix, say $[c_{ij}]_{2 \times 2}$.

$$c_{11} = \sum_{r=1}^{3} a_{1r}b_{r1} = a_{11}b_{11} + a_{12}b_{21} + a_{13}b_{31}$$

$$= (-1)(3) + (0)(1) + (2)(-2) = -7$$

$$c_{12} = \sum_{r=1}^{3} a_{1r}b_{r2} = a_{11}b_{12} + a_{12}b_{22} + a_{13}b_{32}$$

$$= (-1)(2) + (0)(-1) + (2)(0) = -2$$

$$c_{21} = \sum_{r=1}^{3} a_{2r}b_{r1} = a_{21}b_{11} + a_{22}b_{21} + a_{23}b_{31}$$

$$= (3)(3) + (-2)(1) + (1)(-2) = 5$$

$$c_{22} = \sum_{r=1}^{3} a_{2r}b_{r2} = a_{21}b_{12} + a_{22}b_{22} + a_{23}b_{32}$$

$$= (3)(2) + (-2)(-1) + (1)(0) = 8.$$

Hence

$$\mathbf{AB} = \begin{bmatrix} c_{11} & c_{12} \\ c_{21} & c_{22} \end{bmatrix} = \begin{bmatrix} -7 & -2 \\ 5 & 8 \end{bmatrix}.$$

In general, the entry in the ith row and the jth column of the product of two matrices is obtained by multiplying the ith row of $\mathbf{A}$ componentwise by the jth column of $\mathbf{B}$ and adding the results.

Theorem 11. Let $\mathbf{A} = [a_{ij}]_{m \times n}$, $\mathbf{B} = [b_{ij}]_{n \times k}$, $\mathbf{C} = [c_{ij}]_{k \times l}$, and $\mathbf{D} = [d_{ij}]_{n \times k}$ and let c be a real number.
  (i) $(\mathbf{AB})\mathbf{C} = \mathbf{A}(\mathbf{BC})$
  (ii) $\mathbf{A}(\mathbf{B} + \mathbf{D}) = \mathbf{AB} + \mathbf{AD}$
  (iii) $(\mathbf{B} + \mathbf{D})\mathbf{C} = \mathbf{BC} + \mathbf{DC}$
  (iv) $c(\mathbf{AB}) = (c\mathbf{A})\mathbf{B} = \mathbf{A}(c\mathbf{B})$
  (v) $\mathbf{0A} = \mathbf{0}$; $\mathbf{A0} = \mathbf{0}$

Note that the following properties are NOT true in general for matrices:

(i) $AB = BA$

(ii) $AB = AD, A \neq 0 \Rightarrow B = D$

(For example, take

$$A = \begin{bmatrix} 1 & 0 \\ 0 & 0 \end{bmatrix} \text{ and } B = \begin{bmatrix} 0 & 0 \\ 1 & 0 \end{bmatrix}$$

in (i) and

$$A = \begin{bmatrix} 1 & 0 \\ 0 & 0 \end{bmatrix}, \quad B = \begin{bmatrix} 0 & 0 \\ 1 & 0 \end{bmatrix}, \quad \text{and } D = \begin{bmatrix} 0 & 0 \\ 0 & 1 \end{bmatrix}$$

in (ii).)

Definition 12. Let $A = [a_{ij}]_{m \times n}$. The *transpose* of A, denoted A^t, is the matrix $[c_{ij}]_{n \times m}$ where $c_{ij} = a_{ji}$ for all i and j.

Note that the ith row of A becomes the ith column of A^t and the jth column of A becomes the jth row of A^t.

EXAMPLE 13.

$$\begin{bmatrix} -1 & 0 & 2 \\ 3 & -2 & 1 \end{bmatrix}^t = \begin{bmatrix} -1 & 3 \\ 0 & -2 \\ 2 & 1 \end{bmatrix}.$$

Theorem 14. *Let* $A = [a_{ij}]_{m \times n}$, $B = [b_{ij}]_{m \times n}$, *and* $C = [c_{ij}]_{n \times k}$ *and let* c *be a real number.*

(i) $(A^t)^t = A$

(ii) $(A + B)^t = A^t + B^t$

(iii) $(cA)^t = cA^t$

(iv) $(AC)^t = C^t A^t$

§3. Square Matrices

Definition 15. A matrix having the same number of rows as columns is said to be a *square matrix*.

Definition 16. Let $A = [a_{ij}]_{n \times n}$. The entries a_{ij} with $i = j$ are said to constitute the *diagonal* of A.

Definition 17. Let $A = [a_{ij}]_{n \times n}$. A is said to be a *diagonal matrix* if $a_{ij} = 0$ for all $i \neq j$.

Definition 18. Let $A = [a_{ij}]_{n \times n}$. A is said to be the $n \times n$ *identity matrix* (or the *identity matrix* if the size is understood), denoted $I_{n \times n}$ (or I), if A is a diagonal matrix and all diagonal entries are equal to 1.

EXAMPLE 19. Consider the 3×3 square matrices

$$A = \begin{bmatrix} 1 & 2 & 3 \\ 4 & 5 & 6 \\ 7 & 8 & 9 \end{bmatrix}, \quad B = \begin{bmatrix} 0 & 0 & 0 \\ 0 & 1 & 0 \\ 0 & 0 & 2 \end{bmatrix}, \quad \text{and } C = \begin{bmatrix} 1 & 0 & 0 \\ 0 & 1 & 0 \\ 0 & 0 & 1 \end{bmatrix}.$$

The diagonal entries of A are 1, 5, and 9; A is not a diagonal matrix since there are off-diagonal entries in A which are nonzero (in fact, all off-diagonal entries in A are nonzero!). B is a diagonal matrix since all off-diagonal entries in B are zero. C is the 3×3 identity matrix since it is a diagonal matrix and all diagonal entries are equal to 1.

Theorem 20. *Let* $A = [a_{ij}]_{n \times n}$. *Then* $AI = IA = A$.

In other words, any square matrix multiplied on either side by the identity matrix (necessarily of the same size) remains unchanged; I is the identity element for matrix multiplication.

§4. Invertible Matrices

Definition 21. Let $A = [a_{ij}]_{n \times n}$. A is said to be *invertible* if there exists an $n \times n$ matrix B such that

$$AB = BA = I;$$

B is said to be an *inverse* of A and is denoted A^{-1}. If A has no inverse, then A is said to be *noninvertible*.

In other words, a given square matrix is invertible if and only if there exists another matrix of the same size which when multiplied on either side by the given matrix results in the identity matrix (necessarily of the same size).

Theorem 22. *The inverse of a matrix is unique if it exists.*

EXAMPLE 23. The matrix

$$A = \begin{bmatrix} 1 & 2 \\ 3 & 4 \end{bmatrix}$$

is invertible since the matrix

$$B = \begin{bmatrix} -2 & 1 \\ 3/2 & -1/2 \end{bmatrix}$$

satisfies the condition of Definition 21 above (check this!). Hence B is the inverse of A.

Not all square matrices are invertible. (For example, the matrix

$$A = \begin{bmatrix} 1 & 2 \\ 3 & 6 \end{bmatrix}$$

is noninvertible.) Two questions arise at this point. In general, how can we tell whether or not a given square matrix is invertible? If a given square matrix is invertible, how can we find the inverse? One answer to these questions is provided by Exercise 11 in Chapter 2. The reader is referred to any elementary linear algebra book for alternate answers to these questions.

Theorem 24. *Let* $A = [a_{ij}]_{n \times n}$ *and* $B = [b_{ij}]_{n \times n}$ *be invertible matrices.*
  (i) $(A^{-1})^{-1} = A$
 (ii) $(AB)^{-1} = B^{-1}A^{-1}$
(iii) $(A')^{-1} = (A^{-1})'$

Theorem 25. *Let* A *be an invertible matrix. If* B *and* C *are matrices such that* $AB = AC$ *or* $BA = CA$, *then* $B = C$.

Note that the following properties are NOT true in general for matrices with A invertible:

 (i) $AB = CA \Rightarrow B = C$
(ii) $BA = AC \Rightarrow B = C$

(For example, take

$$A = \begin{bmatrix} 0 & 1 \\ 1 & 0 \end{bmatrix}, \quad B = \begin{bmatrix} 0 & 0 \\ 0 & 1 \end{bmatrix}, \quad \text{and } C = \begin{bmatrix} 1 & 0 \\ 0 & 0 \end{bmatrix}$$

in (i) and

$$A = \begin{bmatrix} 0 & 1 \\ 1 & 0 \end{bmatrix}, \quad B = \begin{bmatrix} 1 & 0 \\ 0 & 0 \end{bmatrix}, \quad \text{and } C = \begin{bmatrix} 0 & 0 \\ 0 & 1 \end{bmatrix}$$

in (ii).)

Probability

§0. Introduction

In this appendix, we summarize the elementary theory of probability necessary for a complete understanding of Chapter 5. This summary is intended to be rather concise; more detailed discussions of the topics here may be found in any elementary probability book.

§1. Random Experiments and the Assignment of Probabilities

Definition 1. An *experiment* is the process of making an observation.

EXAMPLE 2. The process of tossing a coin and observing heads or tails is an experiment. The process of rolling a die and observing 1, 2, 3, 4, 5, or 6 is an experiment.

An experiment can result in one, and only one, outcome of a set of distinctly observable outcomes. We are interested here in random experiments, i.e., experiments that generate outcomes which vary in a random manner and which cannot be predicted with certainty.

Definition 3. The *sample space* of an experiment, denoted Ω, is the set of all possible outcomes of the experiment. The individual outcomes, i.e., the elements of Ω, are said to be the *sample points* of the experiment.

EXAMPLE 4. Consider the experiment of tossing a fair coin three times and observing the successive results. ("Fair" means that the two outcomes, heads and tails, are equally likely to occur.) If H denotes heads and T denotes tails, then the sample space of the experiment is

$$\Omega = \{HHH, HHT, HTH, THH, TTH, THT, HTT, TTT\}.$$

There are eight sample points in Ω.

Definition 5. Let $\Omega = \{\omega_1, \omega_2, \ldots, \omega_n\}$ be the sample space of an experiment. A real-valued function P on Ω is said to be a *probability function on Ω* if
(i) $P(\omega_i) \geq 0$ for all i and
(ii) $P(\omega_1) + P(\omega_2) + \cdots + P(\omega_n) = 1$.
The number $P(\omega_i)$ is said to be the *probability of ω_i*.

The definition above only states the properties that a probability function must satisfy; it does not tell us how to assign specific probabilities to sample points in sample spaces. Specific assignments of probabilities must be done in a manner that is consistent with reality if the probabilistic model is to serve a useful purpose. The assignment of probability p to a sample point ω is interpreted as meaning that, if the experiment is performed repeatedly under identical conditions, then the proportion of experiments with outcome ω is approximately p. For example, if each outcome of a random experiment is equally likely to occur (as is the case with a fair coin or an unbiased die), then equal probabilities should be assigned to the sample points.

EXAMPLE 6. Consider the experiment of Example 4. Since there are eight sample points in Ω and since each outcome is equally likely to occur (the coin is fair), the probability of each outcome is 1/8. Check that this assignment of probabilities satisfies properties (i) and (ii) of Definition 5.

EXAMPLE 7. Consider the experiment of Example 4. The assignment of probabilities to the sample points in Ω given by

$$P(HHH) = 1/16$$
$$P(HHT) = 1/8$$
$$P(HTH) = 1/128$$
$$P(THH) = 1/32$$
$$P(TTH) = 1/128$$
$$P(THT) = 1/64$$
$$P(HTT) = 1/2$$
$$P(TTT) = 1/4$$

satisfies properties (i) and (ii) of Definition 5 (check this!); hence P is a probability function on Ω. Unfortunately, since the coin is fair, this assignment of probabilities does not accurately model the experiment.

§2. Events

Definition 8. Let Ω be the sample space of an experiment. An *event* E is any subset of Ω.

Definition 9. Let Ω be the sample space of an experiment, let P be a probability function on Ω, and let E be an event. If $E = \{\omega_{i_1}, \omega_{i_2}, \ldots, \omega_{i_n}\} \neq \varnothing$, then the *probability of* E, denoted $P(E)$, is

$$P(E) = P(\omega_{i_1}) + P(\omega_{i_2}) + \cdots + P(\omega_{i_n}).$$

If $E = \varnothing$, then $P(E) = 0$.

EXAMPLE 10. Consider the experiment of Example 4.
(i) Let E be the event (in words) of tossing exactly two heads. Then

$$E = \{\text{HHT}, \text{HTH}, \text{THH}\}$$

and

$$P(E) = P(\text{HHT}) + P(\text{HTH}) + P(\text{THH}) = 1/8 + 1/8 + 1/8 = 3/8.$$

In other words, the probability of tossing exactly two heads in this experiment is 3/8.
(ii) Let E be the event (in words) of tossing exactly two heads and exactly two tails. Since the coin is tossed only three times in this experiment, we have that

$$E = \varnothing$$

and

$$P(E) = 0;$$

E is an impossible event.
(iii) Let E be the event (in words) of tossing a head on the first toss or tossing a tail on the first toss. Since the first toss of the coin must result in a head or a tail, we have that

$$E = \Omega$$

and

$$P(E) = 1;$$

E is a certain event.

§3. Expected Value

Definition 11. Let $\Omega = \{\omega_1, \omega_2, \ldots, \omega_n\}$ be the sample space of an experiment with $\omega_i \in \mathbf{R}$ for all i and let P be a probability function on Ω. The *expected value* of the experiment, denoted ε, is

$$\varepsilon = \omega_1 P(\omega_1) + \omega_2 P(\omega_2) + \cdots + \omega_n P(\omega_n).$$

The expected value of an experiment is the average value of the experiment after many trials of the experiment.

EXAMPLE 12. Consider the experiment of Example 4 and assume that we are interested only in the number of heads that result from the three coin tosses. What is the expected value of the number of heads obtained in this experiment?

With the additional assumption above, the sample space for the experiment becomes

$$\Omega = \{0, 1, 2, 3\}.$$

We first assign probabilities to the sample points in Ω. The event of 0 heads is $E_0 = \{TTT\}$ and hence

$$P(0 \text{ heads}) = P(E_0) = 1/8.$$

Similarly, the event of 1 head is $E_1 = \{TTH, THT, HTT\}$ and hence

$$P(1 \text{ head}) = P(E_1) = 3/8;$$

the event of 2 heads is $E_2 = \{HHT, HTH, THH\}$ and hence

$$P(2 \text{ heads}) = P(E_2) = 3/8;$$

the event of 3 heads is $E_3 = \{HHH\}$ and hence

$$P(3 \text{ heads}) = P(E_3) = 1/8.$$

Then the expected value of the number of heads in this experiment is

$$\varepsilon = 0P(E_0) + 1P(E_1) + 2P(E_2) + 3P(E_3) = 1.5.$$

Note that it is impossible for the experiment to result in 1.5 heads in any single trial of the experiment. The expected value measures the average number of heads per trial *after many trials of the experiment*. For example, after 1000 trials of the experiment, we would expect that approximately $(1.5)(1000) = 1500$ heads had been tossed.

EXAMPLE 13. On a roulette wheel there are 38 numbers: the integers from 1 to 36 inclusive, 0, and 00. Half of the numbers from 1 to 36 are red and the other half are black. The numbers 0 and 00 are green. What is the expected value of roulette to a gambler who bets $1 on black?

The gambler will either win $1 or lose $1; the sample space for this experiment is hence

$$\Omega = \{1, -1\}.$$

We now assign probabilities to the sample points in Ω. The gambler will win $1 if and only if one of the 18 black numbers comes up; since there are 38 total numbers on the wheel, his probability of winning $1 is 18/38. Similarly, the gambler will lose $1 if and only if one of 20 numbers comes up, one of the 18 red numbers *or* one of the 2 green numbers. Again, since there are 38 total numbers on the wheel, the gambler's probability of losing $1 is 20/38. Then the expected value of the game to the gambler is

$$\varepsilon = (1)(18/38) + (-1)(20/38) \approx -.0526,$$

i.e., the gambler can expect to lose a little over 5¢ per round of the game. For example, after 10000 rounds of the game, the gambler can expect to be losing approximately ($.0526)(10000) = $526. Not surprisingly, games with negative expected values are the secret behind the success of gambling casinos.

Answers to Selected Exercises

Chapter 1

2. a. Maximize $f(x, y) = x + y$
   subject to $x - y \leq 3$
   $$2x + y \leq 12$$
   $$x \leq 4$$
   $$y \leq 6$$
   $$x, y \geq 0$$

   b. Minimize $g(x, y) = x - y$
   subject to $2x - y \geq -1$
   $$-x \geq -2$$
   $$x, y \geq 0$$

   c. Maximize $f(x, y) = -x - 2y$
   subject to $-2x + y \leq 1$
   $$-x + 3y \leq 8$$
   $$x, y \geq 0$$

   d. Minimize $g(x, y, z) = x - 2y - z$
   subject to $-10x - 5y - 2z \geq -1000$
   $$-2y - 4z \geq -800$$
   $$x, y, z \geq 0$$

3. a. Max $f = 20$ at $(x, y) = (4, 0)$
   b. Min $g = 16$ at $(x, y) = (0, 8)$
   c. Max $f = 9$ at $(x, y) = (3, 6)$
   d. Min $g = -3$ at $(x, y) = (2, 5)$
   e. Max $f = 0$ at $(x, y) = (0, 0)$

f. Max $f = 100$ at $(x, y, z) = (100, 0, 0)$
g. Min $g = -425$ at $(x, y, z) = (0, 150, 125)$
h. Let x and y be the number of units of the Monitor and the number of units of the Recorder respectively and let P be the total profits. Then max $P = 10000/3$ at $(x, y) = (20/3, 20/3)$; since fractional magazines are not realistic, the "rounded-off" optimal solution is max $P = 3333$ at $(x, y) = (6.66, 6.67)$.
i. Let x and y be the number of days for the first operation and the number of days for the second operation respectively and let C be the total costs. Then min $C = 4750$ at $(x, y) = (10, 5)$.
j. Let x, y, and z be the number of units of the first formulation, the number of units of the second formulation, and the number of units of the third formulation respectively and let R be the total sales revenue. Then max $R = 475$ at $(x, y, z) = (25, 0, 150)$ or at $(x, y, z) = (0, 50, 125)$.

6. Max $f = 2$ at $(x, y, z) = (1, 0, 0)$

7. 35

8. b. $(0, 0, 0, 1/2)$, $(0, 0, 1/3, 0)$, $(0, 1/4, 0, 0)$, $(1/5, 0, 0, 0)$, $(0, 0, 0, 0)$
    c. Min $g = -2$ at $(x, y, z, w) = (0, 0, 0, 1/2)$

9. c. $(0, 0, 1, 1/2), (0, 1, 1, 0), (3, 0, 0, 1/2), (3, 1, 0, 0), (0, 0, 0, 5/4), (0, 0, 5/3, 0), (0, 5/2, 0, 0),$
        $(5, 0, 0, 0), (0, 0, 0, 1/2), (0, 1, 0, 0), (0, 0, 0, 0)$
    d. The actual extreme points of part c are $(0, 0, 1, 1/2)$, $(0, 1, 1, 0)$, $(3, 0, 0, 1/2)$, $(3, 1, 0, 0)$, $(0, 0, 5/3, 0)$, and $(5, 0, 0, 0)$; min $g = 1$ at each of the first four of these extreme points.

11. a. TRUE
    b. FALSE

Chapter 2

1. a. Maximize $f(x, y) = 7x + 8y - 9$
        subject to $x + 2y \le 3$
        $4x + 5y \le 6$
        $x, y \ge 0$

    c.

t_2	y	-1	
$-1/4$	$3/4$	$3/2$	$= -t_1$
$1/4$	$5/4$	$3/2$	$= -x$
$-7/4$	$-3/4$	$-3/2$	$= f$

2. a. Minimize $g(x, y) = 3x + 6y - 9$
        subject to $x + 4y \ge 7$
        $2x + 5y \ge 8$
        $x, y \ge 0$

c.

x	$-1/4$	$3/4$	$3/2$
t_1	$1/4$	$5/4$	$3/2$
-1	$-7/4$	$-3/4$	$-3/2$

$$= y \quad = t_2 \qquad = g$$

5. a. Infeasible
   b. Unbounded
   c. $x = 4/3,\ y = 0,\ z = 1,\ t_1 = 0,\ t_2 = 0,\ \min g = -4/3$
   d. Unbounded
   e. Infeasible
   f. Unbounded

6. a. $x = 0,\ y = 0,\ t_1 = 1,\ t_2 = 0,\ t_3 = 0,\ \max f = 1$

7. $x_1 = 2,\ x_2 = 0,\ x_3 = 2,\ x_4 = 0,\ t_1 = 2,\ t_2 = 0,\ t_3 = 0,\ \max f = 2$

8. For definiteness of pivots, the anticycling rules were implemented in both problems below.

   a. The final tableau is

t_2	x	z	w	-1	
-1	-1	0	0	0	$= -t_1$
1	1	1	-1	3	$= -y$
-2	-1	0	-2	-6	$= f$

Now t_2, x, and w must be 0 since the coefficients of these variables in the objective function are negative, i.e., any positive choice for any of these variables decreases f. Note, however, that the coefficient of z in the objective function is 0 and hence z is not forced to be 0 in order for f to be optimal. To see what possible values $z \geq 0$ can assume, examine the main constraints of the final tableau (remembering that $t_2 = x = w = 0$):

$$0 = -t_1$$
$$z - 3 = -y.$$

The first constraint gives $t_1 = 0$. The second equation gives $y = 3 - z$; since $y \geq 0$, we have $3 - z \geq 0$, i.e., $z \leq 3$. Hence, all optimal solutions for this problem may be expressed as follows:

$$t_2 = x = w = 0, \quad t_1 = 0, \quad 0 \leq z \leq 3, \quad y = 3 - z, \quad \max f = 6.$$

   b. The final tableau is

t_1	t_2	-1	
$1/2$	$1/2$	$1/2$	$= -x$
$1/2$	$-1/2$	$3/2$	$= -y$
-1	0	-2	$= -g$

Now t_1 must be 0 since the coefficient of t_1 in the objective function is negative, i.e., any positive choice for t_1 decreases $-g$. Note, however, that the coefficient of t_2 in the objective function is 0 and hence t_2 is not forced to be 0 in order for $-g$ to be optimal. To see what possible values $t_2 \geq 0$ can assume, examine the main constraints of the final tableau (remembering that $t_1 = 0$):

$$1/2t_2 - 1/2 = -x$$
$$-1/2t_2 - 3/2 = -y.$$

The first equation gives $x = 1/2 - 1/2t_2$; since $x \geq 0$, we have $1/2 - 1/2t_2 \geq 0$. i.e., $t_2 \leq 1$. The second equation gives $y = 1/2t_2 + 3/2$; since $y \geq 0$, we have $1/2t_2 + 3/2 \geq 0$, i.e., $t_2 \geq -3$ which we already know. Hence, all optimal solutions for this problem may be expressed as follows:

$$t_1 = 0, \quad 0 \leq t_2 \leq 1, \quad x = 1/2 - 1/2t_2, \quad y = 1/2t_2 + 3/2, \quad \min g = -2.$$

9. a. Let x, y, and z be the number of pounds of the first mixture, the number of pounds of the second mixture, and the number of pounds of the third mixture respectively and let P be the total profits. Then $\max P = 900$ at $(x, y, z) = (100, 200, 400)$.

   b. Let x, y, z, and w be the number of towels purchased new, the number of towels washed by the one-day service after the first day, the number of towels washed by the one-day service after the second day, and the number of towels washed by the two-day service after the first day respectively and let C be the total costs. Then $\min C = 570$ at $(x, y, z, w) = (400, 100, 200, 200)$.

11. a.
$$\begin{bmatrix} 1/2 & -1/2 & 1/2 \\ 1/2 & 1/2 & -1/2 \\ -1/2 & 1/2 & 1/2 \end{bmatrix}$$

   b. The given matrix is noninvertible.

   c.
$$\begin{bmatrix} 1/6 & 0 & -1/2 & 2/3 \\ 0 & -1/2 & 1 & -1/2 \\ -1/2 & 1 & -1/2 & 0 \\ 2/3 & -1/2 & 0 & 1/6 \end{bmatrix}$$

12. a. $b_1, b_2, \ldots, b_m \leq 0$
    b. No
    c. $b_1, b_2, \ldots, b_m \geq 0$ and $c_1, c_2, \ldots, c_n \leq 0$

13. b. $x = 0, \quad y = 5/3, \quad z = 2/3, \quad t_1 = 0, \quad t_2 = 0, \quad t_3 = 8/3, \quad \max f = 16/3$

Chapter 3

1. a. $t_1 = t_3 = 0, x \leq 3, y = 2 - x, z = 8 - 2x, t_2 = 3 - x, \max f = 6$
   b. Unbounded
   c. $x = 0, y = 6, z = 4, t_1 = 0, \min g = 14$
   d. Unbounded
   e. $t_1 = 0, 0 \leq x \leq 1/2, y = 1 - 2x, z = x + 1/2, t_2 = x, \max f = 3/2$
   f. $x = 8, y = 2, z = 0, t_1 = 0, \max f = 20$
   g. $t_1 = 2, t_2 = 0, x = x, y = x - 3, z = -2x, \min g = -3$
   h. Infeasible

2. a. FALSE
   b. FALSE

3. $t_1 = 0, 0 \leq x \leq 1/2, y = 2/3 - 4/3x, z = 1/3x + 1/3, \max f = 0$

5. a. The solutions are the same ($x = 4, y = 2, t_1 = 0, t_2 = 0, \max f = 6$).
   b. The solutions are not the same. Canonical solution: $x = 1, y = 0, t_1 = 0, t_2 = 3$, $\min g = 1$. Noncanonical solution: Unbounded.
   c. The solutions are not the same. Canonical solution: Infeasible. Noncanonical solution: $x = -3, y = -4, t_1 = 0, t_2 = 0, \max f = -5$.
   d. The solutions are the same (unbounded).

Chapter 4

1. a. Minimize $g(y_1, y_2) = 4y_1 + 6y_2$
      subject to $y_1 + 3y_2 \geq 1$
      $2y_1 + y_2 \geq 1$
      $y_1, y_2 \geq 0$
   c. Max: $x_1 = 8/5, x_2 = 6/5, t_1 = 0, t_2 = 0, \max f = 14/5$
      Min: $y_1 = 2/5, y_2 = 1/5, s_1 = 0, s_2 = 0, \min g = 14/5$
   d. Yes

2. a. Maximize $f(x_1, x_2) = x_1 + 2x_2$
      subject to $x_1 - x_2 \leq 0$
      $-x_1 + x_2 \leq -1$
      $x_1, x_2 \geq 0$
   c. Max: Infeasible
      Min: Infeasible

3. a. Minimize $g(y_1, y_2, y_3) = y_1 - y_2 - y_3$
      subject to $y_1 - y_2 + 2y_3 \geq 1$
      $y_1 + y_2 - y_3 \geq 0$
      $y_1, y_2, y_3 \geq 0$
   c. Max: Infeasible
      Min: Unbounded

5. a. Max: $x_1 = 0 \, x_2 = 1, t_1 = 0, t_2 = 0, \max f = -2$
      Min: $s_2 = 0, 0 \leq s_1 \leq 1, y_1 = 1/2s_1 + 3/2, y_2 = 1/2 - 1/2s_1, \min g = -2$
   b. Max: Unbounded
      Min: Infeasible
   c. Max: Infeasible
      Min: Infeasible
   d. Max: $x_1 = 0, x_2 = 0, t_1 = 0, t_2 = 1, t_3 = 0, \max f = 0$
      Min: $y_2 = 0, y_1 \geq 0, s_2 \geq 0, y_3 = 2y_1 + s_2 + 2, s_1 = 15y_1 + 3s_2 + 3, \min g = 0$
   e. Max: Infeasible
      Min: Unbounded
   f. Max: Unbounded
      Min: Infeasible

6. b. $b_1 = c_2 = 0, b_2 > 0$, and $c_1 \leqq 0$ OR $b_2 = c_1 = 0, b_1 > 0$, and $b_2 \leqq 0$.

7. b. FALSE

9. b. No
   d. Yes

10. a. Type (ii) behavior
    b. Type (i) behavior
    c. Type (iv) behavior
    d. Type (iii) behavior

11. a. Minimize $g(y_1, y_2, y_3) = -y_1 + y_2 + y_3$
    subject to $y_1 - y_2 - y_3 = 1$
    $-y_1 - y_2 + y_3 \geqq 1$
    $y_1 + y_2 + y_3 \geqq -1$
    $y_3 \geqq 0$

    b. Max: $x_1 = -1, x_2 = 0, x_3 = 0, t_1 = 0$, max $f = -1$
       Min: $s_1 \geqq 0, s_2 \geqq 0, y_1 = 1/2s_2, y_2 = -1/2s_1 - 1, y_3 = 1/2s_1 + 1/2s_2$,
       min $g = -1$

    c. Yes
    d. No

12. a. Maximize $f(x_1, x_2, x_3) = x_1 + x_2 + x_3$
    subject to $x_1 + x_3 \leqq 1$
    $x_1 + 2x_2 = 2$
    $x_1 + x_2 + x_3 \leqq 3$
    $x_1, x_3 \geqq 0$

    b. Max: $x_1 = 0, x_2 = 1, x_3 = 1, t_1 = 0, t_2 = 1$, max $f = 2$
       Min: $y_1 = 1, y_2 = 1/2, y_3 = 0, s_1 = 1/2, s_2 = 0$, min $g = 2$
    c. Yes
    d. Yes

13. a. Max: Infeasible
       Min: Unbounded
    b. Max: $t_1 = 0, x_1 \leqq 2, x_2 = 1 - 1/2x_1$, max $f = -2$
       Min: $s_1 = 0, y_1 \geqq -1, y_2 = y_1 + 1$, min $g = -2$
    c. Max: Infeasible
       Min: Infeasible
    d. Max: Unbounded
       Min: Infeasible

Chapter 5

1. a. Value: 14/9
      Optimal strategy for player I: Play first row with probability 8/9 and play third
      row with probability 1/9.
      Optimal strategy for player II: Play second column with probability 4/9 and
      play fourth column with probability 5/9.

   b. Value: 4/9
       Optimal strategy for player I: Play second row with probability 4/9 and play
       fourth row with probability 5/9.
       Optimal strategy for player II: Play first column with probability 8/9 and play
       third column with probability 1/9.
   c. Value: -1
       Optimal strategy for player I: Play third row with probability p and play fifth
       row with probability $1 - p$.
       Optimal strategy for player II: Always play second column.
   d. Value: $-1/4$
       Optimal strategy for player I: Play first row with probability 1/4 and play third
       row with probability 3/4.
       Optimal strategy for player II: Play first column with probability 3/4 and play
       fourth column with probability 1/4.

2. a. Value: $-5/22$
       Optimal strategy for player I: Play penny with probability 15/22 and play
       nickel with probability 7/22.
       Optimal strategy for player II: Play penny with probability 15/22 and play
       nickel with probability 7/22.
   b. Value: $-5/16$
       Optimal strategy for player I: Play 2 ♠ with probability 13/16 and play 3 ♥ with
       probability 3/16.
       Optimal strategy for player II: Play 3 ♠ with probability 9/16 and play 4 ♥ with
       probability 7/16.
   c. Value: 0
       Optimal strategy for guesser: Guess 'even' with probability 1/2 and guess 'odd'
       with probability 1/2.
       Optimal strategy for holder: Hold 'even' with probability 1/2 and hold 'odd'
       with probability 1/2.

3. a. Player I
   b. Value: 1
       Optimal strategy for player I: Hold 0 pennies in left hand with probability 1/2
       and hold 2 pennies in left hand with probability 1/2.
       Optimal strategy for player II: Hold 0 pennies in left hand with probability q,
       hold 1 penny in left hand with probability $1 - 2q$, and hold 2 pennies in left hand
       with probability q.
   c. 10000
   d. a. Player I
       b. Value: 1/2
           Optimal strategy for player I: Hold 0 pennies in left hand with probability
           1/2 and hold 2 pennies in left hand with probability 1/2.
           Optimal strategy for player II: Hold 1 penny in left hand with probability 1/2
           and hold 2 pennies in left hand with probability 1/2.
       c. 20000
   e. 0

4. $-5/3$

5. Probability of b b = probability of r r = 25/102
   Probability of b r = probability of r b = 26/102

7. a. Value: 0
   Optimal strategy for player I: Always bid with a head and always pass with a tail.
   Optimal strategy for player II: Always see with a head and always fold with a tail.
   b. Value: $-1/6$
   Optimal strategy for player I: Always bet with a jack or a queen and always pass with a king.
   Optimal strategy for player II: Always see with a jack and always pass with a queen or a king.
   c. Value: 23/120
   Optimal strategy for player I: Always bet and see subsequently with a black card, pass with a red card with probability 4/5, bet with a red card and fold subsequently with probability 1/6, and bet with a red card and see subsequently with probability 1/30.
   Optimal strategy for player II: Always raise with a black card, fold with a red card with probability 2/5, see with a red card with probability 13/30, and raise with a red card with probability 1/6.

9. a. $xy \leq 0$
   b. Value: 0

11. a. Value: $1/(4x + 4)$
    Optimal strategy for player I: Play first row with probability $(2x + 1)/(4x + 4)$ and play second row with probability $(2x + 3)/(4x + 4)$.
    Optimal strategy for player II: Play first column with probability $(2x + 1)/(4x + 4)$ and play second column with probability $(2x + 3)/(4x + 4)$.
    b. $-3/2 \leq x \leq -1/2$

Chapter 6

1. a. Min $C = 360$
   b. Min $C = 92$
   c. Min $C = 305$
   d. Min $C = 678$
   e. Min $C = 329$
   f. Min $C = 107$
   g. Min $C = 77$
   h. Min $C = 69$
   i. Min $C = 826$

2. Min $C = 185$

3. a. Parts a, b, c, d, f, and i.

4.

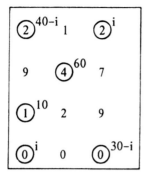

6. a. Minimum-entry method: Cost = 370
   Northwest-corner method: Cost = 370
   b. Minimum-entry method: Cost = 104
   Northwest-corner method: Cost = 94

7. b. Yes
   [Note: Most cycles visualized as involving diagonal movement in transportation problems will result in new basic feasible solutions for the problems provided that the diagonal movement is "reasonable." Since there may be visualizations involving diagonal movement that do not result in basic feasible solutions, we suggest *never* using such visualizations.]

9. a. Min $C = 7$

10. a. Min $C = 76$
    b. Min $C = 14$
    c. Min $C = 37$
    d. Min $C = 16$

11. $x_{11} = x_{22} = x_{33} = x_{44} = x_{55} = 1$, all other x_{ij}'s 0;
    $x_{11} = x_{24} = x_{33} = x_{42} = x_{55} = 1$, all other x_{ij}'s 0;
    $x_{13} = x_{22} = x_{31} = x_{44} = x_{55} = 1$, all other x_{ij}'s 0;
    $x_{13} = x_{24} = x_{31} = x_{42} = x_{55} = 1$, all other x_{ij}'s 0.

12. Min $C = 5$

13. a. Min $C = 25$
    b. Min $C = 28$

14. Maximum rating $= 45$

15. The first man should live with the fourth woman, the second man should live with the second woman, the third man should live with the first woman, the fourth man should live with the fifth woman, and the fifth man should live with the third woman.

16. FALSE

Chapter 7

1. a. $\varphi(v_1) = 1$, $\varphi(v_2) = -2$, $\varphi(v_3) = -1$, $\varphi(v_4) = 0$, $\varphi(v_5) = 1$, $\varphi(v_6) = 0$, and $\varphi(v_7) = 1$.
   b. v_2 and v_3 are sources, v_1, v_5, and v_7 are sinks, and v_4 and v_6 are intermediate vertices

3. a. Max $f = 6$
   b. Max $f = 18$
   c. Max $f = 35$
   d. Max $f = 17$

4. a. One such succession is

$$v_s \rightarrow v_1 \rightarrow v_2 \rightarrow v_d$$
$$v_s \rightarrow v_3 \rightarrow v_4 \rightarrow v_d$$
$$v_s \rightarrow v_1 \rightarrow v_4 \rightarrow v_d$$
$$v_s \rightarrow v_3 \rightarrow v_2 \rightarrow v_d.$$

   b. No

5. a. 2; for example, $v_s \rightarrow v_1 \rightarrow v_d$ and $v_s \rightarrow v_2 \rightarrow v_d$.
   b. 2000; for example,

$$v_s \rightarrow v_1 \rightarrow v_2 \rightarrow v_d$$
$$v_s \rightarrow v_2 \rightarrow v_1 \rightarrow v_d$$
$$v_s \rightarrow v_1 \rightarrow v_2 \rightarrow v_d$$
$$v_s \rightarrow v_2 \rightarrow v_1 \rightarrow v_d$$

etc.

9. a. Min d $= 4$
   b. Min d $= 3$
   c. Min d $= 8$
   d. Min d $= 1$
   e. Min d $= 10$

12. a. ∞

13. a. FALSE
    b. FALSE

14. a. $F = 8$; Min $C = 37$
       $F = 10$; Min $C = 50$
    b. $F = 8$; Min $C = 39$
       $F = 10$; Min $C = 57$
    c. $F = 8$; Min $C = 38$
       $F = 10$; Infeasible

16. Min $C = 93$

17. a. Min $C = 16$

Bibliography

[A1]   A.V. Aho, J.E. Hopcroft, & J.D. Ullman, "The Design and Analysis of
       Computer Algorithms," Addison-Wesley, Reading, Massachusetts, 1976.

[B1]   M.L. Balinski & A.W. Tucker, Duality Theory of Linear Programs: A
       Constructive Approach with Applications, SIAM Review 11 (1969), 347–377.

[B2]   E.M.L. Beale, Cycling in the Dual Simplex Algorithm, Naval Research
       Logistics Quarterly 2 (1955), 269–275.

[B3]   R.G. Bland, New Finite Pivoting Rules for the Simplex Method, Mathematics
       of Operations Research 2 (1977), 103–107.

[B4]   R.G. Busacker & T.L. Saaty, "Finite Graphs and Networks: An Introduction
       with Applications," McGraw-Hill, New York, 1965.

[D1]   G.B. Dantzig, "Linear Programming and Extensions," Princeton University
       Press, Princeton, New Jersey, 1963.

[D2]   E.W. Dijkstra, A Note on Two Problems in Connexion with Graphs,
       Numerische Mathematik 1 (1959), 269–271.

[F1]   L.R. Ford Jr. & D.R. Fulkerson, "Flows in Networks," Princeton University
       Press, Princeton, New Jersey, 1962.

[G1]   S.I. Gass, "Linear Programming, Methods and Applications," Fifth Edition,
       McGraw-Hill, New York, 1985.

[G2]   D.P. Gaver & G.L. Thompson, "Programming and Probability Models in
       Operations Research," Brooks/Cole, Monterey, California, 1973.

[H1]   G. Hadley, "Linear Programming," Addison-Wesley, Reading, Massachusetts,
       1962.

[K1]   T.C.T. Kotiah & D.I. Steinberg, Occurrences of Cycling and Other Phenomena
       Arising in a Class of Linear Programming Models, Communications of the
       ACM 20 (1977), 107–112.

[K2]   H.W. Kuhn, The Hungarian Method for the Assignment Problem, Naval
       Research Logistics Quarterly 2 (1955), 83–97.

[L1]   E.L. Lawler, "Combinatorial Optimization: Networks and Matroids," Holt,
       Rinehart, and Winston, New York, 1976.

[L2]   D.G. Luenberger, "Linear and Nonlinear Programming," Second Edition,
       Addison-Wesley, Reading, Massachusetts, 1984.

[O1]   G. Owen, "Game Theory," Second Edition, Academic Press, Orlando, 1982.

[R1]   N.V. Reinfeld & W.R. Vogel, "Mathematical Programming," Prentice-Hall, Englewood Cliffs, New Jersey, 1958.
[R2]   R.I. Rothenberg, "Linear Programming," North-Holland, New York, 1979.
[W1]   N.A. Weiss & M.L. Yoseloff, "Finite Mathematics," Worth Publishers, New York, 1975.

Index

A

α-path, 195
  backward edge of, 195
  forward edge of, 195
  in relation to path, 205
Anticycling rules
  for simplex algorithm, 60–61
  for transportation algorithm, 181
Assignment problems, 164–178
  balanced, 165
  unbalanced, 164–165

B

Backward edge, 195
Balanced
  assignment problem, 165
  transportation problem, 142–143
  transportation tableau, 143
Basic feasible solutions, 41, 89,
    150
  and VAM, 150–151
Basic solution, 38
  optimal, 43, 91–92
Basic variables, *see* Dependent
    variables
Basis, 151
Beale, E.M.L., 58
Bland, R.G., 60
Bounded above, 16
Bounded below, 16
Bounded subset of $\mathbf{R}^n$, 15

C

Canonical linear programming problems,
    9, 70
Canonical slack linear programming prob-
    lems, 28–29
Capacitated, 185
Capacity
  of a cut, 192
  of edge in directed network, 185
Cells, 143
  getter, 153
  giver, 153
Closed ball of radius r centered at origin,
    14–15
Closed half-space, 12–13
  importance of, for linear programming,
    13
Column player, 119
Complementary slackness, 99
  and optimal solutions, 100
Conservation of flow, 188
Constraints
  main, 9
  nonnegativity, 9
Constraint set, 10
Convex, 11
CPM (critical-path method), 231
Critical-path method, *see* CPM
Cut, 191–192
  capacity, 192
  relationship to dual problem of maximal-
    flow problem, 191, 193

Cut-set, 192
Cycles
  in directed networks, 205
  in transportation tableaus, 151
Cycling, 47, 58–63, 169

D
Dantzig, George B., 27
Dantzig tableau, 27
Degeneracy, 169
Dependent variables (basic variables), 29
Derivation, 206
Destination, 206
Dijkstra, E.W., 207
Directed graph, *see* Directed network
Directed network, 185
  capacitated, 185
  weighted, 205
Domination, 119
Dual
  canonical tableau, 88
  noncanonical tableau, 105
  simplex algorithm for maximum tab-
    leaus, 91
  simplex algorithm for minimum tab-
    leaus, 90
Duality, 87–114
  in canonical linear programming prob-
    lems, 38, 88
  equation, 96
  and negative transposition, 92, 103
  in noncanonical linear programming
    problems, 105
  theorem, 102
Dual linear programming problems, 38, 88
  feasible solutions of, 98, 99
  infeasibility in, 98
  optimal solutions of, 92, 99
  unboundedness in, 98

E
Edges, 185
Egerváry, 170
Equations of constraint, 77, 83
  alternate method for dealing with, 85–
    86
Events, 246
Expected value, 246
Experiment, 244
Extreme points, 15
  in polyhedral convex sets, 15
  upper bound for number of, 20–21, 22,
    23

F
Feasible points, *see* Feasible solutions
Feasible solutions (feasible points), 10
  of dual linear programming problems,
    98, 99
  of transportation problems, 150
Flow, 183
  conservation of, 188
  net input, 187
Ford, L.R. Jr., 198
Forward edge, 195
Fulkerson, D.R., 198

G
Game tableau, 123
Game theory, 117, 135
Geometric method for linear programming,
    16, 22
  disadvantages of, 18–19, 21, 22–23
Graph theory, 185, 230–231

H
Hungarian algorithm, 170
  applied to transportation problems, 178
Hyperplane, 12

I
Independent variables (nonbasic vari-
    ables), 29
Infeasible linear programming problem,
    21, 50
Intermediate vertex, 187

K
König, 169
Kotiah, T.C.T., 60
Kuhn, H.W., 66, 170

L
Linear algebra, 36, 67
Linear programming, 1, 5
  geometric method for, 22
  inadequacy of calculus in, 1
Line segment, 10
Longest-path network problem, 231

M
Main constraints, 9
Management science, 1

Matrices
  equal, 238
  product of, 239
  sum of, 239
Matrix, 238
  diagonal, 241
  diagonal of, 241
  formulation of maximization linear pro-
      gramming problem, 94–95
  formulation of minimization linear pro-
      gramming problem, 94–95
  identity, 241
  inverse, 242
  invertible, 242
  noninvertible, 242
  payoff, 119
  product of real number and, 239
  square, 241
  transpose of, 241
  zero, 239
Matrix games, 117–139
  domination in, 119
  dual noncanonical linear programming
      problems and, 122–124
  fair, 125
  infeasibility and unboundedness in,
      123–124, 124–125
  multiphase, 127
  two-person zero-sum, 119
  von Neumann value in, 125
Max-flow min-cut theorem, 194–195
  duality in, 195
Maximal-flow algorithm, 198–199
  construction of corresponding minimal
      cut of, 199
Maximal-flow network problem, 189–190
  disadvantages of Tucker tableau solution
      procedure, 190–191
  dual problem of, 191
  infeasibility and unboundedness in, 190
Maximization
  canonical, linear programming problem,
      9
  canonical slack, linear programming
      problem, 28–29
Maximum basic feasible tableau, 41
Maximum tableau, canonical, 29, 30
Minimal-cost-flow algorithm, 217–218
  applied to transportation and assignment
      problems, 230
Minimal-cost-flow network problem, 216
  infeasibility and unboundedness in, 217
Minimization
  canonical, linear programming problem,
      9

canonical slack, linear programming
    problem, 28–29
Minimum basic feasible tableau, 89
Minimum-entry method, 143, 180
Minimum tableau, canonical, 29, 30
Mixed strategy (probabilistic strategy)
  for column player, 120
  for row player, 120
Multiphase matrix games, 127

N
Negative transpose, 54
Negative transposition, 54–55
  consequences of duality on, 92, 103
Net input flow, 187
Network problem
  maximal flow, 189–190
  minimal-cost-flow, 216
  shortest-path, 206
Nonbasic variables, see Independent
    variables
Noncanonical linear programming prob-
    lems, 70–86
  equations of constraint in, 77
  matrix games and, 122–124
  unconstrained variables in, 70
Nonnegativity constraints, 9
Norm, 14
Northwest-corner method, 143, 180

O
Objective function, 9
Open ball of radius r centered at origin, 15
Open half-space, 13
Operations research, 1
Optimal solutions, 10
  basic, 43
  and complementary slackness, 100
  in dual linear programming problems,
      92, 99
Optimal strategy, 119
  for column player, 122
  determination of, by dual noncanonical
      linear programming problems,
      122–124
  for row player, 121

P
Path, 205
  in relation to α-path, 205
Payoff matrix, 119
Permutation set of zeros, 169

PERT (program evaluation and review
    technique), 231
Pivot transformation, 34
    application of, to linear algebra, 36,
        67–68
Poe, Edgar Allan, 136
Polyhedral convex sets, 13
    and extreme points, 15
Probabilistic strategy, *see* Mixed strategy
Probability
    assignment of, 245
    of event, 246
    function on sample space, 245
    of sample point, 245
Program evaluation and review technique,
    see PERT
Pure strategy, 120
The Purloined Letter, 136

R
Reduced tableau, 170
Row player, 119

S
Sample points, 244
Sample space, 244
Sensitivity analysis, 99
Shortest-path algorithm I (Dijkstra), 207
    advantages of, 207–208
    disadvantages of, 207–208, 212
Shortest-path algorithm II, 213
Shortest-path network problem, 206
    infeasibility and unboundedness in,
        206
    as special case of minimal-cost-flow net-
        work problem, 217
Simplex algorithm, 23, 27–69
    advantages of, over geometric method,
        63–64
    anticycling rules for, 60–61
    geometric interpretation of, 46–47
    for maximum basic feasible tableaus,
        42
        further restrictions on, 69
    for maximum tableaus, 49–50
    for minimum tableaus, 55
Sink, 187
    uniqueness of, by augmentation,
        188–189
Slack variables, 29
"Solve and replace every occurrence of",
    34, 35

Source, 187
    uniqueness of, by augmentation,
        188–189
Steinberg, D.I., 60

T
Tableau, *see* Tucker tableau
Transportation algorithm, 153
    applied to assignment problems, 165,
        168–169
    applied to noncanonical linear program-
        ming problems, 178
    relationship with dual simplex algo-
        rithm, 143, 153–154
Transportation problems, 140–164,
    177–178
    balanced, 142–143
    formulated as minimal-cost-flow net-
        work problems, 228
    infeasibility and unboundedness in,
        153
    unbalanced, 161
    uniqueness of optimal solutions in,
        179
Transportation tableau
    balanced, 143
    unbalanced, 161
Transpose, 241
Tucker, A.W., 27, 87, 96
Tucker tableau, 27, 29
    maximum, 29, 30
    maximum basic feasible, 41
    minimum, 29, 30
    minimum basic feasible, 89
Two-person zero-sum matrix game, 119

U
Unbalanced
    transportation problem, 161
    transportation tableau, 161
Unbounded
    linear programming problem, 16, 43–
        44
    subset of $\mathbf{R}^n$, 15
Unconstrained variables, 70, 83
    alternate method for dealing with, 85

V
VAM (Vogel Advanced-Start Method),
    144
    advantages of, 143

and basic feasible solutions, 150–151
disadvantages of, 143
Vertices, 185
Vogel Advanced-Start Method, *see*
    VAM
Vogel, W.R., 143
Von Neumann, John, 125

Von Neumann minimax theorem, 125
Von Neumann value, 125

W
Weight, 205
Weighted, 205

Undergraduate Texts in Mathematics

(continued)

Ross: Elementary Analysis: The Theory of Calculus.
Scharlau/Opolka: From Fermat to Minkowski.
Sigler: Algebra.
Simmonds: A Brief on Tensor Analysis.
Singer/Thorpe: Lecture Notes on Elementary Topology and Geometry.
Smith: Linear Algebra. Second edition.
Smith: Primer of Modern Analysis.
Stanton/White: Constructive Combinatorics.
Stillwell: Mathematics and Its History.
Strayer: Linear Programming and Its Applications.
Thorpe: Elementary Topics in Differential Geometry.
Troutman: Variational Calculus with Elementary Convexity.
Wilson: Much Ado About Calculus.

CPSIA information can be obtained at www.ICGtesting.com
Printed in the USA
LVOW091510010812

292530LV00002B/2/A